Bush Wireless

Ian Braybrook

By the same Author
Gweneth Wisewould – Outpost Doctor, 2001
Six Ha'pennies, 2007
The Changing Times, 2011

Bush Wireless
First Published in 2015 by
Marilyn Bennet Publishing
Maine Media
PO Box 677
Castlemaine Victoria 3450
Phone: 0409 333 513
Email: ianandmazza@gmail.com

Copyright © Ian Braybrook 2015

All rights reserved. Without limiting the rights under Copyright, no part of this publication can be reproduced, stored or introduced into a retrieval system, or transmitted in any form or by any means (electronic, mechanical, photocopying, recording or otherwise), without the prior written permission of the writer and the publisher.

National Library
Catalogue in publishing entry

Braybrook, Ian
Bush Wireless

ISBN 978-0-9944370-0-6

1. Radio. 2. Community Broadcasting. 3. History. 4. Biography.

Text design and layout by Level Heading – levelheading.com

Edited by Marilyn Bennet and Bernard Schultz

Internal Photographs: Copyright of the author and publisher
Melissa McArdle, Elliott Midland Newspapers
Front cover: News Ltd. / Newspix
Back cover: Chris Rae

Printed and bound by Griffin Press

Acknowledgements

There were many helpers in the preparation of this book. My friend Brook Acklom was the first person to read the draft manuscript. He encouraged me to continue with it. Robyn Thomas, Ken White, Brad Bridger and Kevin Daw later did likewise. All offered me sincere encouragement and advice. My special thanks go to Marilyn Bennet, my partner, for editing the final manuscript. Her patience and her advice contributed much, far above the love and purpose she gives my life.

Many others have travelled with me on the journey I describe but special mention goes to Jeff Langdon. Jeff took me on board at 3CCC.and put his faith and trust in me, giving me the opportunity to achieve a measure of success in my life. Thank you Jeff.

There are hundreds of others who should be mentioned but it is unwise to do so. It's almost certain that some important names will be missed. Instead I say thank you to all who accompanied me in this fantastic adventure.

Ian

Foreword

I met Ian and his partner Marilyn (Mazza) at community radio station 3CCCfm in 1984, I was the 'new kid on the block' learning production skills and doing on air stuff whilst Ian and Mazza 'the old hands' were handling sales, producing all sorts of programs and presenting on air shows, with Ian managing to find time to do the 'brekkie show' 5 days a week! I had an absolute ball that year, learning the art of radio from those skilled practitioners around me but particularly from 'The Master', my mentor, Ian Braybrook. I drifted out of radio in 1994 and went back to teaching but team Ian/Mazza continued on in the industry establishing and managing 3 radio stations here in central Victoria contributing so much to the local community. And I'm proudly back sharing air time with Ian and Marilyn on their radio station. Ian also tells a good story, read this book and live the story.

Kevin J Daw (KD)

Contents

Introduction · 11

Chapter One · 15
  3CCC and the beginning

Chapter Two · 24
  Harcourt's new radio station, it starts – it stops

Chapter Three · 28
  Some good people, a Listener funds a book, Fire! the Beautiful Harcourt Valley. The station at the station, I get a job, meet some volunteers, a salesman on a pushbike at the station

Chapter Four ·37
  Meet some of the people

Chapter Five ·47
  Some adventures, a fine romance, a mud hut, demolition derby, didgeridoo, a tip launchs

Chapter Six ·57
  Calamity Clegg, a close shave, a Mayor, a Manager and a policeman

Chapter Seven ·65
  An important departure, late news, personalities need not apply, hard selling, Jack Miles and me

Chapter Eight ·75
  3CCC people, Uncle Doug, Three McGowan boys, little kids, embarrassments, Confests and OBs

Chapter Nine · 88
  A bomb threat, some weddings, footy, watching the wheels, tractor racing, a trembling tower

Chapter Ten ·95
  Fishing, motels, movie stars, Catch It, a lump of gold, a porridge addict, a 90-year-old magician

Chapter Eleven · 109
  Many good people, too many Cooks, jazz, musicians, songwriters, feminists and a swagman

Chapter Twelve · 118
   *Slim Dusty, Joe Daly, The P.M. calls, The Olivers from
   Blackwood, a magpie, Langdon gets a fright*

Chapter Thirteen · 129
   Hot dogs, Blue Heelers, a billy goat and a marriage

Chapter Fourteen · 140
   *A Kombi van, Dachshunds, A Country Music festival and our
   Sopwith Camel*

Chapter Fifteen · 149
   Writers, Rockers, Sky Pilots, sightless presenters and Poms

Chapter Sixteen · 159
   Surveys, songwriters and radiothons

Chapter Seventeen · 167
   Morning shows, presenters, Footy, Dad and Dave

Chapter Eighteen · 176
   *Buy Australian, accusations, advertisement, suspension, pain
   and skullduggery*

Chapter Nineteen · 188
   *New beginnings, Education, testing, a dreadful transmission,
   KLFM, huge wins*

Chapter Twenty · 197
   *KLFM to Castlemaine, conferences, from Old Gaol to
   nurses' home, a flag raising*

Chapter Twenty One · 206
   *Census, heritage, gardening, promotions, outside broadcasts,
   generosity*

Chapter Twenty Two · 216
   Autonomy, suspension, haircuts, broken bones, prison, optic fibre

Chapter Twenty Three · 230
   *A shock, a missing link, empty studio, new deal, a pub meeting,
   confusion*

Chapter Twenty Four · 240
   *Building a new station, a community rallies, helpers, LPONs, Old
   Gaol again, good news at last*

Chapter Twenty Five ·250
WMAfm, The Most Outstanding Small Station in Australia, Choosing a name, upgrades, Optus, more helpers, the awards, E.R.P. upgraded, more helpers, pioneer presenters, board members, the right target

Chapter Twenty Six ·260
Growth, good people and bad, footy, you've gotta have rules, an expulsion, pirates, a jail break

Chapter Twenty Seven · 271
Gentrification, graves, the Old Gaol, the epic town division, interviews, new breed, coffee shops

Chapter Twenty Eight · 281
Surprises, awards, a rooster today, a feather duster tomorrow, a sad farewell

Epilogue ·289

Introduction

In this story I give an account of my experience in Community Radio in rural Australia. There are probably many similar stories. In many ways it is biographical.

My 'best before' date has passed but I was once an acceptable radio announcer. These days I'm a far distance from the enthusiastic youth who, in 1959, raced up the stairs of Bill Robert's Vincent School of Broadcasting in Little Collins Street, Melbourne, for my twice weekly lessons.

Bill and his assistant Val Robinson (this may not be her correct name – blame my fading memory!) sweated and fretted over a class of a dozen or so mostly hopeless hopefuls. As far as I know nobody from the class of '59 ever amounted to anything much. Most, like me, didn't last long in the industry. If they ever did manage to land a job, they were banished to remote bush towns to serve their 'apprenticeship'. This included selling advertising, writing copy, gathering and writing news, cleaning the floors and washing the boss's car. Disillusioned, overworked and poverty stricken they went off to find real jobs that paid more than a pittance; the hoped for glamour and fame never eventuating.

In later years I worked with more successful students: Bob Walters at 3CCC and Ian Nichols at KLFM. Bob was the chief newsreader at Channel 9 for many years and Ian Nicholls worked in metropolitan radio. Des Carol, who did voice work for me at WMAfm, was a metro radio man too. All of us wound up on community radio in the bush.

Twenty years went by as I worked in all sorts of jobs far removed from radio, but the lure of radio remained strong.

In 1978 I read an article in our local paper, the Castlemaine Mail, which set me aglow. I fell over myself in response to the appeal for interested persons to join the newly formed Goldfields Community Radio Co-operative.

Thus began the most marvelous adventure of my life. It came at a time of turmoil, unhappiness and uncertainty in my life. It gave me something to aspire to; the opportunity to indulge my long-held passion. Along the way I worked with hundreds of people and the doors of many formerly unknown worlds were opened to me. I thought my education was almost complete, but I had a lot more to learn about people.

My co-worker-volunteers were the motliest crew imaginable: doctors, lawyers, dole bludgers, vets, council workers, farmers, pilots, photographers, laborers, gardeners, secretaries, carpenters, teachers, public servants, hippies, clerks, accountants, financial planners, architects, writers, students, sales reps, politicians, school kids, teachers and more. They represented a remarkable cross section of the people who made up the citizenry of Central Victoria at the time.

We had vegans and vegetarians, communists and fascists, greenies and pinkies, introverts and extroverts, narcissists, know alls and know nothings, the trustworthy and the trustless. There were prima donnas, egos of all proportions, liars, rogues and vagabonds, the loyal and disloyal. Our on-air performances were excellent, good, bad, indifferent, awful and appalling.

This is a story of people; principally the real fair dinkum people who in those days comprised Bendigo and Castlemaine. They made up 3CCC in Central Victoria. These were joyous times that regrettably ended unhappily for me.

In later years I was closely involved with KLFM, also in Central Victoria, but it was eventually to prove to be a bitter disappointment that almost dealt the last blow to my faith and trust in friends. Although successful, KLFM lacked the soul and the pioneering community spirit of Triple C.

In the end, some of the people I associated with lacked decency and honesty.

Then came a huge challenge; establishing a community station from scratch exclusively for Castlemaine and district, completely independent from any other. From this emerged WMAfm which was eventually, sadly, destined to be obliterated.

With the KLFM episode I thought I had reached the bottom of the pit but there was much more to come and with it came great distress.

This is my story of thirty-five years in community radio. There may be slight inaccuracies, but mostly I refer to notes I wrote as it happened, my dairies, letters, faxes and emails; but my memory is not as good as it once was.

I am so glad that I stored numerous press cuttings and almost every communication ever written by me or to me concerning my radio experiences. These have proved invaluable. I have gone through a mountain of paper from a half dozen musty boxes to write this story.

Chapter One

3CCC and the beginning

May 23rd 2013

The Secretary
Castlemaine District Radio Inc.
Box 1077
Castlemaine 3450

Dear Bettie

I hereby terminate my involvement with WMAfm. This includes my membership of the board, my on air activities and my current role as volunteer 'Manager'. This decision is effective immediately.

Recent events have inflicted an intolerable toll on my health and happiness and that of my partner Marilyn, as well as my fellow board members.

I express my bitter disappointment in the actions of a small group of established volunteers in organising what is best described as a coup d'état.

I have always acted in what I believed the best interest of WMAfm from its establishment until the present day. This includes my role in the decision not to renew the contract of former manager Martin Myles.

I wish my successor greater respect and loyalty than that shown to me by the coup leaders and their supporters.

Yours sincerely
Ian Braybrook.

That is how my time in community radio ended. The happiness and retirement plans of my life partner Marilyn and I were ruined.

* * *

My late wife Joan and I, with our two sons Glenn and Dale, moved to Castlemaine in 1973 from Malmsbury, where we had owned the Post Office and Newsagency.

Castlemaine is a country town with a population then as now, of around seven thousand. Somehow it had been given the official title of 'City', something to do with the amount of income from rates I was told.

The town came into being late in 1851, when huge gold discoveries were made at nearby Forest Creek (now Chewton) and Barkers Creek. According to local author and historian Robyn Annear, the early diggers identified the area now occupied by the centre of Castlemaine as Blacksmith's Stone House Flat, most likely after an original occupant.

Castlemaine was then solidly working class and extremely close knit. Everyone knew each other and shared everyone else's troubles. It was a wonderful community. It's different now.

Surprisingly in those 1970s, it boasted seven millionaire residents, at a time when being a millionaire really meant something. The town then as now, largely depended on two major industries, supported by a number of smaller but important ones. The major employers, The Castlemaine Bacon Company, then locally owned by the Harris family but now by multi national giant George Weston Foods, Flowserve, originally Thompson's Foundry and Victoria Carpets, the latter now shut down forever, converted to a boutique brewery and coffee shop. The remaining two, the bacon factory and Flowserve, with the hospital and aged care centre employ about two thousand of our people. The motor car industry, based around hot rod cars, is also a significant employer and large income earner for the town. Castlemaine is recognized as The Hot Rod Centre of Australia. Some say that Art is the big earner for the town but I disagree. I believe it's the Hot Rod related industry that is the bigger by far and it is self sustaining, not reliant on government grants and handouts.

In 1973 when I arrived with my wife and family, Castlemaine was fiercely parochial, a trait it retains to an extent in the present day even though there has been a significant inflow of more recent arrivals, the Hippies of the '70s and the Tree Change folk of the 2000s. These latter are often called 'aristohippies' by old timers, derived from aristocrat, or the 'Latte Elite', due to their apparently well-heeled lifestyle and seeming attachment to coffee shops. We have approximately twenty-four coffee shops in and around town for our seven thousand people.

Nowadays Castlemaine is one of the most cosmopolitan in Australia, home to a variety of artists, musicians, ethnic groups, black and white, rich and poor, the old and young. It is also the centre of Australia's first ever National Heritage Park which is based on the remnants and artifacts of the gold rush and the magnificent Iron Bark forests. Some say that's a good thing, others say it's just the opposite with its rigid rules and regulations.

Property values have multiplied by twenty five times or more since I arrived in 1973, when we paid $12,000 for a three bedroom brick veneer only five years old. It is worth $340,000 in 2014.

Castlemaine is my home and I have loved it and its people. I still do, but it's not the same, and I can't say I love them all anymore.

* * *

It was on a frosty Saturday morning in July that I collected The Mail (established 1854) from Steven's Newsagency in Barker Street and read the article that so excited me. There was a move on to set up a local radio station. Of course I was interested. I had always loved radio and had trained at the Vincent School of Broadcasting almost twenty years before. But my career in commercial radio was brief as I struggled with family commitments, lack of housing in bush towns and a serious lack of money. It was luxury I could not afford and needed a 'real' job.

I waited impatiently for Monday morning to come so that I could call on the contact person named in the article, Dr Jeffrey Langdon, Manager of the Education Centre.

The alternative contact was Justin Shortal, a history teacher at the High School. I was pretty nervous about getting involved. I had a fear of doctors and secondary school teachers, hangovers from my previous disastrous, near death experiences with medical practitioners and ghastly memories of my treatment at the hands of teachers at the Terang Higher Elementary School in the early 1950s.

Upstairs, at number 13 Mostyn Street, above the State Electricity Office and Showroom, was the Education Centre. I had no idea what the function of the Centre was – I still don't know exactly.

On inquiry for an interview with Dr Langdon, the receptionist June Symons (mother of the famous Red Symons of Skyhooks and ABC radio about whom we'll hear more later) directed me to an office at the end of a corridor. I knocked quietly and a voice bellowed for me to come in.

Seated at a large desk, scattered with important looking papers and a large topographical map he'd been studying was the man in question, Dr Jeffrey Langdon. I thought he was a rather fierce looking fellow, with a scruffy short beard and a mop of black hair that stuck out at all angles, this caused by his habit of pulling at the hair as he wrestled with problems. He wore steel-rimmed spectacles in front of penetrating eyes which added to his fierce appearance. I judged him to be about thirty, a decade younger than me. He was casually dressed in T Shirt and slacks, quite unlike my own physician, Doctor Courtis. The bespectacled eyes bored into mine.

'How can I help?' he glowered. He didn't seem very friendly.

I stammered that I was keen on getting back into radio, I had some ancient experience, thought I could be useful, and was offering my service if he could use it.

A change came over him and he extended a hand, introducing himself as 'Jeff'.

I was soon set at ease and we began an hour of excited talk about the proposed radio station.

I later learnt that Jeff was not a medical doctor but had a Masters Degree in Physics and a Ph.D. in Geophysics. He never spoke of this much but I recall him once saying jokingly, that he had studied rocks.

Until recently he had been a secondary school teacher, presumably lecturing students on the creation, purpose and uses of rocks and stones. They are great for breaking windows, kids catapult ammunition (we called them shanghais when I was a kid) and skimming across dams and creeks.

I left his office happily clutching my two dollar membership card for Goldfields Community Radio Co-Operative and full of enthusiasm for the time ahead. It proved to be the best two dollars I ever spent.

Jeff and I were to become good friends and I became his right hand man at the future radio station. I always had, and still retain, the greatest respect for him.

At that time I was working away from Castlemaine a lot of the time, selling door to door, and was not able to attend many of the meetings and functions. All the groundwork was done by Jeff and his closest supporters; people like Daryl Evans, Justin Shortal, Sam Grumont, Phil Rice, Phil Scott, Malcolm Peters, Hugh Elphinstone, Malcom Fyffe and a host of others with whom I had no contact at the time. I take no credit whatsoever for the early days of establishing the future radio station. I managed to attend a couple of fundraising dances and several meetings but mostly I was absent at work.

The long, frustrating and complex work in actually gaining a radio broadcasting license was left principally to Jeff, ably assisted by his technical team and committee. He managed to coerce/recruit a magnificent and talented core group; technicians, engineers, administrators and such. He even gained an honorary Solicitor (and committee member), Kerry McDonald. It was a formidable team that contributed so much toward gaining the hard-won Community Radio License that eventuated early in 1982.

In preparation for the hoped for license, Jeff had again used his particular methods of persuasion, some say coercion, to obtain use of vacant rooms at the former Education Department secondary school building in Templeton Street. Jeff had also somehow gained a federal government grant of $3500 from the Film Commission to buy some studio equipment. With the help of many, a primitive but functional studio was set up there, mostly using second-hand band sound gear, a couple of turntables and a four track reel-to-reel tape recorder.

Daryl Evans was the designated 'engineer' who oversaw much of the installation work and he began tutoring me, among others, in the use of the gear. He was a great bloke who knew his job and was extremely patient with learners such as me. Sporting long hair and a beard he was a left-over from the Hippie era, with corresponding laid back attitudes, often infuriatingly slack and unhurried.

Daryl, as the unofficial engineer and producer, began to record local bands and mock radio programs. Considering the very basic equipment, he did a fantastic job, in particular recording local bands such as Byron Bay and folk singer Kerry McDonald. In the future it became firm station policy to record local music and to give the results worthwhile air time, always having been denied these local, unknown artists in the past.

In what was an amazing coup, Jeff Langdon arranged with Bendigo commercial radio station 3CV (now Gold fm) for a half hour weekly program in their schedule. We called it the Castlemaine Radio Show. It was generally quite pathetic but it was very important to us. Alas, I cannot recall the 3CV Manager's name. Uncommonly for the time, the manager was a woman. God bless her! She gave us learners the opportunity to put together real radio shows and develop the skills that we desperately needed.

The regular anchorman of the show was Justin Shortal, whose smooth, well modulated tone of voice well suited the medium. He became a mainstay of the fledgling radio station later on. He was a real charmer, the envy of many a man; young, ever-smiling and good-looking, he was especially popular with the women. Alas for any female aspirants, he was happily married to Faye and a devoted family man.

He was also an extremely talented entertainer, as I found out later when I saw him perform as a compere and stand-up comedian.

On one occasion, he stepped aside from his scheduled program to allow me to host the radio show and I was most grateful for the opportunity. The half hour program took a patient Daryl Evans four hours to record, allowing for my numerous nervous mistakes.

I was working with a builder friend on a farm at Boort when the show went to air and as I listened I realised what an appalling performance it was. I was a poor substitute for Justin, but it gave me valuable experience.

In my time Castlemaine has always had an abundance of quality musicians. The radio show on 3CV enabled us to feature a number of them; an opportunity previously denied them by existing stations. Bands and individuals like Tipplers All, Mulga Bill's Bicycle Band, John and Viv Adolphus, Faye and Terry White, The Organic Swagman, aka Kerry McDonald, Ray Stanyer, Les Thornton and Ray Lindstrum.

Raising money was always a challenge and Jeff had a brilliant idea for a fundraiser. He called a meeting of interested people at the home he shared with wife Anne, sons Rory and Joe, and Border Collie dog Butch, in Urquhart Street Castlemaine. He proposed to the enthusiastic group that we record and sell a vinyl LP featuring some of the best rock bands in the region! It sounded like a sure-fire winner.

Among the assembled group was Marilyn Bennet, well known as the owner of the Bendigo-based Talent Agency and Musician's Management, The Entertainment Company. She managed two popular bands, Public Enemy and Cruise and she agreed to include them in the project. Another local band, Sharp Toys with Rex Watts and his brother, the late Robbie, Joe Rutledge and my son Glenn also agreed to participate. Daryl Evans agreed to engineer and produce the recording in the Castlemaine studio.

The date was set and the arrangements for pressing the record at EMI and printing labels and covers put in place. Somebody chose the album title: 'Goldfields Rock'.

Daryl was never noted for his speedy work and the process dragged on for months; the band members became impatient and enthusiasm generally dropped away as the weeks went by. By the time the recording actually appeared there was little interest or enthusiasm left.

Finally, Daryl declared the master tape ready and it was promptly dispatched to EMI in Melbourne for pressing. The labels and covers were printed locally and within a month we had a mountain of vinyl albums ready to sell to, what we felt sure, would be a ready market.

It was decided to launch the product at a concert of the three bands. The chosen venue was the Tin Shed at Bendigo showground, a popular venue of the time, in fact the only suitable building in Bendigo back then. And it was a real tin shed, stifling hot in summer and bleak in winter. I saw Jimmy Barnes perform there one summer and it must have been around fifty degrees inside and over seven hundred sweaty bodies were jammed in.

Our crowd at the Goldfields Rock album release was not quite of Jimmy Barnes proportions but we managed about two hundred paying customers, an excellent result as Bendigo folk usually shunned local bands. It was a terrific night as our three bands performed well and the crowd got into it. We actually made a small profit at the door but record sales were very disappointing. At night's end we still had nine hundred and seventy albums left in stock.

Gradually in the months that followed, we managed to unload more and eventually arrived at a balance of seven hundred, around our break-even point.

There seemed little prospect of selling the balance so on Jeff's suggestion, I undertook to sell them door to door for two dollars each on 25% commission. I tramped every street of Castlemaine and I reckon I knocked on a thousand doors. I'm sure that every second home in Castlemaine had a copy of Goldfields Rock by the time I finished. I'm equally sure that they are probably still in mint condition, untouched by any stylus.

Chapter Two

Harcourt's new radio station, it starts –it stops

It was Anzac Day, 25 April 1982 when a large and motley group of two hundred and fifty people assembled outside the former Harcourt Railway Station building.

Not many people have heard of Harcourt, a mere a fly speck on the map of Victoria with a district population at the time about five hundred. The township comprised a general store, post office and service station – not even a pub in those days where the locals could drown their sorrows if the fruit crop failed or the footy team lost yet another match. The area's claim to fame came from the quality of the apples grown throughout the picturesque valley. It was known as 'The Apple Centre of Victoria' in the scant publicity brochures on the rack in Roger and Gail Sellwood's local store.

Nothing much ever happened at Harcourt apart from an occasional bowls tournament at the local Bowls Club and Aussie Rules footy and cricket matches in season. The district had a footy team which rarely won a match, but was enthusiastically supported by the locals. Long serving local, Barry Johansen, President of a dedicated committee and wife Irene, mine hosts of the Northern Hotel in Castlemaine, somehow kept the club together. Barry's family roots were in a Harcourt orchard. His family even had a road named after them, Johansen's Road. He also owned and leased out the Harcourt Tavern and Motel.

This day was a very big occasion for Harcourt – the opening of the town's very own radio station. Few towns its size could boast that. Not that 3CCC would broadcast to the local population alone. The license allowed us to broadcast throughout the region, right across Central Victoria, including the city of Bendigo – a potential audience of one hundred and fifty thousand, a figure not likely to ever be realized of course.

After almost five years of preparation and frustration, Goldfields Community Radio Co-operative was about to switch on the transmitter, a recycled black and white television transmitter donated by BCV8 Bendigo and painstakingly modified by our brilliant technicians Phil Rice and Phil Scott, better known as Scotty. Both were lecturers in Electrical Engineering at what is now Latrobe University but then the Bendigo College of Advanced Education. These two men were the key to getting 3CCC to air and were absolutely marvelous in their commitment and dedication.

Standing on a small lectern in the open car park Jeff Langdon stood poised to utter the official opening words. The Board had recently officially appointed him as Manager and he was actually paid a small salary.

It was a memorable day for Jeff who had laboured ceaselessly to see the dream come to reality.

By his side stood a beaming Justin Shortal clutching a speech in a nervous hand. He had by now been co-opted from the Education Department to act as Schools Liasion Officer for the station, another Langdon coup and initiative! How Jeff managed to gain Justin free of cost to 3CCC from the Education Department I never learnt.

Noon was the appointed time and at 11.50am precisely, the transmitter fired up with the sound of radio gongs, followed by the mellow voice of ex ABC man, Leo Fowler. Gong. Gong. Gong. 'This is 3CCC FM broadcasting on 103.9 Megahertz.' Gong. Gong. Gong.

This soothing message was repeated for the full ten minutes until high noon. The voice of Leo then ceased and on a signal from producer Daryl Evans, Jeff began his speech.

'Hello and welcome to 3CCC FM. This is Jeff Langdon. Today, Anzac day 1982 is the first day of transmission for 3CCC. May the station succeed.'

Jeff stepped aside and his place was taken by a nervous Justin Shortal.

'You are sharing in an historic moment for Community Radio in Central Victoria', intoned Justin. 'With the support of the people of Central Victoria' He added the last bit for no apparent reason. They went on with more but from both men it was the shortest public address I ever heard them make. In the future I was to hear many much longer ones.

With a flourish Jeff signaled for the cross to the studio for our first ever official program. Sweating in the studio was a petrified nineteen year old Aboriginal, Rick Nelson who I was told had come originally from Balranald in New South Wales. He was a friend of our newly acquired Office Coordinator, Sherry-Ann Cox. 'Hello', stammered the nervous lad. 'I'm Rick Nelson and I'm gonna play for youse some of my kinda music.' With a whirring wow as the turntable gathered speed, Blondie hit the 3CCC airwaves of Central Victoria.

With trembling hand Rick closed the microphone, slumping with relief.

We were away! We all cheered and some of us actually wept, then immediately adjourned to the 'big room' to crack a few joyous stubbies – a great Aussie tradition. At last 3CCC was up and running, we could scarcely believe it.

We were not up and running for long however! Two minutes into the broadcast the entire thing shut down and our new audience, estimated at up to several hundred, could hear nothing but hiss – FM Stereo hiss of course! The link transmitter had defiantly thrown itself off course. Our stubbies were set silently and prayerfully aside.

After some frantic corrections by Phil Rice and 'Scotty', the shiny new juggernaut rolled on.

We were heading into the future. But what sort of future? Was there to be a future? Our critics, of whom there were many, thought not.

For better or worse we were steaming into unknown and uncharted waters. Would we founder on hidden rocks or would we keep the ship afloat?

We hoped like hell that we would, but really didn't have a clue. We had a lot learn.

Chapter Three

Some good people, a Listener funds a book,
Fire! the Beautiful Harcourt Valley.
The station at the station, I get a job,
meet some volunteers, a salesman on a pushbike
at the station

It was fitting that Castlemaine become the site of the first ever FM station outside the metropolitan areas. In the early 1930s a local man Gilbert Blake, set up a radio station at his home at 29 Doveton Street. He put recorded music to air, a bit of local talk and even ventured bravely into live music direct to air when he broadcast a couple of items from Thompson's Foundry Band. All this in very limited hours, but it was well received locally. However 3GB did not flourish and before long closed down forever. But Castlemaine was a pioneer radio town. Thompson's Foundry Band is and was an institution in the district, originally formed by workers at the old Thompson's Foundry in the late nineteenth century. Both Thompsons, and the band are still operating, although the foundry is now owned by an overseas company, Flowserve. The band members do not necessarily work at the foundry either.

Jeff Langdon had used his seemingly magic powers and gained a peppercorn lease on the disused Harcourt railway building, transferring the entire operation, such as it was, from Castlemaine eight kilometers south.

It was a wonderful old building, built in 1860 when the Murray River Railway was constructed. It comprised a Station Master's residence of two stories, several administration and storage rooms, two toilet blocks, a washhouse and lamp room. One room was quite large, about ten metres by six and destined to be known as 'The Big Room' where we held our regular Volunteers and Board meetings and regular concerts.

Outside the back kitchen door was a deep well, filled with excellent water. In the residence section at the top of the steep and narrow stairs, we occupied two rooms, one room was the office and the other became a studio. The bottom half was sub-let to Kathy Dawes, the lone mother of a delightful seven-year-old girl named Narrah, sharing the kitchen, bathroom and toilet with soon-to-be a hundred others. Kathy remained astonishingly patient and smiling as her domain was increasingly invaded and overrun by an ever growing crowd of volunteers. She stayed on until the station grew so much that we had to have the extra space.

Before long 3CCC boasted an impressive one hundred plus volunteers; a more disparate group it is hard to imagine. Almost every trade, profession and walk of life was represented and what a terrific bunch of people they were. I learnt so much from and about people that it changed my outlook. It gave me an understanding of differences in people that I could not otherwise have learned. As well, the range and variety of programs was astounding and truly reflected the makeup of the region's population. I learnt from that too.

The variety of ages of our presenters was surprising, ranging from Veronica Ellis at ten or eleven years to Jack Miles at sixty-five and Vic McGowan who was well into his seventies. And who could forget Kath Molitor, a broad accented Pommy in her sixties.

Every conceivable music type and taste was catered for even to the extent of Jacques Sodell presenting a show called 'Possible Music' – a two hour collection of the weirdest sounds; from dripping taps to breaking glass to scraping and scratching noises that Jacques lovingly described as music. One evening Jack Miles, one of our most valued and senior men, was driving home when from the radio speakers emerged the strangest sounds. Jack immediately rang Jeff Langdon at home (and in bed) to advise him that something dreadful had happened to the transmitter, suggesting he get Phil Rice to drive to the mountain-top to fix it. Of course it turned out to be Jacque's regular program but who could blame Jack Miles for his mistake!

Our transmitter was housed in a grey brick structure high on Mount Alexander Regional Park, on a public land site that we leased from the State Government. No such sites are available today due to policies prohibiting these things in Regional Parks.

We built the hut ourselves in a series of working bees, overseen by builder/volunteer David Walters. David was the son of Bob Walters, a retired Channel Nine TV newsreader and one of our volunteers. Bob became a passionate presenter of a wonderful jazz program, and also had the dubious distinction of being a fellow graduate of mine from The Vincent School of Broadcasting.

I don't know where Jeff scrounged the small tower for our dipoles and link gear. However, I do remember us digging trenches through mostly granite in a three hundred and sixty degree circle to bury steel mesh for an earth.

The mountain-top working bees were a real bonding experience and at day's end we would open some stubbies or bottles of wine and, seated on the vast granite slabs and boulders, absorb the beautiful views and ambience of the mountain as we talked of the day and the future. It was a good time.

When we first went to air we broadcast on very limited hours, beginning at 9am for two hours and closing until 4pm. This allowed us to be able to use the studio to train new arrivals, of which there were many. Within a few weeks however, Jeff decided that we would extend our hours to full time, 6am until midnight, and away we went, never looking back. Jeff must have made up his mind on this on the spur of the moment as Sally Clark was winding up her program with the usual announcement that we would now close down until 4pm. There was a pause.

'Oh. No we aren't.' The puzzlement showed in her voice. 'I've just been told by the Manager that we will remain on air.' Jeff had made a decision.

I spent a lot of time around the station and just before we went on air permanently I was given two paying jobs by Jeff. The first was as our Sponsorship Salesman, possibly due to my later fine effort in selling Goldfields' Rock door-to-door! It was on 'commission only' terms, 25% of all I managed to sell. The other was as newsreader for a five days-a-week program titled 'Newspaper of The Air'. I was actually paid eight dollars for an hour per day for this from yet another grant that Jeff had obtained. It was government funded to provide a service to the sight handicapped people of the region and was truly an excellent service. It was really a pioneer of the widespread service now provided in the region by Radio for the Print handicapped, 3RPH. In no time at all I was making an average $75 a week, all up. At the time the average wage was about $350 a week, but I survived.

At 4pm Monday to Friday, I'd slog my way through a half hour of solid reading from the district and statewide newspapers. The other half hour's pay was for preparation time!

I'll never forget how nervous I was when I first opened the microphone to begin that program. I was a bloody wreck, which clearly showed as I stumbled and bumbled my way through it. But 'Newspaper of The Air' gave me fantastic experience and boosted my confidence enormously. Not only that, I actually was paid to do it! Getting paid for work on 3CCC was and would remain a relatively rare experience.

Selling sponsorship was especially difficult for me, with no driver's licence! The fact that FM radio was entirely new to the region was a strong impediment and Community Radio was almost unheard of. At least nothing good was heard of it. There was regular publicity for the activities of Community Radio 3CR in Melbourne and it's notoriously left wing presenter Bill Hartley's support of the Palestine Liberation Army. It was invariably bad publicity that did nothing to enhance the image of Community Radio!

This undoubtedly contributed to the reputation we at 3CCC quickly developed, becoming widely known as pot-smoking, red-ragging, left wing hippies and 'druggos'.

It was totally undeserved. In all my experience I never once actually witnessed any drug consumption at the station except for the very occasional smoke of marijuana. There was consumption of no other drugs to my knowledge and I spent at least twelve hours a day, almost every weekday at work there and a good part of the weekends.

Sure, there were some outspoken left wing people on board but equally there were conservatives, even arch-conservatives like one of our directors, Jack Miles. Me, I have never had even a puff in all my life, but I am political at times; moderately left.

We also had our share of 'Greenies', notably Sally Clark who presented a weekly program on conservation issues. Sally was a terrific person with a heart of gold and we loved her. She kept her private life to herself but it was rumored that she came from a respected, wealthy family. One story told of her attending a high society family wedding at Mount Macedon. It was said that Sally drove up to the church in her rattling, beat-up, smoking old Volkswagen beetle, from which she emerged dressed in her hippy clothes, thus causing great consternation among those assembled. On another occasion Daryl Evans was attending an annual Confest at nearby Glenlyon where half the people attending were completely naked. He was surprised to observe a female that closely resembled Sally emerging from a mud bath. 'I can't be sure under all that mud,' he said, 'but it sure looked like her face.'

Our earliest test broadcasts were made from a caravan perched high on Mount Alexander. I was away at work when this happened but I know from those there that it was enthusiastically embraced by volunteers and was well received 'out there'. Marilyn Bennet (hereinafter often referred to by her nickname, Mazza) was one and she presented a Country Music show. She convinced her friend, 3BO announcer, Brad Bridger to operate the panel for her. Brad and Col Herbert both worked as announcers at commercial station 3BO and their boss, Peter Joseph, had given them strict orders to stay away from the fledgling community radio station. Brad did the panel anyway. Later, when we published a thank-you list of those who helped with the test, Brad's name appeared. His boss was absolutely furious and really got stuck into him. Brad was sacked but was reinstated in a couple of hours when the boss calmed down.

Brad also trained Paul Mulqueen and Sue Wood in panel operation at our studio, another misdemeanor in the eyes of 3BO's boss, but he never found out. Brad became a very close friend as time went by.

There was a lot of work to do in setting up our new studio and office at Harcourt. Our two rooms at the top of the narrow and very steep stairway had a sharp right angle bend in it. Getting the office furniture up there was exhausting. Building the studio was similar and again we were assisted by David Walters. Jeff and Jack Miles helped out and others chipped in but I can't recall names. Finally the studio was built, with a small ante room division from the hallway. As a result there were two studio entrance doors for great soundproofing.

Jeff had somehow raised the money to equip it with good quality gear. We had a Paul Kirk panel, two fabulous turntables, quality microphones and accessories. Our ads were recorded onto cassette, not a great way to do it but it was cheap it and worked okay. Later we added two second-hand cartridge machines which were a marvelous improvement. The studio walls were lined with egg cartons and covered with heavy woollen drapes; acoustically it was very good. There was one large, old style double-hung window that looked directly west over the house occupied by Win and Bob Bassett. In the afternoons the sun blazed in turning the room into an oven – no air conditioning of course! We planted a one metre high Claret Ash beneath it but that was rather futile. When I returned for the twenty-first birthday of 3CCC, long after the station had moved to Bendigo, the tree had just reached enough height to start to shade the window.

My job as sales rep was made more difficult by the fact that I had lost my driver's licence for a driving 'indiscretion'. Stuck eight kilometres from Castlemaine and thirty kilometres from Bendigo, I had the greatest difficulty covering my territory. But I managed by cadging lifts from presenters, catching the occasional bus and using the phone. For transport around Harcourt, where I now resided, I rode a battered old bicycle.

I had previously lived at Guildford, ten kilometres on the other side of Castlemaine, renting a unit at the rear of a former church. Because of my address I became known as The Vicar of Guildford, a title I certainly did not deserve.

In spite of my unlicensed handicap I was able to bring in some fairly good income for the station, three to four hundred dollars per week within the first few months, increasing each week from then on. I am quite proud of that considering that very few had ever heard of 3CCC and even FM radio. As well, community radio was unknown to advertisers, we had no audience to speak of and government regulations restricted advertisements to a miserable forty words with only 'a concise and general description' of the sponsor's business. In other words no inducements to listeners to support a client's business could be offered. The announcements were to state no more than the sponsor's name, address, nature of business (e.g. Gift Shop) and phone number.

Boy was it hard to sell. Principally I had to appeal to the client's community spirit and their support of a community initiative to gain the money. We charged two dollars fifty a spot, and ten dollars a week was the client's average spend. Interestingly, the figure remained similar twenty years later, in fact the 3CCC of 2007, by then called Fresh FM, was selling packages of just one dollar a spot. It is an unsustainable figure of course, but it reflected the desperate circumstances Fresh must have been in at the time.

We continued to grow revenue and after about a year Jeff made me Sponsorship Manager. My role was to be supervision of a proposed new sales agent, write the copy, have the announcements approved and recorded, enter placements on the studio log, keep records for accounts and so on.

Our on-air ad for a salesperson was not exactly a raging success but eventually produced one applicant, Alan Kurzke from Bendigo. Alan was a great bloke, serious about the job and sincere, but he fell by the wayside within six months.

Bev Ellis had been a valuable volunteer for some time and she undertook the job. A dark haired, slim, and attractive thirty-something; Bev was fabulous at it. She was also diligent, competent and committed. Dealing mainly with male business people she was irresistible and the money flowed in. We valued her enormously but her value was lost on some people who simply did not understand how difficult her job really was. A couple of years later, near the end of the era, her reward from one senior female board member was denigration, seemingly supported by management.

John Scarborough from Castlemaine, an earnest and likeable young man, took over the job. John worked very hard and did quite well for a time but eventually departed, disillusioned and angry. He clashed with the then Manager, Gerry Pyne who had initially described him as 'a breath of fresh air' and the parting was in most unpleasant circumstances. John went on to become a financial advisor.

To all those who have ever successfully sold community radio sponsorship under the old regulations, I say well done. At 3CCC at least 70 percent of our total income came through the sales rep's efforts. In my experience I was acutely aware of the responsibility that fell on me and at times it was a crushing burden.

Nowadays, when community radio is allowed full-blown advertising, it is so much easier to sell.

All old-time sponsorship sales people around Australia; I salute you!

Chapter Four

Meet some of the people

It wasn't long before we grew to the stage of needing more space so Kathy decided to move on. (Kathy later married Phillip Rice, our number one engineer)

Alas, we would miss her and Narrah about the place. Quite often when I was on air Narrah would come into the studio and sit on my knee and talk. I think she may have missed having a male in the house and we were very good friends. On another occasion I had another body sit on my lap when on air. Jack Miles had a long haired German Shepherd, a friendly beast. This day, Jack had taken his dog for a swim and Dog was still dripping wet when he came into the studio and leapt onto my lap. Not the best experience when you are on air! Not only wet, but mighty smelly.

We set up Jeff's office downstairs in Kathy's former bedroom and later Bev Ellis, Justin Shortal and I took over her sitting room as an office. It was pretty crowded but better than before. Around this time Sherri-Ann Cox decided to move on and the search for a new Receptionist/ Secretary began. Jeff chose a bright sixteen year old named Bev Stewart; it turned out to be a marvelous choice. Bev came from a conservative farming family from Newbridge, and her mother was quite disturbed by the fact that her daughter would be working closely with only men. (Bev Ellis had not yet come to join the staff.) Later on, her Mum was absolutely mortified when Jeff and Justin took Bev away with them on a weekend conference at Lorne or somewhere in that area. She had absolutely nothing to fear because we all treated her with respect at all times.

Bev Stewart was a great asset to the station and was an excellent, competent worker. We loved Bev, who had found boarding accommodation in Harcourt with couple Peter and Josie Chisholm.

Justin Shortal was our School's Liaison Officer, seconded from the Education Department which paid his salary. His role was to include secondary school students in programs and to teach them the fundamentals of radio, a task he did very well. I got on well with Justin, as did everyone else. Women invariably described him a lovely man or similarly and he was a natural charmer; he was extremely popular all round. As I told you earlier he was also a brilliant compere and comedian. He had done some acting work – 'a bit of TV stuff' as he described it and some TV advertisements, a job he handled with ease with his good looks and winning smile. More importantly he had acting talent and a good quality voice. As Sponsorship Manager, responsible for recording ads, I used his voice as often as possible.

One day I was recording an ad in our tiny production studio, which I often did due to talent being thin on the ground, and struggled to get an ad for a local shoe store on to tape. I got so tongue tied every time I tried to get through the punch line that I eventually had to give up. I think it was Bev Ellis who wrote the copy and protocol said I couldn't change another's work without permission. She wrote. 'Evans Shoex Shoe Store sells shoes of all styles.' Try recording that yourself! I couldn't. Finally I was able to waylay Justin and he agreed to have a go.

'Ah, yes. I see what you mean', said Justin as he pre-read the copy but he sailed confidently through the script until he hit 'Evans Shoex Shoe Store etc.' That's where he became tongue tied. After at least a dozen tries we were both collapsed in hysterical laughter. We had to return the script to Bev for re-writing. Justin's last attempt went like this: '– Evans Shoex Shoe Store shells soos – Oh shit.' Strong language indeed for gentleman Justin Shortal!

The difficulty some people had recording ads was unbelievable at times. A classic case was when one day I gave a script to Christian Boehme, a likeable youngster who aspired to a radio career. He spent over three full hours struggling with a forty word, fifteen second script for a local art gallery. I still have the lengthy reel of tape that he handed to me without a word. There was nothing on it that I could use even though it was common for people who thought they could do it easy, to hand me 'completed' tapes that I had to spend hours editing to link together the good bits.

I was very conscious of my obligation to give our advertisers the best possible product and as a result many of the recorded ads given to me to use never went to air. This caused resentment in the person concerned, who may have spent an hour on the job. My responsibility lay with the client.

I was always under pressure to have ads recorded by a deadline and often there was nobody around the station but Jeff, Bev Stewart, Justin and I. Consequently, talent was thin on the ground. Jeff and Bev were always too busy and more often than not, either Justin or I recorded the ads. As a result almost all of the ads going to air featured our voices. I know that some volunteers resented this but there was little choice. With respect, the vast majority of our volunteers simply did not have the ability, even if they had the presence.

The Education Department eventually decided that they wanted Justin back teaching and not even the best efforts of Jeff Langdon could convince them that Justin should stay. Alas, it was a serious loss to the station and I was left with practically no talent on site at all. There was one bright spot however.

Recently joining our ranks was Kevin Daw, a former school teacher with a big moustache and big voice to match. I was able to use Kevin or KD as he was better known, on many of our sponsorship announcements. KD became a good mate and he developed into a good announcer. Therefore, I used him as often as possible on announcements, which possibly caused further quiet rumblings. Those grumblers had no idea of the requirements for a good voice-over and quality announcement.

KD was popular on air and by mid 1980s he was asked to host our mid-morning show, 'Top of the Morning' and as a regular fill-in for Trevor Penno's popular music show. KD met me on the stairs one day.

'Hey Brookers', he called. 'I'm another Ian Braybrook. I'll be on air as much as you and I'll cop the shit that you do behind your back.' At the time I was doing breakfast Monday to Thursday, a half hour U3A program and The Fabulous Fifties with Marilyn Bennet, who by now was my permanent partner. I was not yet aware of the strength of resentment toward me and KD's message went over my head. There was no indication to me of the trauma that lay ahead. When it came I was a sitting duck.

KD turned out to be a long-serving and loyal volunteer. Over a ten year period he never once missed a show – with one exception – for which he had a pretty good excuse. One dark and wet morning he was driving the twenty-two kilometres from his home at Newstead to Harcourt he splashed into the flooded Muckleford Creek. To quote KD, he drowned the Batmobile; the Batmobile being his treasured 1962 Valiant sedan. Approaching the creek in the dark he was unaware that the creek had risen overnight due to heavy rain and had broken its banks, covering the bridge in almost a metre of water. He plunged into it at ninety kilometres an hour, struggling to control the car, ending up with water up to the windows. He managed to escape unscathed and both he and the Batmobile recovered but it was a very frightening experience.

He was the life of the party, always having a joke. One day I was on air when KD entered the studio dressed in a borrowed kilt, playing the role of one of his characters, Jock McTavish. Unknown to me he had not only removed his jeans but dropped his underpants as well! Standing at the open window, leaning forward, he lifted high the rear end of the kilt to reveal a horrible sight. I almost choked on the microphone but managed to carry on, with our Listeners none the wiser as to what had just occurred. I think that KD was a bit disappointed expecting me to crack up. Great fun as only could be had at 3CCC!

There's a lot more to reading a script properly than meets the eye and it wasn't until Tony Jerome joined us after Justin left, that we had another professional voice apart from KD.

I was quietly excited when Tony turned up but I soon learned that he would only be at the station on Saturdays for the breakfast show. He lived in far-off Shepparton where he had been a commercial announcer for many years.

The first consideration of any radio station has to be its Listeners. I always write that title with a capital L; without them there is no radio station.

Listeners to the shows I hosted were terrific. They wrote me letters, rang me up and showered me with little gifts. I had a constant supply of jars of home made jams, cakes most often delivered, hand knitted dolls and toys came in the mail, twice I received oil paintings. Several wall plaques came, as did heaps of photographs. A potter from Sweenie's Creek even sent me a one-off pottery 'H Bomb', a round cannon ball shape engraved with, in huge letters, 'H Bomb'. He also enclosed a pottery mug with my name on it. I still have both items on display at home. The accompanying note said I should stop mispronouncing Harcourt without the aitch, which I did regularly and deliberately in 'This is Radio 3CCC FM broadcasting from the beautiful 'Arcourt Valley.'

I'm told I was the first person to use the description, 'The Harcourt Valley'. Previously, Stephen Carthew, one of three brothers who operated a car dealership in Castlemaine and who for a time presented Saturday Breakfast, referred to the Barker's Creek Valley on air and I adapted it from that. Pinched it, you might say. Eventually it came into common use and was adopted by all and sundry in Harcourt.

Stephen was known as the Whispering Wombat, behind his back of course, due to extensive use of his soft voice, almost a whisper. This may have been great for appropriate laid back evening music shows but not the ideal style for a breakfast show! Stephen was a nice bloke and talented, but his talent lay in other directions. He later became the Mayor of Castlemaine and President of the Castlemaine Hospital Board.

When Christmas came around I always received a swag of cards and notes. I frequently got mail from listeners who were away on holidays, even one from Europe! A widow, the late Olive (Ollie) Pengelly called us to her home one day and presented Marilyn and me with an original oil painting by a prominent local artist. Ollie was a wonderful person with a heart of gold. She was absolutely attached and devoted to 3CCC, and rang me daily. This is something that occurred frequently with aged listeners and proved a valuable and lasting lesson for me.

Two listeners, Janet and Geoff Postlethwaite, farmers near St Arnaud, delivered to Marilyn a black sheep when she said on air that she wanted one and it was her birthday! Marilyn named the sheep, a ram minus vital bits, Peppi, in recognition of his Peppin Merino breed. Janet and Geoff became and remain good friends. Janet baked and delivered to me a marvelous birthday cake on the occasion of my thousandth brekky show. She was a marvelous friend really.

I had written a book about Dr. Gweneth Wisewould, a legendary GP in the Trentham district. I mentioned on air that I was looking for help in publishing it. Janet, rang me, and without hesitation or any security, loaned me over $3,000. I shall never forget her generosity and the trust she placed in me. After all, I was only a radio friend and she had no knowledge of me other than as a Listener to my shows. She and Geoff were absolutely wonderful; salt of the earth and fair dinkum, hard working farming people. I can never repay such generosity and I will never forget it.

By the way the book was a huge success and I was able to repay Janet without any problems.

Generally 'payola' was restricted to jars of jam, cakes and the odd free feed at the Railway Hotel. Kathryn Gibbons once gave me two small cans of Haggis. I received several small hand knitted dolls which bore the words 3CCC on their jumpers which I still have. The inmates of the Castlemaine Gaol presented me with a beautiful hand painted, framed item which had a photo of Mazza and me, with a black steam locomotive in the background accompanied by 'Ian Braybrook 3CCC fm' in bold red print. I have that displayed in my home studio. I don't know where they got the photo but there are ways and means in jail!

A lady from Bendigo once delivered to me a fabulous pavlova and Milly (Helen) Palmer of Harcourt made me a wonderful fiftieth birthday cake, decorated with a facsimile of my chook house.

I often spoke of my chooks and chook house on air. In fact I once broadcast the breakfast show direct from my chook house. It was pretty famous. I also referred to the Old Castlemaine Gaol as the big chook house on the hill. I had almost all of the prison's ninety-four inmates as Listeners. Some were very special, like Phil aka 'Chad', Ray and 'Shiv' (first names only). Chad helped me to compere one of the shows we put on for the prisoners which featured Chad Morgan. Chad (Phil) brought the house down when he announced that the bar would be open later. Joking of course. Chad (Morgan) got a fabulous reception and drew great cheers when he said, 'Can I take you blokes with me to all my jobs.' We were most saddened to hear that Ray died soon after his release. I heard later that he was allegedly murdered by a former fellow inmate. I never heard any more of that.

I still have several items and cards handmade by Ray as gifts to Mazza and me.

When I was hospitalized with serious burns in 1984 my ward was decorated with an amazing one hundred and eighty get well cards, twenty of them from prisoners. The kindness and generosity of our Listeners will always be with me.

It was a Saturday in June; I was in our garage cleaning down an old VW motor I had arranged to sell to a bloke from Bendigo. I had a two litre bucket half filled with petrol and an old paint brush. It's a good way to remove grease and such. I had the garage door wide open but it was dark inside so I slung an electric lead-light over the rafters. As I worked I heard a plunk sound and turning I was confronted with a terrifying wall of flame. The lead-light had fallen and the spark from the bursting light globe set the petrol fumes alight. I got such a shock I jumped backwards and in the process tipped the bucket of petrol down the front of me. In a flash I was on fire. Terrified, I tried to beat out the flames but couldn't. Fortunately Mazza was outside cleaning windows and saw me all aflame. Driven by terror I began to run to try to extinguish the fire but it was hopeless. Mazza bravely chased me down and threw me to the ground, rolling me over and somehow stopping the blaze. She helped me into the bathroom, put me into the bath and run the cold shower over me. She then phoned our neighbor Yvonne Ford, a nurse. Together they stripped the few remaining scorched rags from my body and continued the shower of cold water whilst awaiting an ambulance. My clothes had been burnt from me, including a pair of overalls of which remained only the press studs. I won't describe the details except to say that I suffered horrific third degree burns to my legs, groin, left hand and arm. My prized tackling piece was badly scorched and swollen but thankfully intact. My testicles swelled to the size of baseballs. Mazza and Margaret one of the nurses, had a great fun time fashioning a sling for them. They laughed, happy in their work, but I didn't laugh a lot. I did have a laugh when Bev Ellis played a special request for me – Jerry Lee Lewis's 'Great Balls of Fire'. One thing I did do in my stay in hospital was lose my modesty!

Many weeks later, much of the time in indescribable agony, I was released from hospital, still with very raw wounds, but on the mend. My neighbour, Ian Foster a nurse at the hospital and my old friend Dennis Zepnick, also a nurse, took me home and made me comfortable. I was still in serious pain and daily swallowed bucketsful of codeine tablets. This had earlier caused me to have the worst case of constipation in history, relieved only by nurse Ian, utilizing gloved digital assistance. It was no fun (for either of us). I named Ian 'Goldfinger' after that.

I always try to look at the bright side and I was able to relate a tale to my family and friends about my 'pioneer' penis transplant job; the first ever. It was a great success, I lied, but the problem was that the only compatible donor available was a nineteen-year-old African-American from Alabama. The picture it painted usually drew a laugh.

I returned to my job on breakfast a week after I went home, having the greatest difficulty ascending the stairs but determined to. I was unable to wear trousers, but got into baggy shorts okay.

In September the annual Pere Awards were held at Rafters, a newish restaurant in Bendigo, and I wanted to attend. Mazza arranged for a loan of David Keith's kilt for me to wear and off we went. I was able to stay a couple of hours before discomfort forced us to go home, but it was a memorable night for me.

I am sure I owe my life to Mazza for her quick action. If she hadn't stopped me I would have run till I dropped, in my desperate effort to escape the fire. No wonder I love Mazza.

The broadcast from my chook house was a success and went for four hours! It was not really from the chook house of course, but again the magic of radio and sound-effects records does wonders; 'The Theatre of The Mind'. It all came from our living room. My guests included Bart Ford, my former landlord, a laconic small-time farmer from North Harcourt. With his natural slow drawl he presented as the popular image of the Aussie farmer, a real live Dad from 'Dad and Dave'. He talked of his sheep and apple trees and gave his predictions for the weather – 'When the rain comes from the north-east boy, it lasts for three days.' He called every male 'Boy' and every female 'Girl'. Nobody found it offensive. He was terrific on air and the audience loved him. I also had John Scott the Postmaster, Dick and Shirley Gibbs from Bendigo and Anne and Rob Hadden, local nursery owners. Mazza also played her ancient out of tune piano and we had a sing-along. It was awful but great fun.

Chapter Five

*Some adventures, a fine romance, a mud hut,
demolition derby, didgeridoo,
a tip launch*

Marilyn and I came together through 3CCC. I used to call on her at her business The Entertainment Company of Bendigo; my main focus initially was to get her to sponsor the radio station. After much convincing I eventually signed her up. At the same time I felt a strong attraction to this beautiful thirty-eight-year-old.

I suggested it would be appropriate for her to co-present with me 'The Entertainment Guide' program, 6 o'clock Tuesday evenings, and she accepted. Marilyn, 'Mazza' as she became known, read out the info and I operated the panel and turntables. I had my eye on her but the problem was that she was married with two children.

One June day in 1982, Jeff and Anne Langdon invited the two of us to dinner at their home and as soon as we finished on air we drove to Castlemaine. We had a very pleasant dinner with Jeff, Anne, Joe and Rory. Marilyn and I formed a bond that night and have been together ever since. It was a very rocky road we took to get there but we finally made it.

Soon, Marilyn and I moved into a farmhouse in North Harcourt that we rented from a wonderful old farmer, Bart Ford and his wife Yvonne. They had two young sons, John and Aaron. The family was salt of the earth and we became extremely good friends.

After a time Marilyn and I had decided that 3CCC was to be our life and we bought a six acre block on the edge of Harcourt. We did this with money she had got as her small share of the sale of the matrimonial home. I, of course, had no money. We managed to borrow the money from the Bendigo Building Society to build a mud brick house. It took a heap of hard work as we did much of it ourselves, ably assisted by Marilyn's father, Gordon Boyd, a retired builder. Looking back it seems impossible that we built a house on six acres for under $40,000.

We named it Stonehurst after Mazza's mother's family home on the farm in north-east Victoria where, as a kid, she spent her school holidays. It was our beautiful home and we loved it, and we prepared to stay in Harcourt forever.

Marilyn has always been at my side and she came to love 3CCC almost as much as I did. She contributed hundreds of volunteer hours each year and she would do all sorts of things to get a different angle on a subject. For instance on one occasion she undertook to ride as a passenger in a beat-up old bomb of a car in a demolition derby at Bendigo Showgrounds. Dressed in the compulsory protective gear she hung a tape recorder around her neck and sat in the passenger seat. The car was owned and driven by Harcourt Service Station proprietor, Ray Rice. The object of these mad car races appears to be to do as much damage as possible to the opposition vehicle, forcing them from the track. Crashing into each other at high speed is mandatory.

As the old Valiant crashed and bashed its way around the track, Mazza recorded her graphic impressions of what was happening. She emerged from the badly bent car, obviously grateful to have survived the terrifying experience. Later, we listened to the tape. Unfortunately, the explosive roaring of the engine and the clashes of metal to metal obscured much of the commentary. What remained decipherable contained far too many expletives to ever be put to air!

On another occasion we spoke with the owner of a reopened gold mine at Barry's Reef, near Blackwood. A flamboyant American, the man bore the splendid name of J.P. Morgan, not *the* J P Morgan of course. After a few drinks with JP at the Blackwood pub one night, Mazza accepted his offer of a tour of the mine next day. I went along and, aided by torchlight, we made our way about two hundred metres along a tunnel into a hillside. Near the end of the tunnel we came to the main shaft.

'C'mon let's go. We ride down on that' said JP, indicating a large metal bucket attached to a cable over the shaft. The cable wrapped around a winding drum driven by a rowdy diesel motor.

I was mortified.

'No way, I'm not going down on that. How far is it?'

'Only three hundred and fifty feet, it's quite safe,' drawled JP.

'I'll go', said Mazza. 'You stay here. Give me the recorder.'

I'm no hero and have a morbid fear of heights and of being shut in so I readily hung the recorder around her neck and pushed 'record'. Mazza stepped onto the rim of the bucket with JP.

'Okay. Let her go, pal,' yelled JP to the engine driver.

With that the bucket began its dizzy descent. Mazza shot a quick glance at me.

'Shit!' she cried and disappeared from view.

An hour later she reappeared, covered in mud and dripping with water and sweat. She was so relieved to be back safely, swearing that she'd never do it again. She had experienced an amazing tour through the accessible ancient workings of the long-abandoned Sultan mine where new work was being carried out. Most of it below the level being worked remained flooded, as it was one hundred years before when the mine was forced to close.

A new entrance had been constructed by digging the tunnel into the hillside. In her fear she had completely forgotten that the tape recorder was rolling and the forty five minutes recorded revealed a valuable insight into her experience and reactions. It was seriously hilarious and edits of it went to air on our next show. It was a brave effort and Mazza really should have received an award for it!

She was also the 'anchorman' for a historic live to air from the Central Deborah gold mine in Bendigo in 1987. To our best knowledge it was the first time any such broadcast was attempted. The technical work was done by our new Manager Gerry Pyne, a whiz at such things.

Mazza did all the underground comment and interviews whilst I remained safely on the surface operating the equipment. It was a broadcast that received good publicity and raised awareness of 3CCC to new heights.

Mazza and I did a little country music act where we played the part of hick country singers. I was Frisky T Slim and she was Sassy I Sue and boy, were we hick! With the help of Jack Haynes and Mick Ahearne on backing guitars we recorded several songs in duet. I also played the part of Syrus T. Gildersleeve the Third, their money-grabbing Manager.

We suggested to Jeff Langdon that it would be a good stunt to launch Frisky and Sassy's latest recording, Don Gresham's 'Iddy Biddy Putty Cat' and 'Country Tips', (the latter written by Peter McAndrew and Mazza, with apologies to Kevin Johnson) at the Castlemaine rubbish tip. Jeff thought it a great idea and we proceeded to set it up.

At that time, the tip was the disgusting pile of foul and rotting garbage still common then. I got permission from the CEO of the council and invited MHR Neil O'Keefe, our member of Federal Parliament, to officiate at the launch. O'Keefe, a good bloke with a sense of humour, readily accepted.

On the appointed day we set up the mobile studio, better known by all of us as 'The Truck', for that is what it was, complete with portable generator. We were in the middle of the tip, surrounded by huge mounds of indescribably disgusting and festering heaps and proceeded with the launch ceremony. We were all dressed appropriately in dinner suits and evening gowns. Present were Bev Ellis, Edith 'Calamity' Clegg, Peter McAndrew, Jeff Langdon, Daryl Evans and Neil O'Keefe. Frisky and Sassy were resplendent;

Frisky in dinner suit and bow tie and Sassy in her old wedding dress.

It was all very serious as we went to air, Neil O'Keefe congratulated the couple and Jeff interviewed the recording artists and their Manager, Syrus T. Gildersleeve the Third, who made it known that he had chosen the tip for the launch to 'save on distribution costs'.

When news of the event filtered through to Melbourne, following front page publicity in district newspapers, the huge-circulation Sun News Pictorial asked us to set up a repeat performance for them to cover. We happily agreed and the result was million dollar free publicity – a two page centre spread in what was the biggest circulation daily newspaper in Australia. It was fantastic.

There were some people around the station who frowned on our methods of gaining publicity. It seemed that they regarded such brash commercialism as impure and not fitting for a community station. The fact is that it worked, and worked well.

I never missed an opportunity to gain publicity for the station and was given a pretty free hand by Jeff. The efforts of those we involved resulted in our little community station being one of the best known (and respected) in Australia. We had hundreds of them come and go in my time there. Some lasted for one show, some, like the bearded, blue-singleted Bikie who was scheduled to do a half hour weekly show never started. He was arrested in the car park as he parked his Harley Davidson on his way to the studio and never seen again.

Gerald Harney (not his name) stayed for a few months. He appeared from nowhere, was aged about sixty five and a smooth talker. He was President of the Pensioners' Party and conducted The Pensioners' Hour until one day his distraught wife called in to explain that he could no longer be with us. It was alleged that he had absconded to Queensland, taking all the Party's funds with him. That was the end of The Pensioner's Hour and, incidentally, The Pensioner's Party.

James Lopez, a homeless teenager who was based at the Bendigo Salvation Army hostel, blew in one day on his motorbike and stayed for a couple of months – and I mean stayed! He would hang about the station all day, getting under everyone's feet. He wanted to help but had no idea how to go about most things. I gave him little tasks to do that kept him out of our way for short spells.

He would often sleep the night downstairs in the big meeting room.

One very dark morning I arrived at 5.30 for the breakfast show and as I snapped on the record library light the globe blew, plunging me into blackness. I stumbled around flicking my cigarette lighter to find some records.

In the darkness I had the strangest feeling! I was not alone in this room! My hair actually prickled and I was truly frightened. I had often thought of the possibility of intruders – thieves or even murderers – as I entered the dark and empty building. One of my strongest fears was that I could be seized by some lunatic, forced to broadcast his messages and held as a hostage. Let's face it, it could happen and it would have been easy.

I stood stock still in the darkness. Yes! There was another person in the room! I sensed it rather than heard it. My heart thumped. Suddenly I heard movement. I lit my lighter, fearful of what may confront me. A voice came from a dark corner. 'Oh. Good morning, Ian. I slept here last night, too tired to go home. I hope I didn't frighten you.' It was James!

'Christ. You frightened the shit out of me, you bastard.'

Soon after that, this lonely lad left us. He went without a word and we never saw him again. I wonder what became of him.

So much happened around 3CCC that it's hard to know where to begin and end. Peter McAndrew played a song from The Pogues that contained the 'F' word. Jack Miles took the album and with a three inch nail scratched it so it could never play again. McAndrew was not happy. And Jeff was furious.

There was the working bee we called and two people turned up, Mazza and me and it was a Saturday afternoon when our beloved footy teams Essendon and Collingwood were playing and we missed it. Ah, such sacrifice we made!

How about the time we broadcast a concert by Dire Straits naughtily lifted from TV. We nearly had a hysterical fit when the phone rang and a voice announced that he was X from the Broadcasting Tribunal. It turned out to be no less than station supporter John Brumby, the future Premier of Victoria.

Daryl O'Brien and Alan Clarke conducted the Vet Show (Alan was the vet and Daryl, Shire Ranger) and it was very popular. They regularly argued on air about the virtues of each other's preference in music and it was good fun.

All sorts of people dropped into 3CCC, nothing really surprised me. We once had a visit from two Aborigines, Trevor and his wife Una. The man's aboriginal name was Na Gun which he explained meant buried beside a spring in dreamtime. Mazza and I were fascinated by them and together they went to air with us on The Fabulous Fifties show and played the didgeridoo and guitar superbly. Not exactly 1950's music but extraordinary for sure. We never saw them again.

Triple C always had several Christian broadcasters who fitted in well with the rest of us. Colin Coles was a minister in the Uniting Church and he had a great sense of humour, always with a happy yarn to spin to his listeners. He was a big fan of the Fabulous Fifties show which ran immediately before his light-hearted program. Colin was close to retiring age, which he did before my time at Triple C ended. Rev. Phil Salvin, a man of about sixty-five, from the Anglican Church was another with much fun and good humour within. He once was co-compere with me of a concert for inmates of the Castlemaine Gaol (always spelt in the old English way, not 'jail'). Phil had a small farm out of town and had a bright red ute to carry hay to his stock. It was the tiniest ute in existence, a Daihatsu or similar. One bale of hay would be its capacity, but Phil loved scampering around in it. Not the sort of vehicle most vicars would drive! Rev. Ron Wood was another from the Anglican Church, a softly spoken and warm-hearted man, about forty five years old, a far more serious character than the others.

I once called Barry Hansen, a well known presenter at TV8 for some reason or other. Ashley Buckle answered and I heard him call 'Hey Barry, Ian Braybrook wants to talk to you. Are you in or out to lunch?' Ashley came back, 'Sorry, Barry is out to lunch.' You don't forget those things and it's a reminder to cover the mouthpiece properly.

To the disappointment of some, 3CCC generated little controversy in those first years. Its most publicised detrimental activities came from administrative blunders in my latter time there. Perhaps the most interesting reactions both within the station and outside came from the introduction of The Faggots and Dykes Show, presented by members of the gay community. I didn't share the bitter opposition of some of our people, notably Jack Miles. My objection to the show was the poor taste, very coarse language and schoolboy smut of the initial presenter who called himself Ian. It was not his real name and I won't reveal it here. I was not too keen on him as an individual, I saw him as a disgusting, dirty minded person, and I'm no prude! A sponsor, a big time builder from Bendigo, approached me at my Hot Dog Harry stall at the Harcourt Market and told me he had heard the Faggots and Dykes Show when driving home from Melbourne. He expressed his disgust at the poor taste of the presenter and cancelled his sponsorship on the spot. But that's the way it was back then. There was much fear abroad of HIV being spread by homosexuals, so much so that Jack Myles took to drinking coffee from disposable paper cups. It didn't bother anyone else that I am aware of, but that was typical of Jack. At the time the Faggots and Dykes Show ran a station fundraising disco at the hall at tiny Franklinford. Gerry Pyne attended as a guest but decided to stay outside the hall. The disco raised a disappointing $102.

I am proud of the fact that every one of the over twelve hundred breakfast shows I did was unpaid, although some volunteers were sure that I got paid for it. To give me time for all the myriad of jobs I had to do, I had Friday off from breakfast and for a time 'Ian' conducted the show.

We had established a regular music format for breakfast to ensure continuity. The first hour was country music. Consistency is vital for listener retention as anyone with any knowledge of radio knows.

'Ian' was apparently not a team player and chose to ignore the station policy. One early morning at 6.15 I was mortified to hear disco music. I went to the phone, 'Where's the country music?' I snapped.

'There is none this morning, Ian,' he replied in a most condescending tone.

'We have a music policy and if you can't adhere to it you can f... off as far as I am concerned.'

He hung up in my ear. I was furious.

'Ian' reported the incident to Gerry Pyne, by now having replaced Jeff Langdon as Manager. Gerry discussed it with me and suggested that I talk with 'Ian' and sort it out. Gerry agreed on the policy issue and said he would contact him to put him on the right tram.

The next day, Saturday, 'Ian' was part of a crew doing a live broadcast from the street in Kyneton, so I drove there to see him where I sought him out and apologized. We parted amicably – my apology accepted and I felt we had a good understanding of each other and the format. The matter was closed.

I was shocked to read in the minutes of the next Board meeting a strong censure of me for my action, based on a letter of complaint lodged by 'Ian'. I felt betrayed as I believed we had an understanding. It was also unknown for complaints about one volunteer against another to go to Board level. It was a Managerial matter.

I must mention that I had been appointed Volunteers' Coordinator a few months before. It was really only a title and I never took it seriously. I was found guilty of 'unbecoming conduct' for one in that exalted position and issued with a strong reprimand.

I presumed that Gerry had put forward the fact that 'Ian' and I had settled the matter amicably ten days before and I failed to see the necessity for the Board to be involved at all. I was quite annoyed and angry about this, but I kept my mouth shut. I'd been put on trial in my absence, without notification or opportunity to speak in my defence.

As it turned out it became par for the course in the Board's future dealings with me. I had enemies, but as yet didn't recognize it.

Chapter Six

Calamity Clegg, a close shave, a Mayor, a Manager and a policeman

Apart from the response and reaction to The Faggots and Dykes Show, the most controversy generated by on-air activities involved Jeff Langdon when he was Manager. He had an acid tongue and wasn't afraid to use it if he felt it desirable or necessary. On one occasion he heaped scathing criticism on a very prominent local family allegedly involved in what was termed 'bottom of the harbor deals', a famed and scandalous taxation minimization scheme. As a result we were threatened with potentially bankrupting legal action. This caused quite a flurry and deep concern especially with our legal eagle, Kerry McDonald. Jeff was a little sheepish about it all, especially as he was supposed to set the standard for the rest of us. Fortunately, the litigation never eventuated.

Community Radio is all about 'real' people, that's the basis of its existence. 3CCC had hundreds of them come and go and my contact with them changed my attitudes and outlook considerably. The surprising thing is that such a diversity of people got on so well and had few disagreements. Phillip Edmunds, our Writer in Residence, called it 'Unity in Diversity'. Phil had been employed for a year under a grant scheme that Jeff Langdon ferreted out of somewhere.

Sam Grumont, husband of Pat and father of Danielle and Zachary, was a teacher and a mate of Jeff. Sam presented a modern type jazz show once a week. He was the biggest Miles Franklin fan I ever came across. I had never heard of Miles Franklin pre-Sam. It was just one of a thousand things that 3CCC taught me.

Sam was also the Mayor of Castlemaine for a time and it was during this period that he was helping Jeff to paint the interior of his house. Jeff told me the following story.

One night, many glasses of red into the project, the pair decided that they needed another ladder and Sam suggested that he borrow one from the school where he worked. At 1am they had jumped the fence and were struggling with the borrowed ladder across the school yard when a loud voice called. 'Halt. Stop or I'll shoot!'

It was the security guard and it was obvious to him that he had surprised thieves at work.

Ignoring their drunken protestations, the guard held the two at gunpoint as he rang the police. The constabulary soon arrived, placed the prisoners in their van and whisked them off to the police station. The police Sergeant was called in from home to conduct the interview and, being woken at this hour, was in a foul mood. He turned a deaf ear to Sam's garbled story and commenced to type the charge sheet in readiness for the thieves' statements.

Jeff, typically smart-arsed when half pissed said jokingly, 'I can see the headlines now. Mayor and Radio Station Manager charged with theft and fined eight dollars for pinching a ladder.'

He giggled and Sam grinned agreement.

The unhappy Sergeant did not look up from his typewriter. 'The charge will be burglary and the penalty is up to ten years.' That settled the two lads down a bit.

Eventually the school cleaner was woken and called in and reluctantly confirmed Sam's yarn that he had permission to borrow a ladder.

The Sergeant, as reluctant as the cleaner and in no hurry, finally released the two villains.

I have already spoken of my admiration for Jeff Langdon. He was and is a very talented and intelligent person. We remain good friends. The son of an onion/dairy farmer from the Colac district of Western Victoria he excelled at school and earned a scholarship to the prestigious Ballarat Grammar. He went on to Melbourne University where he studied science, gaining a Masters Degree in Physics, culminating in a PhD in Geophysics. Jeff could have gone on to an academic career as he was offered jobs by the University of New England and a college in the U.S.A. Instead he moved to Castlemaine to work out a bond as a teacher. From there he was appointed the Director of the new Education Centre in Mostyn Street and that is where I met him.

Jeff Langdon was a man of action. 'Forget the theories, it wastes time. Get in and do it and achievements will follow.'

Running a community radio station is a very difficult and different job. You are dealing with all sorts of people with all sorts of ideas. Always waiting in the background are those who believe they can do it much better. Big egos abound.

Jeff always felt the biggest problem for small-town community radio was the lack of people. He hoped to eventually achieve an audience of ten percent – maybe even fifteen! We never did quite that but we did pretty well. I reckon we had five percent at one stage, but it's a guess. My view is that gaining five percent is a significant achievement. I believe that WMAfm Castlemaine, that I was to manage later, peaked at that in 2012. Not huge, but I figure a cumulative audience of three hundred and fifty to four hundred was about as good as it could be. It most likely declined after that.

When Jeff finally left 3CCC, we presented him with a caricature done by local artist Stuart Billington and a set of scales engraved 'Goodbye Jeff and thanks for keeping the balance.' Jeff actually wept. He looked at me and patted me on the shoulder, tears in his eyes. 'It's been a great five years, Thanks.'

Country music was always a big part of 3CCC and provided us with some unforgettable characters; chief among them was 'Calamity' Clegg.

Her real name was Edith, Edie to most and nicknamed Calamity by me for her disastrous performances on air. This approaching-seventy-year old retired Chief Nursing Sister made every mistake in the book and added a few new ones to boot!

Edie closed her microphone when it should have been open and opened it when it should have been closed. She mis-cued her vinyl records (pre-CD era). Played them at the wrong speed, started tapes at the end instead of the beginning, stumbled and stuttered through her words. Sometimes she completely lost her way and often cried out loud in despair. She pushed wrong buttons and it was not unusual for her to have two things going to air at once. Sometimes the level of her music was so low it was inaudible. She carried on phone conversations with the microphone open and chatted happily over the music with 'live' visitors to the studio.

Edith was indeed a real calamity; a true-to-life radio disaster that drove Manager Jeff crazy but her listeners absolutely adored her! Many of them believed her bumbling was all part of her act – that nobody could be that bad – but our Calamity was as bad as she sounded. I loved her too and frequently ran to her rescue on air.

Calamity knew almost every country singer in Australia. She visited them in their homes and when they toured through had them stay at her home in Bendigo. She attended Country Music Festivals and events far and wide across Australia, always armed with her trusty (and misused) portable recorder. Sometimes she even managed to actually capture an interview, which I had to spend hours editing. Her visits to the Annual Tamworth Country Music Awards each year was such an adventure for her; a chance to catch up with all her 'idols'. She would come home with a swag of recordings by all these unknown artists – some good and some very bad!

She despised modern Country Music, especially American which she refused to play. 'Australian or nothing' was her motto.

She had the distinction of having a song written and recorded about her. Don Gresham was the man, the song, 'Calamity Clegg from 3CCC'. It got a lot of air play at 3CCC but, precious little anywhere else!

Calamity happily banged, clattered and bumbled her way through about seven years of radio before finally retiring in 1989, having developed a strong dislike for the new guard at 3CCC. She then astonished us all by marrying her first love, a retired horse trainer, Colin Sprague, and moving to live at Port Fairy. Marilyn and I visited a dying Calamity in hospital just before the end. It was dreadfully sad. She is gone now and with her went one of Australian Country Music's most loved women. Vale Calamity Clegg!

Country music was very popular in the bush and by 1984 we had about fourteen hours a week of it on air. It brought us many loyal listeners and some good presenters. People like Estelle (real name Edith) Bunn who came to us first as a panel operator for Fred Paynting. Fred was totally blind and loved his Country Music. A bloke called Fred Floyd, a popular Bendigo Country Music identity, took over Estelle's role as panel operator when she later had to give up the job and he did it for a number of years.

Let's describe Estelle as mature-aged and she continued presenting CM on KLFM aged well into her seventies. She was meticulous in her preparation and presentation. There was none of this wandering in with an armful of recordings to do a show! Estelle spent more hours preparing her program than she actually spent on air. It was quite amazing and a credit to her. When people rang her on air for a request she always declined, often quite snappily. Her program was already full. She only took requests on notice for inclusion in subsequent weeks.

Estelle Bunn was a no-nonsense person who would quickly tell anyone where to get off, be it our Manager or a Listener. Estelle passed away in April 2015 aged ninety.

Eddie Ford was a staunch CM fan who presented a weekly program. He was the publisher of a motor magazine and had a remarkable collection of 1950's American cars. Fabulously preserved or restored he kept them in his private museum at Newstead, sixteen kilometres out of Castlemaine. They are either there or crammed into farm sheds and include a pink Cadillac once owned by the legendary Johnny O'Keefe. Marilyn and I once took Slim Dusty, his wife Joy, sister-in-law Heather and daughter Anne to see Eddie's collection. They were most impressed and Slim even indicated that it may be a good last resting place for his 'Old Purple' Ford sedan that carried him for so many thousands of kilometers. It didn't come to pass unfortunately.

Eddie was a man of few words who played three songs back to back, mostly American. He would briefly announce the titles and artists and play some more.

'Good stuff!' One could hear the cries of the audience who often tire of the lengthy outpourings of knowledge and description from presenter-buffs on Community Radio.

Fred Paynting was totally blind and a bit of an ocker, which showed in his style. He would typically begin his show with. 'G'day, this is Fred Paynting with a country music show and I hope youse are gonna enjoy it.'

How does a blind man know when the microphone 'open' light glows and it's time to speak or shut up? His panel Operator, Estelle Bunn (later Fred Floyd) had a unique way with Fred. She would reach across the panel with his walking stick and jab him in the ribs. This was his cue to speak or shut up.

'I often felt like belting him over the head with it.' Estelle once confided

Fred had a beautiful Seeing Eye Labrador dog named Paul. Paul would diligently lead Fred from his car to the station, along the train station platform at 3CCC at Harcourt, to the entrance door, up the stairs and into the studio. We used to watch admiringly at first but soon got used to it. Sometimes Paul would get a little confused and make a small mistake. When he did Fred used to go nuts at him and flog him with his leather lead. We hated to see this and were unhappy when it occurred. We knew better than to interfere with a Guide Dog's duties and stayed quiet.

'I wish the dog would bite the bastard', muttered John Scarborough after witnessing one such incident.

'Or lead him over a cliff', added Bev Stewart.

We didn't have to wait long for Bev's wish to come true. Paul did lead Fred over a cliff, albeit a small one. Jack Miles had repositioned a safety sign which directed visitors away from the platform area to an entrance on the other side of the railway building. Fred's usual path down the platform was blocked by the sign so Paul dutifully led his master around it, staying close to the usual route. Unfortunately there was space for the dog between the sign and the platform edge, but not for Fred. He went flying over the edge, collapsing in a heap among the stones and rail tracks a meter below. Looking from a window Marilyn saw this event, called us in the offices and we all ran to help, expecting blood and broken bones at least.

It was a long and nasty fall. Luckily Fred was bruised but not badly injured and was able to continue to the studio to present his show.

Back inside we quietly applauded Paul the dog, and Jack Miles, for relocating the sign. Justice had been served!

The platform could tell a lot of stories. One Christmas, the Kyneton crew of David Sprigg and Ross Oliver organised a Christmas party on the platform. They lined up two rows of trestle tables, making it pretty crowded with the one nearest the platform about a metre from the edge. Before we began we checked with V Line to ensure that no trains were due to pass. We got the all clear, and the party began. To our horror, about thirty minutes in, a train came hurtling down the track on our side of the line. They went through Harcourt at 120 kilometres per hour, the fastest stretch on the line. Good God! Somebody had given the wrong information. The terror stricken people seated on the platform side were trapped on the edge. Most of them stood up and held onto whatever they could as the rest of us watched in terror, expecting the worst. Somehow nobody was hit or fell and the party resumed, albeit a little subdued. It was very close to a dreadful disaster.

Here's one of those lovely true stories. We espied a little mongrel dog wandering down the track without a care in the world, when a steam powered locomotive came trundling into sight. Seeing the little dog the driver slowed to dog pace and followed the little feller until we were able to coax him from the tracks. The driver gave a big grin and a wave and opened the throttle for Bendigo.

This is a fair dinkum story too, in fact all the stories I relate are true. For example George, had presented two heavy rock shows then rang me one morning to say, 'Sorry mate I can't do any more shows. I'm in jail!'

Chapter Seven

An important departure, late news, personalities need not apply, hard selling, Jack Miles and me

We relayed a breakfast news service off-air from 3RRR in Melbourne and it was never on time – always late – and it annoyed the crap out of me. I quite often had up to four minutes of lead-in music as I waited for the cross. The crew at TripleR had no consideration for us as the duo of presenters prattled on with their usual garbage. Fair enough I suppose, it was their news service, but it was discourteous at least.

One time, Kevin Daw was doing breakfast for me as I took a week's break. As he waited impatiently for a cue to cross for the 7.30 news, the phone rang. He was in a flap and left the microphone open. His big booming voice came loud and clear over the music.

'Ring me in a minute mate. These Triple R bastards are giving me the runaround – always late – they give me the shits!'

In May 1987, Jeff called Marilyn, Bev Stewart and me into his office, asking us to sit down. I felt that something was brewing but was not prepared for what came next.

'There's something I want to tell you before I announce it', he said. 'I've taken a job as Manager of a Health Centre. I finish here in a month.'

He may as well have dropped a bomb on us! We were shocked.

'F...!' I groaned.

'Shit', said Bev.

'Oh no', said Marilyn.

We stood in silent disbelief. We had never imagined that Jeff would leave us.

It was a dark, gloomy day as we struggled to come to terms with a 3CCC without Jeff.

'I'm getting right out', he said. 'I won't even join the Board for twelve months – assuming I can get elected.' He grinned.

'I want to give the new manager, whoever it is, a clear go without Jeff Langdon looking over their shoulder.'

I was appalled. I couldn't imagine 3CCC without Jeff – but the die was cast.

It was not only the end of an era; it was a signal of the beginning of the end for me. Soon he was gone and he took another important friend with him.

Jeff's replacement was Gerry Pyne, a likeable young bloke, married to Margaret and a father. He was a Telstra technician who also had a good knowledge of new-fangled computers that some saw as a vital future tool for radio. Correct as it turned out, who can imagine a radio station computer-free today?

There came about a debate by the board of a request from my old adversary Neil 'Ian' Cowan, that a volunteer's time on air be restricted to 6 hours a week, aimed at me of course. To my surprise the board rejected the idea. I had been convinced it was a set up to cut me down. The Board ruled that, although the idea had appeal, it was dangerous to adopt such policy. What if a temporary fill-in was needed over a week-long period or similar?

Thus this attempt to downgrade my presence failed. By now I knew that KD's prediction was right and that some person or persons were out to lower my profile and reduce my influence. They needed a rule or policy to justify the move.

I loved doing breakfast. I had dreamed of it since I was a seven year old living in the wild bush country around Blackwood, where my father bought our first wireless set. Sure, there were times when sacrifices had to be made. For example, I couldn't sit up at night with Marilyn watching TV as I had to go early to bed to rise at 4.30am. But I had always been an early riser, like milking cows at daylight or 7am starts in the shearing sheds. It's the best time of the day for sure. I often likened it to opening a brand new jar of Vegemite, where nobody had had the chance to dive a buttery knife into it. And the friends I made! Hundreds of my Listeners became my radio friends, sending me letters and small gifts. I had ninety-four in the old jail for a start. I received no pay but it was the most enjoyable time of my life.

I had difficulty grasping this possibility. I am not a conceited person as any who know me will attest, but I was aware that I had a good audience, was popular with listeners and generally respected. I was competent and reliable – devoted to the station and its success. Why would people want me out?

As it turned out it was my high profile that did me harm. There was considerable resentment in some, particularly because of my popularity and what they saw as my publicity seeking. I plead guilty to the latter but always for the station, not personal.

But as Board member Phillip Edmunds once stated, aimed at me. 'Triple C does not need personalities.'

I thought that to be a revealing and amazing statement coming from a radio station executive!

I felt under serious pressure and it was affecting my on-air work. I was tired, nervous and unsure of myself but I don't think our listeners noticed. I found it difficult to sleep and I had constant headaches. My Doctor told me I was suffering from stress and tension.

'I'm surprised, Ian. I thought it was pretty relaxed at 3CCC.'

I told him the truth.

Marilyn was also tense and unhappy, totally unlike her. She developed lumps in a breast and was sent to hospital for their surgical removal and biopsy. Thankfully, it was all clear.

Her surgeon said, 'Tension and worry can sometimes seem to bring these things on.'

Within a week of Jeff's departure, Bev Stewart announced that she too was leaving. Jeff had offered her a job as his secretary and she had accepted. It was a great shock to me and totally unexpected. We had been a small close-knit staff who worked happily together, understanding each other very well. It was a sad occasion.

Nicki Bright, another personable and competent young woman took Bev's place and we got on very well, but 3CCC was not the same.

Within a year Bev Ellis had also gone. Her replacement, John Scarborough, became a good friend. John arrived full of enthusiasm and youth and got stuck into the job. He did well but found it difficult to sell our product. He also felt that he did not get proper support from the senior management. I helped wherever I could and we were good friends. He trusted me. At the time community radio could not broadcast commercials. All that was permitted was a bland forty word announcement which offered the Listener no inducements or incentives to buy. We could simply give a 'concise and general description' of the business. This amounted to the business name, what they did or sold and their address and phone number. Nothing more. I knew all about that as I was the original sales rep. It was bloody hard! To a large extent we had to rely on the goodwill of business people and a small number were enthusiastic supporters. Most business people however wanted a bit more bang for their buck and it was hard to convince them of the worth of what we had to offer. Who could blame them? But what we offered was very cheap and we did reach a good number of Listeners; perhaps between five hundred and five thousand, depending on the program appeal and time of day. We charged just $2 an announcement on a three month contract, usually no more than $10 a week. On 25% commission it was pretty hard for a sales rep to make a living! So, after six months of trying hard, John quit, unhappy and disillusioned, he also did not get along with the manager of the time.

I was sorry to see him go, especially when I met the replacement the board selected. He was a big-noting smart arse, who will be unnamed. He bragged of what he would do and to my annoyance heaped scorn on his predecessor, John. Fortunately, he didn't last long, finding the going too tough even for one with his majestic talents.

Justin Shortal had recently departed, called back to school, so, apart from Jack Miles, I was the last Langdon era person left standing.

Things were changing at 3CCC but a lot of water went under the bridge before the end.

* * *

Roy Tyrell was a professional stand-up comedian and a friend who used to drop in whenever he passed through. One time he accepted our invitation to come from his home in Melbourne to compere our inaugural in-house awards night – The Pere Awards. They were a tongue in cheek affair – a send up of the prestigious, formal and stuffy annual National Pater Awards backslap.

In 1985, Justin Shortal and Marilyn prepared an entry for me in the Pater Awards and to my delight and astonishment I was selected as one of five finalists in the Country Radio Personality section.

Jeff, Mazza, Bev Ellis and I attended this glittering night of nights in the then magnificent Southern Cross Hotel Ballroom. We camped at the cheapest hotel that we could find, somewhere upstairs at the back of a dingy building in Spencer Street.

As we entered the ballroom we were met by a lovely lady who congratulated me on making the top five finishing with, 'but it's a shame you didn't win.' It sort of took the gloss off the rest of the night for me.

The Ballroom was packed solid with bursting egos, wives and girlfriends – a sort of Logies night for radio. Anybody who was anybody was there and I met a number of radio names that I had long respected – notably Eric Pearce and John Laws. Both were perfect gentlemen who treated Marilyn and me as equals.

Not so gentlemanly were a couple of others. Michael Carlton gave a speech for some reason dotted with uncalled for coarse language, possibly it was acceptable in his regular circles but it shocked us people from the bush.

John Laws gave him and his ilk a generous serve when he graciously accepted an award – a real put down, skillfully aimed, but not obviously connected to the villain, but we all knew who he referred to.

When Derryn Hinch got up and spoke about his Porsche being damaged by vandals, it became too much for the alcohol influenced Jeff and he hurled loud abuse at Hinch. Fortunately, Hinch didn't appear to hear it. We three fellow travelers cowered with embarrassment and felt like sliding under the table that we shared with the Punter to Punter team from 3RRR. The next day on their excellent Punter to Punter program they gave Jeff a very public but humorous spanking – much to the chagrin of the good Jeffrey.

Our 3CCC Pere Awards were much more fun and we packed the dining room at the Harcourt Motel for the first ever event.

Marilyn and Bev Stewart spent countless hours of their spare time making up trophies from scraps of timber gathered from the Castlemaine Technical College carpentry school room. They glued the odd shapes together and painted them gold – over one hundred and fifty of them on the first occasion – one for each guest, with some guests being multi-award winners!

We had a great night with Roy Tyrell as compere. He added a bit of real class to the event. It was broadcast live to air and, as usual, the difficult audio and technical work was done by Daryl Evans – he was a wiz at that – frustratingly slow and late at times, but nevertheless a wiz!

The place was packed with people having a good time. Mazza and I even did our Frisky Slim and Sassy Sue act – Country Music at its worst – to considerable applause. I suspect that we are both attention seeking hams.

Roy Tyrell had spent years on the road and could tell some great stories; like the one about Dave Peekin, (not his real name) an egotistical Country Music singer who thought he was God's gift.

Always out to make a grand entrance he stopped the bus the entertainers travelled in as they approached outback Tamworth in late afternoon. He'd spotted a sign post that read 'Tamworth 1.2 Km'.

'I'll jog the rest of the way,' he announced, donning his green silk shorts, white singlet and runners, confident that his arrival in Tamworth would be well publicized and appreciated. He didn't know that some local joker had inserted a decimal point in what was originally 'Tamworth 12 Km'.

The road is very quiet out that way with very little traffic to hitch a ride with. To the delight of the troupe a sweating, exhausted Dave, having jogged all the way, staggered onto the hall stage at 8pm just in time to perform.

Roy related to Mazza and I the story of an after-show barbeque put on in a country town by another very well known Country Music star. On stage at the end of the show he invited anyone interested to attend a barbeque at the EZ Motel. We'll call him Charlie Merton, and he was partial to large quantities of grog.

The next morning Roy went into Charlie's motel room to be confronted by a horrible sight. The bathroom was awash with blood. It was everywhere and in the washbasin floated a long-dead Yellow Perch.

At first Roy thought a murder had taken place but it turned out that a drunken Charlie had wanted some fresh meat for the barbie and a local bloke went out the road, siezed and trussed a sheep and took it back to the room. Here they cut its throat in the shower and butchered it for chops.

The unit was a disgusting mess and after cleaning the room to the best of their ability the entertainers slid quietly out of town.

Charlie was a regular pisspot, always half drunk. He once bought himself a lovely new Ford Falcon sedan on a visit to the city, bright red with all the extras. He proudly drove it to a club, got drunk and took a taxi to his motel. He was either sensible enough not to drive or, more likely, forgot that he had bought the car. Next day he could not remember where he had been or where he left the car.

In spite of a concerted search effort by his pals and the police, Charlie never saw the car again.

Roy's brother, Norm, was the bass player and road manager for a popular show. Following an after show booze-up the troupe was being driven in their small bus back to the motel. Norm was leaning against the door, clutching an opened bottle of champagne. Nobody noticed as the door flew open and Norm disappeared backwards into the night. Fortunately they were traveling at a snail's pace.

Half an hour later Norm arrived at the motel, bloody and bruised, but relatively unscathed, still clutching his bottle of champagne!

We had heaps of visitors to 3CCC – some I recall quite clearly. Ted Egan A.M. for instance. One day he was passing through the district when he decided to drop into this radio station he had heard so much about, spouse Nerys Evans was with him as always. The two stayed for a couple of hours chatting with Mazza and me over coffee in our kitchen. Ted is a fair dinkum Aussie, who has done much work for indigenous people in the Northern Territory, his adopted home. Ted was born in Melbourne and raised in suburban Coburg. In 1932 he left home, age fifteen, and went to the Territory in search of work. He stayed. The people grew to love Ted and thought so much of him that the federal government made him the Administrator of the entire territory, a position he held from 2003 until 2007. Along the way Ted recorded about forty music albums, accompanied by nothing more than a Victoria Bitter carton which he thumped with his hands as accompaniment. Good people Ted and Nerys.

There once was an itinerant recorder player who wanted to do a live broadcast. He played two recorders at once – one up each nostril! Disgusting, but he could really play quite well. I put him to air but not sure if our description of his playing method went down too well.

A young Country singer named Colin Thompson called in to see me one day looking for help in promoting his show. I was pleased to help and taped an interview with him which I put to air next day on Calamity Clegg's Country Music program. Col gave us several of his recordings to give away and we gave him lots of free promotion.

I thought the lad was a bit ambitious as he had booked and paid for the five hundred seat Golden Twin Cinema in Bendigo, expecting or hoping to pack the place with a one night concert performance. Slim Dusty and John Williamson filled the theatre with ease but I was not so sure about Colin Thompson who was quite unknown in our region.

After two weeks of solid promotion a sad and disillusioned Col called on me again. He'd had to cancel the show. There had been only eight bookings – four of them from our giveaways.

Col went back home to Gippsland, but I am happy to say that he has since achieved considerable success. He was a most likeable young man.

John Cain was the recently elected Labor Premier of Victoria and he accepted Jeff's invitation to attend the Official Opening of 3CCC in July 1982. It was a big event with many speeches, live music and a general good time, all broadcast direct to air. I landed the job of speaking with the Premier. It was the occasion of my first big-name interview, but John Cain was a lovely bloke, putting me at ease, and I had no trouble at all. I soon learnt that the bigger they are the better to interview. Some time after this Neil O'Keefe, our local MHR, arranged for me to interview the Prime Minister, Bob Hawke on a visit to Castlemaine. It was a breeze. The P.M. was friendly, smiling and helpful and it was a real scoop for 3CCC. I got a few slaps on the back and was very pleased with myself.

Marilyn had purchased a Red Flowering Gum tree for the Premier to plant to commemorate his visit and the opening of the station. With due ceremony the Premier planted the sixty centimeter sapling on the west side of the building in a prominent spot.

We named it The John Cain Tree and it grew and flourished, soon three meters tall, much to the pleasure of Mazza, until one day a big wind came and blew it out of the ground.

We sadly cut up the remains and Jeff kept a metre long piece of the trunk which he labeled 'The John Cain Tree' and displayed in his office. This happened in the summer of '84.

In the Spring, I was mowing the grass when I noticed new shoots appearing on the site of the departed tree. Sure enough! The John Cain Tree was re-sprouting. A piece of root had remained in the earth and it had begun to grow.

The John Cain Tree again leapt skyward and flourished in spite of lack of care and several attempts by various drivers to flatten it with The Truck.

It may still exist but if it does remain today nobody would know of its significance as the promised brass plaque didn't eventuate.

Some years later, when he was under serious pressure to quit, I related this story to John Cain.

He laughed. 'Perhaps there's a message in the story of The John Cain Tree.' He resigned as Premier shortly after.

In 1992 I wrote: 'People came and went at 3CCC but it is my hope that The John Cain Tree will always remain. Perhaps it will outlive the station itself.' It did.

Chapter Eight

3CCC people, Uncle Doug, Three McGowan boys, little kids, embarrassments, Confests and OBs

We had a lot of fun at 3CCC. Of course there were many serious times, but overall it was fun. For me, life was great; I had the love of a beautiful woman, we were building a new home together and I was doing a job I absolutely loved. What could be better?

Eighteen-year-olds Tim Borchers and Gavin McDougall started their duo show at 4.30 in the afternoon and were notorious latecomers, usually bounding up the stairs at the last minute. More than once I had to put their first record to air as they screeched to a halt in the car park.

One such day I locked the entrance door and Justin Shortal and I took over their show. As Tim and Gav hammered at the door Justin adopted the role of Gav and I became Tim. For ten minutes we prattled on while a frustrated pair listened to the monitor downstairs at the back door. We sent the boys up mercilessly until somebody unlocked the door for them. They took it in good humour but continued to arrive late.

We decided to try to revive the 'Fifty and Over' radio show which ran on 3UZ back in the 1950s. I contacted Kevin O'Gorman ex-3KZ. He was unsure who compered the show but thought maybe John McMahon. Mazza rang Bert Newton who gave her McMahon's number. He was delighted and thought it a great idea; however he said it was Doug Elliot who had been compere. There was no bigger name in radio and TV than Doug Elliot, Uncle Doug, as everyone called him. John told me that Doug was ill with cancer and lived at Murrabit in northern Victoria.

I wrote to him c/o Murrabit Post Office and in due course he rang me. He was quite keen to do it and I arranged to meet him. As it turned out he was by then staying with his daughter Wendy at Walmer just up the road from Harcourt. I met him, his wife and nineteen year old grandson there on Saturday 6 May 1988 and conducted a long interview with him; probably the last interview ever. Sadly he died before we could get the first episode of Fifty and Over off the ground. How I wish I had kept that interview where we discussed the golden days of radio.

I had been on air regularly for five years and feeling pretty pleased with myself when an aging gentleman visited. It was Sunday afternoon and Jack Miles was on air. The gent made it clear that he wanted to meet Jack.

'Who are you?' he grunted over his spectacles. Expecting recognition I replied, 'I'm Ian Braybrook.'

'Do you do a program?

'Yes, I do a couple,' I said.

'Huh!' He grunted. 'I've never heard of you. Where can I find Jack?' Now that brought me down to earth!

Jack was a popular figure, not only around the station but with listeners, especially of the older variety. Always a gentleman, his devotion and commitment to 3CCC was unsurpassed and only once in many years did he miss a show – on 16 December 1986. He suffered from severe migraine headaches and often went on air in serious discomfort. On that day however he had to surrender and rang me to fill in for him, which I gladly did.

Jack was the ultra-conservative right winger and often the typical grumpy old man but we all loved him. He epitomized the dedicated volunteer that established 3CCC.

Jack eventually sold his home at Welshman's Reef and moved to a coastal town in NSW. In 2007, with great sorrow I heard of his death there. When told, Jeff Langdon wrote a touching memorial letter to the Castlemaine Mail, which was published.

The Sunday afternoon program with Jack, Vic McGowan and Calamity Clegg and later Paul Mason and Tony Bell, was one of our most listened to periods. Old fashioned people presented old fashioned music and Sunday 'arvo' developed a large following.

Vic McGowan was in his late sixties when he started with us having recently retired from his profession as engineer and moving to Glenlyon. His son Keith was well known for his work on Metro radio but Vic did not see much of him, so he told me. Vic and his wife Bib became great supporters.

It all began for Vic when he bought tickets in a raffle we ran and he won! He came to collect his prize, a donated oil painting, and stayed for about ten years.

Vic was a third generation radio announcer – but in reverse. His son Keith, a legendary overnight announcer at 3AW and Keith's son were professional radio announcers. Vic was the last of the boys to start – and he did it well. In 1989 we almost gave up on him. His health deteriorated until he could no longer make it up the stairs to do his show. His doctor ordered open heart surgery to replace damaged heart valves.

In those times, it was an operation still largely being pioneered and we had serious misgivings about Vic's survival chances. We need not have worried. In less than a month he returned, climbed the stairs with ease and went on as if he had never been absent. Dogged by other serious health problems Vic battled on for another three years before retiring from radio and lived on at Glenlyon for over a decade more. His son Keith passed on in early 2014 and 3AW lost one of their pillars.

'Vet Talk' with local veterinarian Alan Clark and co-host Daryl O'Brien was a popular weekly program. Alan, with his soft voice and sophisticated taste in music contrasted sharply with Daryl's ocker, gravelly voice and preference for Lesley Uggams and Mitch Miller and they provided good fun for listeners. They frequently 'clashed' over the music selection and heaped scorn on each other. Nevertheless it was an interesting program where Alan provided information and solutions to a myriad of problems with all sorts of animals. Daryl was one of the originals with 3CCC and I believe is still presenting on radio in Bendigo.

We all have embarrassing times on air – one of my worst was when I played a Pete Best's Beatles song called 'Shooting Rabbits'. I'd never heard it but the rural Aussie title appealed to me.

It was 8.20am, peak time. Suddenly the band stopped the music and a loud voice bellowed 'F... the rabbits!'

I was dumbstruck! Our listeners were mostly conservative country people and I expected the phone to start ringing. Nothing happened, so I guess the listeners, like me, couldn't believe what they had heard!

Another time I was reading something or other and couldn't quite focus.

'Hang on a minute while I adjust my testicles,' I said. I couldn't believe I'd said that and have no idea how it slipped out. One of the first rules in radio is 'Do not draw attention to mistakes or f... ups.' I didn't. Nobody complained.

Kids often provide a laugh. One day Mazza and I were presenting 'The Fabulous Fifties' when Bev Ellis ushered in a group of visitors from the Dunolly Primary School. As usual we spoke to the kids on air. Marilyn asked one bright eyed seven-year-old if she would like to send a cheerio to her sick mother – asking 'Which hospital is she in?'

Without hesitation the girl replied. 'She's locked up in the Psych. Centre!'

Another girl offered a cheerio to her friend Kylie who couldn't come today, 'because she had nits in her hair'.

Then there was the little girl of five whom I interviewed in a group at the Elmore Field Days. This little darling left me speechless with her response to some nice words I proffered about the pullover she was wearing. Looking sweetly and seriously into my eyes she said. 'My Nanna knitted this and she died.' Such is life!

During an Outside Broadcast in Castlemaine, Mazza brought the six year old sister of volunteer Doug Scobie's current girlfriend to the microphone. When the girl caught sight of Doug in the group she called in her loudest voice, 'That's Doug Scobie and he's going to marry my sister.'

This astounding news was broadcast to Central Victoria as Doug cowered in a corner. He wasn't and he didn't.

Probably my worst embarrassment came when I interviewed the members of The Drifters, all large African Americans. They are quite famous and have been around for half a century. Someone, probably Jeff Langdon, had organised for them to visit 3CCC as they passed through on their way to Bendigo. It was mid afternoon and the studio was not on air. Jeff sprung it on me, 'The Drifters are here and you'll need to interview them.' With that, the group trooped in and we went straight to the studio. I was not in the least prepared and quite nervous because of that. We went directly into the interview and I hadn't a clue what to ask them. We began and soon after I was getting lost for words. In the back of my mind I knew that the legendary Clyde McPhatter had been their lead singer. I knew he was no longer with the group. 'Ha,' I thought, 'Here's a good and reasonable question.'

'What's Clyde McPhatter up to these days?'

There was a stony silence until one of the very large, bristling, glowering men said gruffly and simply. 'He's dead.'

Oh my God! What a fool I was! I really had known that Clyde had died, but simply forgot in my confused panic. Obviously the three Drifters hadn't forgotten and he was just as obviously a good friend. I struggled through the interview somehow but was a bloody wreck. The Drifters knew for sure that they had been dealing with a backward bush-bred idiot; one who had insulted them and the memory of their friend.

McPhatter had in fact founded The Drifters around 1953 and was their lead singer. He was probably the most imitated and influential man in Doo Wop and R&B and this fool from 3CCC hadn't a clue. McPhatter had died in 1972, about eleven years before my appalling interview with the survivors of The Drifters.

One day we set up the truck, the gear and the monstrous tower for an OB from the Easter Fair in Bendigo. Nobody had thought of a place to plug in for electricity and all the nearby shops were closed. Trevor Thomas and Daryl Evans went on a scrounge walk and eventually found a power point at the rear of a distant shop. We ran a series of leads for one hundred meters and did the job, albeit a late start.

We did an extended OB from Daylesford – two days in the main street. Interviewing passersby was always interesting! One never knew what reaction would come, mostly it was horror and refusal to speak but sometimes rewarding. The presenter on the street had to be innovative and try for a laugh when things dragged. One time I approached an electrician drilling a hole in a shop wall. Excuse me. Why are you drilling a hole in this bank's wall? His reaction was one of some surprise and I won't write his response here. Something about f.....g idiots.

The overnight was quite funny as Katherine Gibbons turned up at midnight and so did Johnny from Dunolly. A roster stuff up. The two had not exactly been bosom buddies in the past. There was an unpleasant, heated exchange that went direct to air that ended in both sharing the van all night. To add to the event there was only one shared microphone; all quite cosy, but a bit sweaty.

Alf Hooley had a guest on his show, a female environmentalist with strong views. She ripped into the spa water of Daylesford and Hepburn, claiming that every spring was contaminated by the activities of miners! Now that didn't go over very well with the locals who largely depended on the spa water to attract tourists. The expected blast from the local businesses and Council did not eventuate, thank God.

My turn came for the breakfast shift at Daylesford. My beloved VW Kombi had earlier lost one light so I had arranged with Gerry Pyne to use the station car for my early start. I arrived at the station at 4am but no car was there. Gerry had taken it the night before to a do at the Theatre Royal and he had forgotten me completely. With Mazza on board I had to drive forty-five kilometres through darkness and thick fog in a VW Kombi, notorious for bad lights, with one bad light. I used to say that I had to get out and light a match to see if the lights were working! That trip was no fun, believe me.

I went off to the first Down To Earth Confest weekend at Glenlyon Sports Ground, toting my portable recorder and, on this occasion, my camera. The Confest was attended by many thousands of people who shared an interest in natural healing, healthy food, massage and such like. The weather was perfect – the sun was not too hot, the sky was cloudless and the wind did not blow. Our own Vic McGowan, an actual Glenlyon resident, was one that I met there, browsing he said. Me, too.

The first thing I noticed was that most of the visitors didn't wear clothes – in fact it held my attention quite firmly. There were hundreds of women in all sorts of poses without a stitch of clothing. I stared hard. I'd never seen anything quite like it. There were also a huge number of naked men but I didn't see any reason to envy them – except for the boy aged about fifteen laying flat on his back receiving massage from a naked waif before a largish mixed audience. I couldn't help noticing the lad's vital rigidity and I felt sorry for him. What a predicament to be in. I noticed that he wasn't the only one in various stages of this condition among the males receiving massage. I also observed a number of females in massage positions not usually on show. I didn't get any interviews, but I did get some good photos, which I sold to a magazine.

Not wishing to appear too different I purchased a purple sarong, stripped to my jocks and put it on. I also bought a large terracotta and leather boot-laced badge to hang around my neck. With my already long hair I really looked the part.

Nobody took a lot of notice of me as I wandered about laden with recording gear and a camera, although I felt really conspicuous. At days end I made my way into Daylesford, parked at the bottom of Vincent Street and made my way to my brother Ken's restaurant and takeaway. There were many strange looks and some hostile glares from passersby as I walked up the street, bare-chested, sarong clad, with open leather sandals and my large terracotta badge. Daylesford was unlike the town of today, it was very conservative back then.

Ken and his wife Dot were aghast when this horrible apparition appeared in their crowded, respectable restaurant, amid the unbelieving stare of the clientele. Later, when they recovered, Dot and Ken were actually highly amused and we had a good laugh. It was really very good fun.

We returned to the Confest a couple of years later when Daryl Evans went along with The Truck (Mobile Studio) to record bands playing there, notably Mi Sex, Canned Heat and No Fixed Address.

The Confest was a flop but the recordings were superb and we used them on air for a number of years. They were among the most popular recordings that Daryl ever made.

Oddly we didn't do a lot of OBs from our home town of Harcourt. Apart from a historic broadcast of a local football match, there were only three others that I recall.

I wanted to do a live broadcast of Saturday breakfast from the town's hall where a history display was being put on by the locals. Jeff gave me the okay, but I had to set the gear up myself which I did on the Friday evening.

I arrived at 5.30 in the morning and was on tiptoe on a chair making an adjustment when it shot out from beneath me. I fell heavily and toppled down the steps at the rear of the truck to the ground, damaging my back quite badly. I could barely make it back into the truck to operate the panel. I managed to get through the program, although in a lot of pain. Happily the event was judged a big success. Thereafter for a couple of weeks I was unable to sit down for long and conducted my radio programs mostly standing up! My back is still a problem many years later.

The OB from the Castlemaine Show one Saturday morning went okay until we tuned into Punter to Punter on relay from 3RRR. Those fellers good naturedly rubbished Jeff something awful for his behavior at the Pater Awards night. Jeff must have got out of bed the wrong side and didn't see any humour in it at all. Angered, he sped toward Harcourt to give them a blast and silence the program; driving too fast he was pulled over by the cops and issued a heavy ticket. He came back grumpily to the show grounds and meantime we had lost the keys to the truck. Jeff was furious. Then Doug Scobie stood on the truck cabin roof to wrestle the tower into place and the roof caved in! It was not Jeff's best day – or ours. But we did find the keys.

This reminds me of another agonizing on-air experience. I would stand at the open studio window to have a smoke. The rules said 'no smoking' but it was largely ignored, especially by me, and I was the only person in the building early morning anyway.

The windows were old and heavy and they were controlled by concealed heavy metal weights attached to cord that held the window up when opened. One early morning I was at the window contentedly puffing on a cigarette with hands outstretched across the sill. Without warning the cord broke and the window crashed down hard across my wrists. The pain was excruciating as I struggled to free myself, certain that I had broken bones. Somehow I got free; my wrists swollen to twice their size and the pain was awful. I trembled with shock and pain but managed to get through the program. It turned out that no bones were broken but I was in pain for a couple of weeks.

Mazza had the worst injury of all. It was near Christmas as we presented our Fabulous Fifties show. We had two guests in the studio, sponsors from Spa Kitchens of Creswick – Peter and

Alan. They had brought two bottles of champagne and we were having a happy on-air Christmas party.

Mazza had to venture downstairs. The stairway carpet was badly worn and frayed and her foot caught in it at the top step. She crashed heavily; head first down the stairs to the first landing. We heard her screams from the studio and dashed out to find her in a heap, half conscious and crying. Peter and Alan rushed her off to the hospital. I, alone at the station, had to stay on to complete the program.

Mazza had hurt her neck and shoulder, a legacy for today, but she came back smiling from the hospital three days later.

The lads at Spa Kitchens were great supporters and we became good friends. We once went with them to a country music festival at Gordon, near Ballarat, where Alan lived. We met at his place for a barbeque and drinks after and it was a great day. Our friend Donna Fisk was one of the entertainers and so was Frank Ifield. This was before he lost his voice for many years. Mazza conducted her first ever interview with him. Frank was a good subject and a professional so her choice was a good one. Mazza was rapt!

Our first ever attempt at a live broadcast from a horse race meeting was a ripper! It was the Kyneton Cup day, a huge local event. We got off to a bad start. Jeff drove The Truck into the course via the main entrance where a large Welcome sign hung suspended over the archway entrance – or it did until Jeff ripped it down as the tower on top of the truck tore into it. The sign and the archway hit the ground and splintered into kindling wood.

Amazingly nobody seemed to notice this disaster as Jeff drove casually on. Unchallenged and undetected he parked The Truck in the appointed spot.

We had arranged to take the race descriptions off-air from 3UZ by placing a microphone in front of a radio speaker. We planned to fill in between races with Mazza, Bev and I making various comments and interviewing jockeys, trainers and so on. Daryl was to be our panel operator/producer as usual.

We cranked the transmission tower to its full height and to our horror found that the hill behind us prevented our microwave signal from reaching our transmitter at Mount Alexander.

We moved The Truck to another spot – same result. We were stuffed and our credibility shot to pieces. Bev was distraught, having sold lots of advertising space for this highly publicised, first ever for Central Victoria. Somehow we had to get by.

It was thirty kilometres from the track to our studio and Jeff had a brilliant idea. We would tape our 'live' interviews and comments on thirty minute tapes and Bev could ferry them by Ford Laser to Harcourt where Jack Miles in the studio would put them to air. He would also put the race descriptions by 3UZ to air from there.

We went through the entire day and nobody was any the wiser, in fact race officials congratulated us on the superb coverage.

You would think that we would have learnt from this experience but there was another to come. Heavy rock band, Darkcide, was doing a show at the Theatre Royal in Castlemaine and we secured the rights to broadcast it live. We set up the gear and The Truck at the theatre to find that our microwave signal was blocked by yet another hill! But we had learned a very valuable trick at the Kyneton races. The theatre was then run by Ray Lindstrum, himself a musician.

Daryl taped the show on half hour tapes and Jeff ferried them to Harcourt and put them to air. The only difference was that we were an hour out of sync with the actual event.

As we left the theatre at night's end we noticed the occupants of a car parked beside us. The driver flipped on the radio and the puzzled astonishment showed on the faces as they listened to live performances that they had seen an hour before.

We got away with that one, too!

We were involved in a number of concerts at the Theatre Royal back then, nights, long remembered. Eric Bogle was a sensation and his show a sell out. We shared a beer and a barbeque at the station the afternoon after the show. Ronnie Gilbert from the fabulous 1950's folk group, The Weavers, came to town with Judy Small and it was an incredible night. American folkie legend Tom Paxton was another great act that brought people from all around the district to the old, slightly crumbling Theatre Royal. The Battlefield Band from Scotland was also a fabulous night as was the Aussie group, The Cobbers. We had many great nights like that in those days.

On one occasion Peter Sarsted of 'Frozen Orange Juice' fame and Doug Ashdown, 'Winter in America', put on a show. Next day they called on Mazza and me at our mud brick home for lunch. I will always remember how much Peter loved the place. He had never been to anywhere like our lovely property before.

Darkcide was one of the most popular bands to come out of Central Victoria for a number of years and several times they gave their services free of charge as fundraisers for 3CCC. They were a top class heavier rock band deserving of bigger things, but maybe arrived on the scene too late, after the era was closing. Darkcide contributed several thousand dollars to our coffers.

Oddly enough they did not get a lot of support from the rank and file of 3CCC. On one occasion, a 3CCC Christmas party, over three hundred Darkcide fans filled the ancient Castlemaine theatre and netted us over a thousand dollars after expenses, and a split of the door with Ray, the venue operator. Only two people from 3CCC attended – Mazza and I.

The Darkcide boys, Glenn, Steve, Andrew and Rick, were disappointed at that lack of support from our people that night and more so when not a word of managerial thanks went their way. After three weeks Bev Stewart offered to type a letter of thanks, which I signed; the least we could do.

Another time, Doug Scobie took up the Darkcide offer and organized a fundraiser at Bendigo College. Bendigo was well known for shunning things local, including musicians, so it wasn't a shock when the students stayed away in droves. To the embarrassment of Doug the gig lost three hundred dollars, but it wasn't the organisers' fault.

'That's Bendigo,' he said.

Darkcide's leader and singer-front man was my son Glenn Braybrook. I was proud of him, but some people hated me playing his music too often, which I confess I did.

Chapter Nine

A bomb threat, some weddings, footy, watching the wheels, tractor racing, a trembling tower

So many things happened at 3CCC! We had a new transmission tower, which soared skywards around thirty meters installed on the mountain, I recall watching with horror as Jeff ascended it to the top, no safety harness, to fix an antenna problem, almost hanging by his fingernails. I felt sure that he would fall. A good community radio station manager does more than sit in an office!

One time Marilyn was the organiser for Free Entertainment in the Park (FEIP) at Rosalind Park in Bendigo. It was an all day and into the night affair with several local rock bands performing. She had managed to get together all the then radio stations serving Bendigo (excluding the ABC) to promote the event and share the role of compere. She selected me to represent 3CCC. There was a huge crowd and I had never compered a live show before and was very, very nervous. I had no problems waffling on when broadcasting but a real live audience was a different matter. I got through but it was not a good performance. I have since overcome that fear and am comfortable talking to crowds these days.

The FEIP day was a huge success. One of the highlights was the tight trousers worn by the 3BO DJ, Mike Marshall (not his real name). He obviously dressed to the left. I was also surprised to see my son Glenn, singing with Darkcide, climb onto the sound shell roof and bare his bum. But there you go!

One day Marilyn was at work in my office when she answered a phone call. There was an ominous silence and then a dark voice came through 'I've planted a bomb in the building.' Nothing more. Poor Mazza nearly dropped the phone in fright and she rushed into Jeff's office.

'A bomb. Jeff! A bomb!' she cried. 'Someone has planted a bomb here.'

Jeff looked up at Marilyn from his paperwork but said nothing.

'Jeff there's a bomb! What'll we do?'

As calm as could be Jeff said quietly. 'You look after it,' and went back to his papers. He was not one to panic, our Jeff, who obviously dismissed it as a crank call. Which it turned out to be, but it worried the heck out of Marilyn and me for a few hours. There was no explosion. No bomb.

Jack Miles did not often swear but one day he and I were recording an ad in the one and only studio. It was early days when we opened at 10am, closed at noon, re-opened at 4pm and closed at 10pm. Halfway through the recording a train roared through the station, the driver blasting the horn. 'Bastard trains,' said Jack. We then realized that the transmitter was still on and Jack's expletive went to air. He was very embarrassed and fretted that he would be in trouble with the authorities! I think they had more important issues to worry about.

In the early years we would do outside broadcasts (OBs) from anywhere the fancy took us – agricultural shows, trade fairs and shopping centres – even on the roadside in small townships plugging into the power from a farmhouse. Sometimes we were far from electricity supply and used a portable generator.

The Dunolly Goldrush was one such spot, an event set in the bush some five kilometres out of town on a former goldfield, surely a unique site for a radio broadcast! We conducted two successful broadcasts from there, using portable generators for power and a prayer or two to line up the transmission Yagi with our tower on far-off Mount Alexander. Don't ask me how we did it, but it worked!

Highlights of those Dunolly broadcasts were the direct-to-air of actual wedding ceremonies. Each year a couple was found who were prepared to take their vows there. One was a wedding which included four children from previous marriages. The kids actively participated in what was the most memorable wedding service I have ever witnessed.

One day I received a letter from a bloke named Bruce McKenzie of Trentham. Bruce enclosed one of his poems and asked if I could read it on air. I was very impressed and did so next day. The response from Listeners was extraordinary. I had five phone calls asking for more. Bruce continued to send me his works and I continued to read them. Eventually Mazza and I decided that we should meet him and, one day, unannounced, we called on him. As a result he and his wife Faye became very good friends and ultimately Mazza published three books of his poetry, all of which sold well. I likened Bruce to Henry Lawson and Banjo Patterson, fair dinkum, he was that good. Sadly Faye passed away in 2009.

Anne Swaby was another listener who became a friend. She presented us with her complete album collection which was a valuable addition to the library in those vinyl days. She used to write me great letters, back in the days when people still wrote them!

In 1985 we broadcast our first ever football match. When Bev Ellis proposed that we broadcast a description of the local team, Harcourt Lions, doing battle with arch rivals Campbell's Creek, Jeff jumped at the chance. It was to be the final match of the season.

Our team of broadcasters was selected; Jeff Langdon, Phillip Edmunds, Bev Ellis, Marilyn Bennet and Julie McHale, a local school teacher. I was to give 'special comments' due to my alleged brilliant background with the Mudflat Murderers of Williamstown and to conduct various interviews.

I have no doubt that it was an appallingly amateur broadcast as our inexperienced team tried their best to be professional, struggling with names, positions and techniques. It was hilarious, as we learnt that footy commentators are really highly skilled in their craft.

The half time interview with dedicated Lions supporter, Andrew McSporren, (the multi-talented Justin Shortal) was a highlight of the day as Justin played his role to the hilt.

In any event, history was made on that August day in 1985. The Lions, who had not had a win for the year, bolted over the line as winners! The team gave the credit to our presence there. Club stalwart, Steven Adamson, best known as Wonder, was pretty excited and kept repeating in a loud voice, 'Three Triple C IS football.'

From this humble beginning many years ago came 3CCC's regular broadcasts of the Maryborough–Castlemaine League matches. This was eventually dropped in favour of the bigger Bendigo Football League, a service that continues to this day. This caused considerable resentment locally, but they still talk about that famous first broadcast and the associated win for the mighty Harcourt Lions!

Some years later a youngster named Andrew Hudson began broadcasting footy on 3CCC. He went on to become a top AFL TV commentator. A young fellow named Michael Nihill was footy fanatic. He tried very hard to be a professional commentator-expert and even sent audition tapes to EON and FOX in Melbourne, but didn't quite measure up. He gets full marks for trying.

Another live broadcast that is engraved in my memory because of a near disaster, was the Steam Engine and Tractor Rally from Bendigo Showgrounds. It was the annual gathering of enthusiasts from all over displaying and demonstrating their loved and pampered machines.

A special event was put on for our benefit, a vintage tractor race. Three old machines were selected for our drivers, Marilyn Bennet, Bev Ellis and Calamity Clegg, who between them did not know one end of a tractor from the other. After quick lessons they felt that they knew how to steer the monsters and, hopefully, how to stop them!

The five hundred metre circuit was roughly defined by white markers as the large crowd of onlookers was told to move back.

The race was terrific fun and certainly the biggest attraction of the day as the three competitors roared around the track at five kilometres an hour. I would clamber onto the tow bar at the rear, clutching a microphone on a one hundred metre lead that Daryl Evans had hastily made up. After getting a few rushed words from the driver I'd jump clear and dash for safety as the next machine lumbered toward me.

On the second circuit Calamity lost control and missed the turn careering straight into the crowd, narrowly missing several spectators and parked cars. An attendant caught up and jumped aboard and got Calamity back on track. Meantime Marilyn had hit the lead.

As Bev went by on her third pass I jumped on board, chatting happily. To my horror Bev missed the turn and headed into the crowd and car park, toward the main arena. My one hundred metres of microphone lead quickly came to an end and gave way with a sharp snap – ending my graphic description of what was happening in mid-word. Bev careered on, in panic and completely in loss of control of the tractor. The attendant finally caught up and got aboard, taking the wheel and getting Bev back on track.

The crowd cheered as a beaming Calamity Clegg roared across the finish line in first place, twenty metres clear of Bev and fifty clear of Marilyn, who had struggled badly in the race. It was a fun time that exemplified the attractions, capabilities and appeal of Community Radio.

It was a long way from the Steam and Tractor Rally at the Bendigo Showgrounds to our transmitter on Mount Alexander and we had had to crank our twenty metre tower to its maximum height to get a signal to the mount. At the best of times the tower was a precariously balanced affair, attached to the rear of The

Truck on a swivel and secured with only a small ten millimetre bolt at the base. The half-tonne steel structure would sway alarmingly in even a moderate wind.

I stood at the rear interviewing the Secretary of the Steam Society. Thank God I was oblivious to what near disaster was building around me.

It was essential that the vehicle did not move in either direction so The Truck wheels were chocked with wooden wedges. Somehow the chocks at the rear wheels moved and Marilyn, Daryl and Bev, seated at the panel in the vehicle, were horrified when the unit lurched and rolled backwards.

It moved only thirty centimetres, but that was sufficient to cause the tower to whip and sway in a terrifying manner.

We will never know why the tower did not come crashing down on the crowd assembled there and no one had any inkling of how close they were to a disaster. How the bolt holding the tower did not snap is one of life's mysteries

It was not until I had concluded the interview that I was told what had happened. I was shocked and never again had any confidence in the stability of that tower.

One day Jack Haynes, one of our producers employed under a government training scheme, was driving The Truck, complete with tower, to a site in Melbourne. I think Daryl Evans was with him. As he moved down busy Nicholson Street, Fitzroy the lights at an intersection unexpectedly turned to red. Jack hit the brakes hard and the tower, perched high on the roof of The Truck, slid rapidly forward. It hung a full five metres ahead of the cabin and narrowly missed the car in front. It took the sweating, cursing Jack and his passenger, thirty embarrassing minutes in peak traffic to get the tower back onto the roof. Motorists and pedestrians gave the lads a really hard, good natured time, but nobody offered to help. Another time Daryl backed the truck into a Mini Minor, almost demolishing it, but the insurance covered it. Once he drove into Ray Rice's service station for fuel and the tower atop the truck hit the servo roof and took a great lump out of it. Ricey took it all well.

The Truck was involved in a number of other memorable adventures as time went by.

Peter Fairthorne was returning in The Truck from a job in Bendigo. As he sped down Big Hill, a descent well known to locals who use the Calder Highway, Peter was horrified to see one of the rear wheels roll past him. He thought, 'Good thing it's a dual wheel vehicle' but when he finally drew The Truck to a stop he discovered that the second wheel had also come off. Somehow he and The Truck survived without a lot of damage but it took a marathon effort by a small group of our volunteers to retrieve the wheels from a distant paddock and refit them to The Truck.

Through contact with Bert and Joy Oliver at Blackwood we organised for Mazza to present a weekly program titled The High Country, sponsored by local businesses, which celebrated all that's good about Blackwood and district. It featured Australian music of laid-back country or folkish type and was well received.

On one occasion Marilyn and I were headed for Blackwood to conduct a recorded 'live' broadcast. We had to abandon the journey when The Truck developed the most alarming wheel wobble. We returned to 3CCC at ten kilometres an hour where it was discovered that some part of the steering had come adrift.

We actually recorded a broadcast from The Truck at Blackwood some time later as part of the annual Easter wood chop carnival. We had a great time and were hosted like royalty by the town's people. It was a wonderful experience.

Chapter Ten

Fishing, motels, movie stars, Catch It,
a lump of gold, a porridge addict,
a 90-year-old magician

I rose at 7.30 one Saturday morning and was surprised to hear Ken Tester on air. He had started at 11 the night before and his midnight relief didn't turn up, so Ken valiantly stayed on. Neither did Neil Cowan arrive at 6am for the breakfast show – so Ken stayed on. To his dismay two guests of Cowan's arrived at 7am carrying guitars for a live performance. The hapless Ken had to somehow put them to air, something he had never done before. He phoned me for help as he managed to put the live act to air while I rang all around trying to find a fill-in for Ken. No luck, so eventually at about 8.30 I went in and took over. At 9.06 after the news, I put the tape of Glenn Heyne and me doing the gardening show to air and went home to finish my breakfast.

Speaking of news reminds me that for a time we took news on relay from 3RRR. They were always late and cared not for the time, content or length of the news. One time I clocked the 7.30 news from 7.27 to 8.12. Forty-five minutes for a four minute news service! Amazing and annoying? Yes and bloody infuriating, but it was given free so we did not lodge a complaint.

There were some wonderful people that went through 3CCC in my time there. Trevor Penno, a thirty something son of a farmer from Taradale, a tiny township fifteen kilometres to the south, was a quiet and sincere bloke. As well as farming he played in a small country dance band, The Taratones. Real bush dance music – it was marvelous in its simplicity and nostalgic appeal – a piano, sax and drums. He presented mostly rock style music including The Beatles, his favourites; 'The Fab Four' as he constantly told us.

Derek Gibson, professional photographer, was a competent, fastidious announcer who loved to talk with his on-air guests. Interviews of forty-five minutes were not uncommon, not everyone's cup of tea, but he was popular and did a professional show for a number of years. He later went to Bendigo's KLFM. Derek did me several favours at 3CCC and I have not forgotten them.

Ross Rankin was another good bloke, heavily involved in the early days. I liked Ross and was a bit miffed when he made a few scathing comments in a letter to me in which he sarcastically referred to 'the Ian Braybrook Fan Club', a reference to my popularity with listeners.

Les Harding lived with his wife Ros and son and daughter at Wellington Flat, on the eastern side of Mount Alexander. He was a Listener and came to an open day at the station and I convinced him that he should train to present a program. He took me up on it and I put him through a crash course. He was pretty good on air. I named him Rock Harding, movie star, when he obtained a role as an extra in the movie, 'Kangaroo'.

Rock and Ros became very good friends and we spent a lot of time together. One time they got a temporary job looking after the Harcourt Motel owned by Barry and Irene Johansen. As the motel was on the way to 3CCC I used to drive my Kombi past the reception office before 6am. The drive-through had a loud alarm to rouse sleeping managers of new arrivals, and I also drove as noisily as I could. One morning as I left the driveway Rock leapt into view and hurled a large paper bag full of flour onto my windscreen! It was raining lightly and the Kombi looked like a ghost ship. Rock collapsed with mirth and we shared a huge laugh. Cleaning a dough mixture from a Kombi is not a lot of fun, however.

One day Rock happened to mention how he hated, in fact detested, cooking breakfasts and especially disliked making up compote of fruit for guests. On April Fool's Day Mazza and I conspired with Ros to set Rock up.

Assisted by Ros, Mazza and I made a booking for Mr. and Mrs. Smith for the night of March 31st, saying we would be very late arrivals and please leave the room unlocked. At 5.30 in the morning Mazza and I sneaked into the motel room. We had arranged with Ros to put our breakfast order onto the spike for Rock's early morning start. We ordered everything on the menu, bacon, sausages, chops, tomatoes and eggs, toast, coffee, juice and the dreaded compote of fruit, set for 7am sharp, the earliest possible time. Come 7.15am there was a knock at the breakfast slide and a weary voice called, 'Breakfast'.

I called out, 'Thanks Rock! You're a bit late.' There was a short period of silence and then a screeching 'You bastards!' Poor Rock actually began to cry real tears. I let him in and he put his arms around me and wept, saying over and over, 'You bastards.' Mazza and I felt bad to have so upset him but we all soon got over it and with a beaming Ros immediately on the scene we all sat down to a hearty, huge, and very happy breakfast.

Rock often rang me when I was on air putting on a sexy female voice making all sorts of lewd suggestions. I went along with him but he was really a poor female impersonator. He never did know that I knew it was him. Maybe he'll read this and find out.

Hard times fell on Rock and all sorts of strife. He went broke, his wife Ros left him, went back, left again went back and finally the marriage fell apart. We eventually lost contact when they moved interstate. In January 2015, I answered a phone call and to my astonishment and joy Rock was on the other end. He had tracked us down via Facebook. Mazza had twice rejected him as a Facebook friend as she did not recognize his Facebook name or the photo of some old man. Finally he got through with a strongly worded message that yelled. 'IT'S ME. IT'S ROCK.' She arranged for him to make a surprise call and I was rapt.

Bill Strong never set foot in the station but was a regular on the breakfast show. He was a well known local fisherman and each Friday he would phone in with advice, tips and comments and information where the fish were biting. It was a popular segment. Like the man himself, the advice he gave was sincere and genuine.

Bill and I once ran a competition for the best fish caught for the week. The prizes were several boxes of Catch It (try saying that!), an artificial bait. Over six weeks we received only two entries, both from people Bill and I knew. It was an embarrassment that we quietly faded away. We didn't do it again!

An on-air competition often drew little or no response. We would usually make up some sort of winner's name and go forward. However, in one instance I was astonished at the response.

I jokingly offered a jar of Vegemite as a prize for a correct answer to something or other and received fifteen calls in a few minutes. From then on I gave Vegemite away frequently, paying the costs myself. Eventually the drain on my limited resources grew too much but I wanted to continue with a winner. I thought I'd give Kraft, the makers, a try. I phoned their marketing manager and, lo and behold, he readily agreed to donate some product. I was astonished to see a truck arrive a few days later with a pack of two hundred and eighty-eight very large jars and they were to come with regularity thereafter.

Over a couple of years, where we had trouble giving away much more expensive prizes, I gave away hundreds of jars of the magic concoction. Figure that out!

My good mate Kevin Daw, KD, is loud, boisterous and friendly. He was presenting Top of The Morning and promoted his weekly show Open Country. 'It's pretty boring this week; produced by Ian Braybrook. That's a pity. It gets better next week when I start

The Best Of – or is it the least worst of?' I rang him from home to object, joking of course, and he started raving merrily on air that he was going to end it all – jump from the window etc. etc. Bev Ellis ran up the stairs and told him to control himself. She was serious. Earlier I had buzzed KD from my office and we shouted back and forth in our 'funny voices' at each other. A delivery man came in and couldn't believe his ears. 'You must have a lot of fun here,' he grinned. We did.

I loved the time he was in the studio presenting and putting to air a taped reading of the book Gold! Gold! by a local author Cora McDougall. It told of the struggles of the goldfields people and the discoveries of gold. Suddenly the tape dropped from the machine and rolled across the floor. Of course the story stopped instantly and there was total silence. Quick as a flash KD opened the mic and cried. 'Christ. She's fallen down a mineshaft!'

He was aware, as was I that our Board members rarely, if ever, listened to 3CCC and once he said, 'If you want to get hold of our board members ring 3CV or the ABC and get them to broadcast a message. They'll be listening to them.' Risky talk KD!

Musician, Mick Ahearne, our Live Music Co-ordinator, was a lovely bloke, sincere to a point of sometimes being painful and completely dedicated to his and other's music. When he had a serious disagreement with our by then manager Gerry Pyne, and quit in anger I was pretty distressed. Mick was a good musician but his attempts to be an announcer were bad. I liked Mick a lot.

John Hannaford (not his real name) a Social Worker from Bendigo was a quiet and gentle man who presented a half-hour Health Talk show once a week. Most times his show was pre-recorded in our tiny production studio and part of my job was to operate the equipment.

One such day John shyly handed me a tape. 'I wonder if you would record a message for me for Anna? She's working in Queensland and I miss her terribly.'

I readily agreed and listened somewhat embarrassed as John poured out his heart to his love so far away. Not too much later Anna ended the romance and I wondered just how bad John must have felt.

I had some wonderful Listener friends. Edna Medley, a perhaps fifty-year-old, lived with her husband near the Harcourt Cemetery and she was a regular phone caller when I was on air. She particularly loved my description of the shopping centre of Harcourt as 'Flat Cat Flat' due to a cat being killed on the road outside the shop. She thought it was hilarious! Nobody else did, I am sure. Anyway she rang one day and asked if she may call and take a photo of our mud hut that I was always talking about. When I got home that morning, there she was, camera in hand, waiting for me to come home for breakfast. I posed for her at the front of the hut and she snapped away. A week later she delivered a hand painted plate bearing the image of the mud hut and me in the foreground. I have to say it was no great work of art but I still treasure it.

Our neighbours at Harcourt were Nicki and George Brereton and their two kids, Megan and Andrew. We became firm friends and still visit each other although they now live in Adelaide. Megan when she was about ten actually recorded a piece for me. I was always impressed with the item 'Yes, Virginia, there is a Santa Claus'. It was a piece of inspired writing in 1897 by Francis Church, an editorial writer of the New York Sun, in response to a letter from eight-year-old Virginia O'Hanlon. Megan read the part of Virginia. I still use it on air at Christmas.

Across the road from the on-air studio lived Bob and Win Bassett. Bob worked as a contact trench digger. From my perch on the first floor I looked directly at their house. Although I couldn't see inside the house I pretended I could. I usually described what they were having for breakfast and many mornings I told of Bob heading off to work with his Thermos full of porridge. You see, he had a serious addiction to porridge, or so I said, and had to have a regular fix. He had even attended the local branch of Porridge Anonymous at the ANA Hall. Poor Bob got hell from his workmates, most of who listened to 3CCC breakfast. It was all good fun and Bob and Win loved it.

Graeme Stewart from Moliagul, an Aboriginal, often called to see us and he really enjoyed what we did. He quietly told Mazza that he loved her! It always impresses me the number of friends we made through being on 3CCC. He was one.

Speaking of Aboriginals, for a time we had the Aboriginal Co-Op Show. It didn't last long as the presenters only turned up occasionally and when they did they operated on what I call Aboriginal Time, that is, a complete disregard for the clock.

The mention of Moliagul recalls a regular Listener named Ian who lived in a caravan in the bush outside the town. His only companion was a milking goat. Ian used to ring me quite often and told me of his gold discoveries, for that was what he did for a living. It seemed like a pretty good living judging by the things he told me.

One day Mazza and I were broadcasting from the steps of the old market in Castlemaine when a man approached me and introduced himself as Ian from Moliagul. He was not what I had envisaged, being quite well dressed and clean shaven. I expected a dirty, untidy, bearded older man. I guessed he was about thirty-five years old. He called me aside and drew from his trousers pocket a large piece of quartz that simply bristled with gold – at least as much gold as quartz. He handed it to me. 'It's not to keep but to let you hold and look at. I want it back,' he grinned. It was beautiful. 'How much is it worth?' I queried, amazed.

'Oh, about twenty thousand,' he said casually. 'But it's not as good as the one I found a few weeks ago. I got almost one hundred thousand for that.' He seemed quite unexcited about it all, more excited at meeting Mazza and me he reckoned. He was one of the many characters I met through radio.

Jack Flett was another. Jack was a ninety-year-old magician, also a veterinary surgeon, ex-champion footballer and museum curator from Dunolly. He was a terrific talker and spinner of yarns. In a two hour interview I recorded in his tumbling down house, I am still unsure whether he told me any truth or not. According to Jack he was a wonderful footballer and an amazing magician. He even showed Mazza, her son Glenn (aged ten) and me his magician's suit. It was a beat up old raggedy thing, multi-coloured and not exactly clean. Jack said his other job was entertaining primary school kids, hence the suit. He was also a vet, he assured us, having learnt the profession from a traveling vet he camped with at a fishing spot at Lake Hindmarsh one time. Without blinking an eye he told us how he had helped the vet put up his tent and showed him how to catch a fish. In return the man taught him the trade. Vets who have struggled through six years at university would be quite impressed! But, Jack was a wonderful vet able to cure most anything, so he said. I still have some of the recordings I made that day, there were six small reels in all, and I hope to place them in Jack's Dunolly museum one day. He was one of the most remarkable characters I ever encountered. Young Glenn never forgot his meeting with Jack and neither has Mazza. Or me.

Bob Savige was a builder from Bendigo who loved music. He became heavily involved in 3CCC and did a great job around the station. He helped out wherever he could. A tall, quietly spoken and friendly man we were sorry to lose him when he moved his family to Melbourne. Fred Langenhorst, a tall blonde man in his thirties was a regular presence at the station. He was our bookkeeper and did a marvelous job keeping us on track financially.

Lorraine Foley was one of my favourite people. A divorcee approaching middle age she was a warm personality both on and off the air.

At her beginning, with only sixty minutes training, Jeff advised her that she was ready and would be on air next week. Panic stricken, Lorraine set up her own 'studio' at home using salt and pepper shakers for knobs and Frisbees for turntables. Her cartridge machine was a foot stool!

She told me that she had to do well to prove to her family that she could do it; that she felt that they often put her down. She showed them and us that she was capable when she went on air for the first time and presented an almost mistake-free show.

Lorraine developed into one of our best presenters and we were good friends. She was a great asset to the station – a most willing worker outside of on-air work, an area that many volunteers showed little interest in. Unfortunately after several years she became disillusioned with the direction of the station and she quit. Dedicated and competent people like Lorraine Foley are hard to find and her departure was a considerable loss. Lorraine passed away in mid 2013.

Almost everybody used their real name when they went on air but not Chris Spencer. Not that he wanted to hide his identity he just liked the name he adopted. Chris was about thirty and he sported a large red beard. He called himself The Moonlight Knight and was so softly spoken as to be sometimes inaudible. Nevertheless he had a good following and his dedication to music, especially the local variety, is legendary. We all liked Chris and he spent many years with the station. Eventually he produced a great CD featuring many of the recordings of local bands made originally by Daryl Evans at 3CCC.

We had several former announcers and radio and TV presenters doing voluntary work from time to time. Gene Fisk was one. Gene was very well known around central Victoria, having worked at both of the Bendigo commercial stations, 3BO and 3CV, over a long period. For a time he lived next door to my mother in Napier Street, Maryborough where I also met his daughter Donna. At the time we had him with 3CCC, he was working at 3GL Geelong after a stint at 3UZ Melbourne when it was all country music. Gene also performed a good type of country music and recorded a large number of songs. He was pretty good, too. Each week he sent me a taped program entitled 'Progressive Country Music' recorded at 3GL, where he was production chief. It was a very good show but amazingly was soon dropped on order of the Board as being too professional. I was stunned and so were Gene and a lot of others, but weird things happen when you have people running a radio station that know little about radio!

For a time one of the Central Victoria's best voices, Col Herbert, worked for us at 3CCC. He had worked at both Bendigo commercial stations among a number of others, TV included. Jeff hired him as a Producer under a government funded employment program that he had dug up somewhere. From the start Jeff and Col did not see eye to eye and after a few months Col departed. It was rather disappointing as Col's mellow tones added a bit of class and professionalism to our station. Col and I remain very good friends in spite of future occurrences.

Another bloke that did a long stint with us was Glenn Heyne from Daylesford. Glenn was a professional gardener/nurseryman. As well as hosting radio garden advice shows he worked as a regular announcer. At the time he was at 3AW (and later at 3UZ) in Melbourne.

One day Bev Ellis told me about Glenn whom she had met in his shop at Daylesford and had indicated that he may be interested in helping us. I had often thought that a gardening show would be a good thing and jumped at the chance.

I went to see Glenn and he readily agreed provided I became his panel operator. Being a city announcer he didn't have a clue about that aspect of radio, it was done for him.

We cleared him an hour on Saturday mornings, eight to nine, and it was an immediate success.

It turned out that I was to be more than Glenn's panel operator as I became more and more part of the show. It was terrific fun.

Glenn and I joked and yarned our way through the allotted hour and the response was amazing. Huge numbers of people would ring in with their questions about numerous problems in the garden. We couldn't put them to air, lacking the seven second delay, but I took them, often live on air as part of the fun.

I was amazed at Glenn's knowledge. Every week I'd slip a ghastly, impossible question I fabricated into the mix and to my astonishment Glenn came up with a credible answer – even if he made it up on the spot and it was total crap. I never once caught him out.

He was a good bloke and couldn't do enough for us – personally for Marilyn and I and for 3CCC. He and wife Peta with daughter Clare became good friends. Marilyn even became Glenn's Manager for a time. He once invited me to do a telephone segment, with him at 6am Sunday mornings on 3UZ in which I played the yobbo bush whacker from Harcourt. I did it twice but was not comfortable with it and the time slot didn't help so, in mutual agreement, we pulled the pin. I don't think I was very good.

Eventually Glenn's commitment to his shop and to 3UZ became too much and he had to give up his role at 3CCC. It was an unhappy day when the last show went to air.

Glenn sometimes couldn't make Saturday mornings and we recorded the show through the week in the evening. On those free Saturday mornings Marilyn and I sometimes had a stall, selling home grown plants at the Wesley Hill market. This supplemented our very meager income.

I always had a radio tuned to 3CCC, monitoring as part of my job and it was no different at the market. We had our car beside our stall with the radio on and I had the chance to listen to Glenn with myself as the tape rolled to air.

It is a crowded market and once you get your car inside there's no getting out. There was no public phone anywhere and it was long before mobile phones so you can imagine my concern as our first ever recorded program went to air. What if something went wrong?

It was 8am and the program started. I couldn't believe my ears as garbled gibberish emerged from the speakers. Struth! The bloody tape had been put on backwards! This gibberish went on for an amazing ten minutes as I ran about in a frenzy, completely frustrated, with no phone and no way to get the car out.

'What's the matter with the idiot who put it to air?' I cried to Mazza in despair. 'Surely they can hear it!'

After an eternity the garbage stopped and the voice of 'the idiot', John Dixon, came, on apologizing for a technical problem. Then followed another ten minutes of music while the operator figured out a way to correct the mess. Finally the unfortunate John must have worked it out and the gardening program re-started. It was about twenty minutes into the program and in mid sentence; a debacle, no other description suits.

On another similar occasion Mazza and I had a stall, again at the Wesley Hill market. It was 7.50 am when I remembered that I had agreed to put the Glenn Heyne tape to air at eight. There was nobody at the station as the previous show, a Christian program presentation, was on a tape and put to air by the overnight announcer before he went home. I panicked. There was no way I could get the Kombi van out and there was no mobile phone in those days.

One of our presenters, Dennis Stingells, also had a stall, selling pumpkins from the back seat and trunk of his trusty Ford V8. His stall was on the roadside and his car accessible so I rushed to him for help. He willingly shut up shop and I roared off in the Ford full of pumpkins.

They were the fastest pumpkins in the west as I sped over the ten kilometres to the studio. I was still one minute away when the tape ran out and I was treated to the dreaded sound of dead air. I made record time as I dashed up the stairs to the studio, put some sort of music to air and cued the Heyne tape.

In all we lost only four minutes but, as any radio person will tell you, just four seconds is a very long spell of dead air, let alone four minutes!

Exhausted, I returned to the market and gave Dennis his car and his pumpkins back. Dennis reckoned it was the funniest thing he'd seen in a long time, but I wasn't laughing at the time.

The Gardening Show aside, the only other shows I have ever done that beat it for personal enjoyment were The Fabulous Fifties with Mazza (Marilyn) Bennet. We had so much fun presenting these shows and it rubbed off on our audience who felt they were a part of it. We regularly flew around town in our ancient Sopwith Camel with its dope covering falling to bits and engine sputtering and threatening to stall, describing outrageous scenes as we went. We attended race meetings, beach events, parties and workplaces – all in our imagination, of course – accompanied by appropriate sound effects. It was just wonderful. I abused Mazza for her tardiness, incompetence and eating habits, all very sexist, and much more. Mostly our audience loved it all but we drew some unpleasant responses from a couple of women who told me in no uncertain terms that I was a sexist pig! I'm sure that they had no sense of humour. Marilyn was quite happy to be a part of it and thoroughly enjoyed her role. Male chauvinist pig that I was I even made her spin the propeller to start the Sopwith Camel as I relaxed in the cockpit yelling orders. I told outrageous stories of the adventures of my ancestors and of my ability as a footballer with the Mudflat Murderers and at cricket, as Mazza listened incredulously and made sneering remarks. Not a word of truth in any of it. We played nothing but good old style rock and roll because we loved it. We loved to quote from an article in the Bendigo advertiser of around 1956, written by an anonymous columnist named Barnabas. Viewed in more modern times his ravings were hilarious. *'Rock and Roll seems to drug their senses, losing what little balance they have, it's proved baneful effects should be classed with the use of marihuana and similar dangerous drugs.'* Barnabas then says he is not straight laced and narrow minded and *'This sound is monotonous, tom tom like, inducing an hypnotic state where the wildest excesses are possible. Like dervishes of Arabia they work themselves into a state of frenzy often culminating in a form of epileptic seizure. It should be removed without hesitation or apology. An animal frenzy that knows not what it is doing.'* The tirade went much further. Yes, they did print this stuff in the 1950s. And Mazza and I loved to stress Barnabas's points! We later transferred the Fabulous Fifties to KLFM where it became Bush Wireless with an even bigger audience.

The stairwell was covered with a photographic history of 3CCC. The entire collection was destroyed when the station moved to Bendigo.

Premier John Cain declares 3CCC officially open in July, 1982 (we opened on April 25th).

With government minister Race Mathews, Paul Murphy, Julius Porlai, Jack Miles at 3CCC in 1984.

3CCC – The Station at the Station, Harcourt, Victoria.

My Kombi van, faithful servant of 3CCC, signed by Roger McKellar free of charge.

Mazza and I doing a broadcast from the Bendigo Easter Fair.

I give our friend, bride Bev Stewart away to John Sutherland at Murrabit on the Murray.

Bev Ellis and me pictured in 2015.

Rosemary Mckenzie and Jeff Langdon at a 3CCC function.

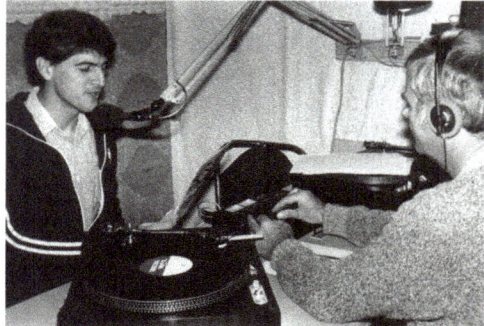

Brad Bridger recording a spot for 3CCC in our production 'Studio'.

Mazza and me at a formal station function.

With Justin Shortal at a Deb Ball in Bendigo. Justin was M.C.

Guildford Gus aka Dennis Zepnik at the microphone at 3CCC.

Two aging gentlemen seen in Castlemaine.

Mazza with JP Morgan at his gold mine at Barry's Reef, near Blackwood.

With Aussie legend John Williamson at The Truck 3CCC.

In party mood at 3CCC. On my right is Johnnie Devlin and Lonnie Lee. Dennis Knight to my left. Others are the band and crew.

L to R: Norm Tyrell, Col Elliot, Rodney Vincent.

Ted Egan and his wife Nerys enjoying a beer in the kitchen at 3CCC.

With Slim Dusty at Clarkefield on the set of 'Slim Dusty–The Movie'.

An outside broadcast from the Dunolly Gold Rush.

Doug Scobie, Mazza, Peter McAndrew and me at the launch of Frisky and Sassy's new record. Castlemaine Tip circa 1985.

Me and Calamity Clegg do Buttons and Bows. Mazza is M.C. 3CCC party.

Comedian Roy Tyrell and Edith Clegg (Calamity) at 3CCC Pere Awards.

Mazza and me in dinner suit and gown for record launch at the tip.

Mazza and Slim Dusty at Clarkefield.

The 3CCC Morning Music Club team: Jack Miles, Lorraine Foley, (at rear: K.D., Catherine Gibbons, John Khuen), Vic McGowan, Trevor Penno, Noel Tamblin.

The Delltones with Mazza on her 40th Birthday. Ted Earnshaw sneaks in at rear.

Me, Aussie singer/songwriter Kevin Johnston and Daryl Evans at 3CCC.

My 50th birthday cake made by Helen (Milly) Palmer. Reads 'Silly old coot, master of lies and crap.' and much more.

In earnest conversation with my good friend Les 'Rock' Harding.

Comedian Roy Tyrell, Mazza and me entertaining at a 3CCC live-to-air function.

With John Jones (Jonesy of 4GC breakfast) at Pater Awards at Southern Cross hotel. He let me hold his award.

With Jeff Langdon at a Pere Awards night, I had to wear a kilt. I was recovering from serious 3rd degree burns and could not wear trousers.

M.C Justin Shortal, Sassy Sue and Frisky T. Slim at a Pere Awards night 3CCC.

Sassy seated in lap of embarrassed John Brumby. John was to becomePremier of Victoria.

With Eric Bogle at a 3CCC barbeque.

With Doug Ashdown and Peter Sarstedt at our home at Harcourt.

Mazza with Frank Ifield.

Two country stars, Frisky T.Slim and Chad Morgan.

Chapter Eleven

Many good people, too many Cooks, jazz, musicians, songwriters, feminists and a swagman

As I previously stated there were hundreds of people who passed through 3CCC. Brian Havenhand of Bendigo had a close connection and involvement in the early days as did Leo Fowler. Leo played an important role, co-coordinating the technical development of the station. Jack Miles was an important person, a retired State Electricity Commission worker, he had a good knowledge of radio and electrical things and worked at 3CCC almost every day for eight or nine years before retiring to the south coast of New South Wales where he passed on in about 2005. I liked Jack very much in spite of our political differences! Along the way he and his wife Betty were divorced, but remained good friends.

Jack's domain was the former lamp room on the passenger platform where he stored all sorts of bits and pieces necessary to keep the radio station going. He was one of the workers who helped David Walters, son of Newsreader Bob, to build our upstairs studio. I helped where I could but I am no carpenter or technician! He was also one of the many who early on chipped in and helped to construct our transmitter hut atop Mount Alexander. Now that was hard work folks, but after the day's effort we would often sit and gaze across the wonderful landscape sipping on red wine. It was good reward for effort.

Others involved in our first years on air were Kerry Martin and Stuart Gibson, with his broad Scottish accent, both of the Students Union at Bendigo College. Kerry got into hot water for an on-air indiscretion and was suspended for two weeks – nothing really serious but she did use the forbidden F word.

June Symons helped a lot with her typing of the numerous documents and odds and ends so necessary and churned out by the truckload by Jeff Langdon. June was husband of Don who presented a jazz style show for many moons and had the softest, almost inaudible voice with a slight lisp.

Kerry McDonald was the Organic Swagman who, with Rod Willaton, presented a folk music show. He was also our Solicitor and a member of the Board for some time. His wife Brenda and twelve year old daughter Jaala also presented programs. Veronica Ellis, daughter of Bev and John Ellis was another twelve-year-old who went to air. The two were remarkably grown up and competent.

Melissa Clark was a very attractive teenager who tried very hard but she had the softest voice. One day I could stand it no longer and went into the studio.

'Why don't you bring your voice levels up? You know how to do it? We can't hear what you're saying.'

'I don't want them to hear what I'm saying. I don't want them to hear me.' I was flabbergasted.

Others I clearly recall are Trevor Scott, Ted Earnshaw – a good mate and a bit of a sad sack, Laurie Hill, John Beavis talented singer-songwriter and Clive Willman. Ann Conway was a popular presenter and Country singer who eventually helped set up Phoenixfm in Bendigo.

David Keith's Scottish music program was a must, well presented and David often left the mic open and sang along. On another occasion he loaned me his valuable kilt but that's another story. David Robb presented his favourite music, Reggae, and it was a popular show with many. Caroline McKenzie-McCarg was another polished presenter and Jean Wyldbore was popular with a program that focused on tourism. She also researched and presented a significant recorded program on the history of the Theatre Royal, which she got me to produce.

The Symes family, Stan, Heather and daughters Michelle and Rachelle were avid listeners and often called in to see Mazza and me. They usually stayed for several hours eating into the time we should have spent on other work, but they were great people.

Nancy Pond was another who worked very hard and quietly behind the scenes. She and her husband Glenn lived at Yandoit, a considerable distance from Harcourt, but Nancy regularly attended the station, working as a bookkeeper and typist. She had previously worked at 3AW in Melbourne so her knowledge was extremely valuable.

Pat (Patricia Moloney) came from Trentham, notoriously damp spud country, to present a program. She was quite articulate and before long sought and won a seat on the board. She worked hard at it, especially as she suffered considerably from serious and debilitating arthritis and carried a stick as support. She was popular all round and made worthy contributions to the running of 3CCC.

Paul Mason and Tony Cook drove all the way from Melbourne to co-present a Sunday afternoon program, 'Stepping out with a Memory'; nostalgic music from the 1930s and 1940s. Paul in particular had a fabulous knowledge of the music and was extremely popular with our senior audience. In fact Sunday was a top day, with Calamity Clegg's country music, followed by Jack Miles with nostalgia and then Vic McGowan with more of the same. Paul and Tony followed them, rounding off a very good day for older folk.

There were two Tony Cooks at 3CCC, the other a bearded, long haired, good natured hippy type from the Chewton Bushlands. He bore no resemblance whatever to the Melbourne Tony Cook, but there was some similarity to a third Tony Cook, also from Chewton Bushlands! The first mentioned Tony Cook was regularly seen at bush dances and the like dancing the night away, usually solo. He loved to dance. Sadly he died early in 2015.

Two others who may have been classified as 'Hippies' were Team and Christine Henderson, responsible citizens and parents as well as talented musicians and all round entertainers from Taradale. (Many years later Christine was elected to our local Council, becoming Mayor and their son became a volunteer at WMAfm). 'Hippy' was a title locals gave to anybody with long hair who dressed and behaved non-mainstream.

Rosemary McKenzie and Anne Langdon presented a feminine type show called Fairplay. Neither were rabid feminists but they called for fairer treatment of women generally.

Phil Campbell was in his early teens, a mate of another aspiring announcer, Brad Geier. Both lads came from Bendigo, thirty-four kilometers distant to present their shows, a pretty big effort involving dedicated parents. Phil was the typical DJ type who adopted the big voice and style of commercial announcers prevalent in the eighties. He loved what he did but as far as I know he never made the big time. About the youthful Brad Geier we will have much more later.

From Melbourne came a great bloke named Ian Jorgenson to co-host a fabulous show with Daryl Evans. The two, put in hours of work in preparation for the Saturday evening Southern Star Show. It was very well produced and probably the best regular program ever to come out of 3CCC. Ian contributed a good deal to 3CCC behind the scenes I believe.

Sam Grumont was the jazz guru of the station and really knew and loved his music as did our blues specialist, the suave and knowledgeable Julius Porlai Junior. 'Dr Jules', an accountant, was well liked around the station and served as an excellent member of the Board for some years. His program, 'The track of the Blues', was well listened to by blues lovers all over Central Victoria. I still see him from time to time and he is still playing the blues on a station in Bendigo.

Rex Watts and his brother Robbie didn't do anything on air but were nevertheless attached to the station through their wonderful music. Sadly Robbie passed away at an early age. He was a brilliant guitarist who, with Rex and Joe Rutledge, worked with my son Glenn in Sharp Toys and later with some top Australian bands.

Who could forget Frank Stowe! Frank was the first one to present a regular program on 3CCC, Jazz on Saturday. His program started at noon and it began at exactly noon no matter what. It was not unusual to hear the preceding program, Punter to Punter, relayed from 3RRR Melbourne, cut off in mid sentence because the clock struck twelve! This annoyed the crap out of a lot of us but Frank didn't consider it odd! I understand that almost thirty years on, Frank is still presenting Jazz on Saturday on Fresh fm, the remnant of 3CCC in Bendigo, and no doubt on the stroke of twelve! The first time Frank went on air from the Bendigo studio, at the old fire station, he was not familiar with how things worked. At twelve o'clock he crossed back from 3RRR and began his show. We were treated to ten minutes of dead air. Frank had not been shown how to properly switch to the studio and went merrily on his way, all by himself until somebody went in and fixed the problem. If ten seconds of dead air is eternity what is ten minutes?

Speaking of Frank, I readily recall Frank Callahan and his wife Margaret of Ballarat. Frank was an accomplished musician who could play just about any instrument. He worked as 'Frank Callahan's One Man Band' and indeed he was. Frank was no longer young but he never lacked enthusiasm or never lacked work. He was much in demand at dances throughout the area. We came to know Frank and Margaret quite well following his coming to the station many times and having Daryl Evans record dozens of his own songs. Frank sold hundreds of his excellent cassettes at the numerous dances he performed at. His signature song must surely be 'Ballarat' which is still in use in the area in promoting his beloved city of Ballarat.

Scott Hall was a Castlemaine School Teacher who loved to get on air and he presented some excellent music shows before calling it quits. Lots of people come and go in community radio.

Felicity Say was a real charmer, well spoken and well educated, she was said to be the daughter of the legendary broadcaster Norman Banks, who was the mainstay of Melbourne's top station 3AW for many years. Norman was extremely popular and drew a huge audience. He is credited with beginning the now annual event of Carols by Candlelight in Melbourne's Alexandra Gardens. Felicity obviously inherited his well modulated tone of voice and, when I was searching for a woman to read a serialised version of a book, I asked her. She readily accepted, although it was a major task. The book was 'Outpost – A Doctor on the Divide', written by Trentham's legendary physician, Gweneth Wisewould, fifteen years before. I volunteered to be the producer. Felicity and I spent many hours in the tiny production studio as she read her way through what I finally edited into twenty, ten minute episodes of the wonderful story. The serial was broadcast in the morning show and was very popular. It was beautifully read by Felicity.

Keith Johnstone was with us for a time and I remember him mainly because of a live-to-air interview he conducted with an eighty-four-year-old woman. She was very deaf and he had to actually YELL at her. It was really quite hilarious and topped off when she made a derogatory remark about the town council. 'And you can leave that in,' she said defiantly. 'It's already in!' shouted Keith.

One of our volunteers, a ragged hippy-looking type whose name escapes me, was pulled up by police who discovered a car full of white powder. No doubt the constable thought he'd caught a drug dealer/user but it was in fact flour, as the bloke ran a small flour mill. The copper was a little miffed it seems as he then followed the man into town and booked him for some minor driving offence!

Youngster David Breakwell was a drummer in a small time local band; he joined us and presented a very good music program for a time. He was outstanding because of his enthusiasm, which stays in my memory. He never did join big time of music, but he certainly wasn't alone in that! Trevor Thomas was another presenter who stays in my memory because of his enthusiasm and good approach to broadcasting.

Another ex-ABC man was Maldon resident the late Peter Baster. Peter had been a journalist with the ABC and each week, without fail, he delivered a reel to reel tape ready for me to put to air. It ran for only about ten minutes and featured news from Maldon and information from the Country Fire Authority. Peter was a worthy contributor, fastidious in what he did.

Mal Peters was another man who made a major contribution to the early development of 3CCC. He was president in 1983 and his stated aim was to make 3CCC the best in Australia. He typified the determination of the people that made up the station in the early days. I am uncertain but I believe that he eventually moved to Queensland.

Farmer/School Teacher Malcolm Fyffe, was also a valuable contributor for a number of years. His manner and demeanor were more like the laid-back farmer than anything else. Nothing seemed to bother him. I held him in high regard and he was a strong supporter and mentor to me in later, troubled times.

Unfortunately some of the people involved along the way have faded from my memory. Probably I had little to do with them when they were at the station and some I rarely saw as they presented programs at night or, like many, didn't last long.

Sherri Ann Cox from Maldon was a young woman who was our very first Office Coordinator, a job she did very well. 'Office Coordinator' was another title for 'Jack of all trades' and involved just about every job you could think of – from typing and answering the phone to going on air and organizing volunteers. It was a demanding position and Sherri was good at it. Regrettably she left us after a relatively short spell and was replaced by the sixteen year old red headed farm girl from Newbridge, Bev Stewart.

Bev was absolutely wonderful. She did her job with patience, competence and never fading good humour although she was often placed in stressful situations. We all loved her.

John Sutherland, a farmer's son from Teal Point, near Murrabit in Northern Victoria, loved her in a different way and Marilyn, Jack Miles, Bev Ellis and I eventually attended Bev's marriage to John, a most memorable experience described elsewhere.

We had some weird and wonderful characters at Triple C. Margot Archibold from North Harcourt, a big, bustling woman, famous with us for her saveloy soup, was sacked, reinstated and then sacked again, the last time forever. She was of determined character and was not afraid to speak her mind – a trait which got her into trouble and ended her involvement with 3CCC. She was also a passionate devourer of garlic, even kept it in her shoes, in the belief that it was a cure-all. When she vacated the confines of the studio you certainly knew she had been there! With her husband Jim she ran a service station and local shop that specialized in frog bits and pieces, alongside the Calder highway at Fogarty's Gap road turn off to Maldon. Jim unfortunately died prematurely whilst alone feeding cattle on the property and it was some time before he was missed. Not much later the entire shop and servo was demolished to make way for the new Calder Freeway.

Slade Pullman was different, to say the least, and Peter Schofielding (not his real name) was a real creep. He seemed to appear everywhere. One day he came across Bryan Roberts playing the organ outside Kmart. Bryan was a professional, and was being paid for his work. Peter did not know that Bryan was already one of our best presenters. He congratulated Bryan on his playing and said he would use his influence to get him on air at 3CCC. Bryan just smiled and said, 'Thank you.'

Chapter Twelve

Slim Dusty, Joe Daly, The P.M. calls, The Olivers from Blackwood, a magpie, Langdon gets a fright

'Hey, Ian,' called Bev Sutherland, 'you're wanted on line three. It's Bob Hawke, the Prime Minister.'

I laughed. Bev was at it again. We were always kidding each other.

I picked up the phone. 'G'day Bob, how yer going?' I spoke as if the PM called me every day.

I was stunned when a serious voice intoned. 'It's David Nihill here, from the Prime Minister's office. I'm responding on behalf of Mr. Hawke to your letter asking him to record a greeting.'

You could have knocked me over with a feather! I had forgotten that I had written to the Prime Minister asking if he would record a birthday greeting for our upcoming fifth birthday.

David Nihill went on to explain that the PM was unable to tape the greeting but if I could come to Canberra he would be pleased to arrange it for me.

I was impressed! It was difficult to imagine that a Prime Minister would actually do that for a hick radio station in some place called Harcourt he'd probably never heard of.

Slim Dusty was coming to Castlemaine to perform at the basketball stadium, part of the biennial State Festival. I had had a fair bit of contact with Slim and Joy since Mazza and I spent a day with them on the Clarkefield set of the Slim Dusty movie. I had conducted a lengthy interview with Slim in preparation for a 'Special' there as we sat together in my old VW.

I used to smoke about thirty cigarettes a day and as we sat and talked in the confined space I nearly choked Slim with my clouds of smoke. I was then unaware of his aversion and bad reaction to cigarette smoke. I learned that later, but Slim was too much of a gentleman to complain or ask me to stop puffing.

When Mazza and I arrived at the Castle Motel in Castlemaine where Slim and his group had already unpacked, Mazza mentioned to Slim that he had a lot of fans resident at the old folks' home, 'Alexander' and suggested an impromptu visit. Slim readily agreed and Mazza immediately drove us to the complex.

We visited several of the Hostels and the residents (and staff) could scarcely believe their eyes.

I think this action from Slim says a lot about the man and explains why he was so loved by so many Australians. Put simply, Slim Dusty was a good bloke.

Slim and I had a mutual friend, Joe 'Trumby' Daly, a rugged outback individual with a heart of gold and a real talent for writing bush verse. Slim recorded over thirty of Joe's works over the years, beginning with 'Trumby', the poignant story of a black man who died because he couldn't read or write. Joe had named it 'Jacky' but Slim considered that inappropriate and changed it to 'Trumby'. Joe's words always came from the heart and were completely descriptive of the outback and its people that he so loved. He had spent all of his life working in the outback, working with cattle mostly, but for a time on the Moomba gas field in South Australia. He eventually retired to Broken Hill.

Joe loved Slim and they became good friends, visiting each other whenever they could. Joe's brother, Ron, died at an early age and once when Slim visited he went with Joe to Ron's grave at Broken Hill cemetery. Joe told me that Slim shed real tears as the two of them stood at the graveside.

Joe, wife Kaye and the five children once called to see me at 3CCC whilst on a trip to visit my brother Alan at Dunolly. They were close friends for the many years that Alan lived and worked at outback Tibooburra. Alan, by then married to Tessie and with a baby daughter Eileen, decided to move to 'civilization' and tried Dunolly. He lasted a year before moving back to the scrub, Broken Hill. I suspect that a verse which painted a vivid picture of the outback life that Joe wrote and posted to Alan had something to do with this.

Alan bought a house on the edge of Broken Hill and he and Joe lived in adjoining streets there, two hundred metres apart. They remained lifetime good mates.

On this visit Justin Shortal conducted a wonderful interview with Kaye and the children in which Kaye played the guitar and the kids sang. It was a lovely radio program, one of the most memorable I have heard. Sadly, I fear it was lost from the archives of 3CCC, where I placed the recording for preservation. I had interviewed Joe separately. A couple of years later a company published Joe's wonderful book of his verse, a copy of which he presented to me. I hold it with pride and sorrow for the memory of a great Aussie bloke.

Joe passed away at Broken Hill in 2007, outliving his mate Slim and leaving his best mate, my brother Alan, very unhappy.

Bert and Joy Oliver were from Blackwood in the Trentham district. They had the distinction of being the only known listeners to 3CCC in the small forest hamlet about ten kilometres to Trentham's south. They also became our good friends, calling to see us whenever they were nearby. On one occasion they called in to say hello and stayed for a week! Bert was a returned World War II digger. Taken prisoner by the Japanese at Singapore he was one of the many, including my older half-brother Ron Collard, who were forced to work on the infamous Burma railway in Thailand. Sadly, Ron did not survive and died at Hintock Camp aged nineteen in July 1943. Bert was a small, thin man, and he said that this was what saved him from death on the railway. He explained that many big men fell away and died. Like many of those who shared the horrors Bert did not speak of them but one day I managed to coax him to do so. Hopefully his story on tape is preserved along with numerous others in the archives of 3CCC, the remnant of which is now Fresh fm Bendigo. Bert and his wife Joy shocked everyone by moving to South Australia very late in life. We thought they would never willingly leave Blackwood.

I cannot forget Donald McTavish, (not his real name) a light plane pilot in his forties, he called on me one day expressing his desire to train in announcing and to get on the radio. He was the most disastrous pupil I ever had. At the controls of a plane he may have excelled but at the controls of a studio he was hopeless. I simply could not teach him. He could not grasp the technique at all. For weeks he confused one knob or switch with another and I gave thanks that I would never have to fly with him! Eventually I gave up on him and handed him to a nonplussed Doug Scobie. Doug also gave up on him after a few weeks and Donald never did take off on the airwaves.

One of our oddest visitors was a young Magpie, who we named Hector. Hector hopped into the production studio one day when Phil Campbell was at work recording a show. Hector flapped himself onto the mixing desk quite unconcerned and stared fascinated at Phil's production process. Young Phil could not believe what he was seeing. 'It may be country radio,' he told me, 'but this is ridiculous.'

Hector must have been somebody's pet for he lived happily in my office for two weeks, with breaks outdoors. Hector perched mainly on the telephone answering machine which soon became spattered with unmentionable waste and filth. One of my jobs was to clean it every day.

Hector appeared to be fascinated with the machine; perhaps it was the recorded voice of Gavin McDougall, after whom Marilyn named the bird. We had nicknamed Gavin as Hector Pascal because at the time he gave the weather reports on Bendigo TV Channel 8, a play on words. I fed Hector with meat scraps and such and he seemed quite content. He settled in to be one of the crew. Regrettably one morning I found him dead, slumped feet up beside his beloved answering machine.

Maybe it's constant ringing, or even perhaps the sound of Gavin's voice, had a disastrous effect on him. I suspected suicide. Gavin went on to be Chief of Staff at Chanel Nine TV News and was last heard of as Director of Public Affairs at the Australian Consulate in Hong Kong. Now that's a community radio success story!

The list of odd types and acts goes on! Like the confident, important sounding male, whose career was thankfully brief, who spoke knowingly of George Gershwin and his sister, Ira! Fred Paynting, Country music presenter, although sadly blinded in a car smash, was able to present a show with the aid of a panel operator. He caused considerable mirth in the office downstairs when he said, 'I can't get used to this daylight savings.' What about the new chum who introduced the popular orchestra leader as 'Bert Kamper*fart*'. The list is huge!

Jeff Langdon had a good sense of humour – combined with an acid tongue. A woman, claiming to be a financial supporter of the station, once wrote to the paper complaining about Jack Miles singing praise of Queensland's controversial Premier, Joh Bjelke Petersen. Although he was at the other end of the political spectrum, Jeff went on air and got stuck into the woman quite mercilessly, ending with: 'I suggest that you keep your money. We defend the right of anyone to express an opinion on no matter what. That's public radio lady. You can do us all a favour and listen to another radio station.'

I was in the habit of reading bits on air from our in-house publication 'Voltalk', put together by Phillip Edmunds and edited by Catherine York-Moore. There was never anything earth shattering, just items that I figured our Listeners would be interested in. Certainly I read nothing that was strictly for our volunteer's eyes. I knew that our audience felt part of the family and I believed that was our greatest strength. A regular feature was the announcement of 'The Volunteer of the Month' as chosen by the Board. One time the editor lodged a strong objection to me quoting from 'her paper'. She said it was a breach of copyright and ethics. She threatened legal action and suggested that she would report me to the Australian Broadcasting Authority. This was pretty serious stuff.

When the manager Gerry Pyne approached me clutching the letter he told me he feared damage to the station and I had better cut it out. I was astonished and angry. It was an absurdity. I could quote from any publication on earth, provided I acknowledged it, but not from our in-house journal! I rightly felt it was a lot of crap.

Next morning I was still upset and related the story to our listeners. I hedged around a direct quote by saying, 'I usually reveal our Volunteer of the Month as published in Voltalk but I am now forbidden to do so pending possible legal action. However I say a special good morning to Susan Trigg.'

That evening Jeff defiantly introduced a new segment to his 'Schlock Show' an interesting talk program that examined all sorts of current issues. It was co-hosted by a man I then held in some regard, the very relaxed and amiable – Al Watson. Al was a pharmacist who resided at a tiny dot on the map, Sandon. The new segment was introduced with a rousing fanfare as Jeff seriously intoned, 'We now present Readings from Voltalk.' He went on to read the Editor's scribbling about breach of copyright, breach of ethics, legal acts, Broadcasting Authority etc. etc. It was Jeff at his sarcastic best. I loved it!

No comment or further complaint was heard from The Editor of Voltalk.

We later did a live-to-air broadcast of live music from Al Watson's home. I didn't attend what was a very happy celebration but listened at home. It was awful radio, but fun for the participants.

Several years later I went into a chemist store in Bendigo where Al was working. I was surprised to see him and greeted him with 'Hello Al. Good to see you. They've got you working mate,' a common enough greeting in Australia. I was shocked when Al went right off and in a rage hurled the most vitriolic abuse at me. Apparently he was upset at the perceived inference that it was rare for him to work! Of course my remark intended no such thing. I slunk from the shop, injured and embarrassed.

Jeff Langdon's biting tongue often got people off-side and sometimes landed him in trouble. It was not always intentional. One time there was a dramatic response. Jeff had obtained another grant to employ one or two people and he was conducting interviews with applicants. One was a woman in her thirties who lived with her husband in the then trendy Merrifield Street area of Castlemaine. When she volunteered her address Jeff responded with something like: 'Oh. That's the trendy north end. Do you live in one of those rustic old humpies that are falling down?'

That didn't go down too well with the woman who was quite likely very proud of her old home. The interview went downhill from there and the woman left in a huff.

At lunchtime a half hour later Marilyn, Bev Sutherland, Jeff and I were in the kitchen devouring our pies and cream buns when there was a loud thumping on the locked door behind us. It was more like kicking than knocking.

A male voice bellowed. 'Langdon! Langdon! Are you there Langdon? Come on out here you lump of shit I want you.' It appeared that Jeff had a visitor.

We sat in stunned silence as the hammering continued. Jeff turned a little pale.

'Who the hell's that?'

It became pretty obvious when the voice called. 'You have insulted my wife, you bastard. Come out here, you prick.'

The thumping and yelling continued as a slightly nervous Jeff moved to the door. 'Uh oh, Jeff,' I thought 'You're in serious trouble here.'

Squaring his shoulders Jeff cautiously drew the door open, confronting a livid face that snarled at him in fury. The man lunged at Jeff, seizing him by the shirt. Jeff struggled free and stepped back holding the man at arm's length.

'Hang on a minute man. Hang on. What's the trouble?'

'The trouble is, you bastard, is that you humiliated my wife.'

We sat agog in the kitchen not daring to go outside. Like true cowards we left Jeff to his fate!

The two grappled their way out of our sight – the shouting continuing. We huddled in the kitchen straining our ears.

Jeff must have called on his best negotiating skills because the noise gradually subsided. After a few minutes a tousle-haired Jeff returned to his lunch.

His face erupted in a wide grin. 'I'll have to watch my mouth in future. I don't think that lady will be working for us.'

Jeff seemed to get in the poo quite often for one reason or another. Like the time good hearted Margot Archibald brought us a big pot of soup for our lunch. It was ghastly, with great lengths of saveloys and a bit of carrot floating in murky water. We called it saveloy soup and it was inedible. Jeff took the pot and emptied its entire contents onto the garden bed at the back door. Guess what? Who should call in but Margot, who couldn't miss the pile of savs and carrots outside the door. She didn't say a word but her face said it all as Jeff shuffled quickly into his office.

At 2 o'clock one morning Jeff's phone rang. Struggling to wake he answered the call. A voice came loud and clear 'Langdon. You're a F...g C...t!' Nothing more. That call really troubled Jeff – but only for a day – he had a thick hide.

I think it was Jeff (and maybe Kerry McDonald) who decided we should fly the Eureka flag, an idea I fully appreciated. It flew for a day and disappeared overnight. Whilst a replacement was being sought we were hit with vehement protests from the Castlemaine RSL. 'Why fly that rag? Why not our Australian flag? I fought under that flag for King and country,' and all that. They were ultra-conservative back then, I'm afraid. Undeterred up went the new one. It too disappeared. Never one to give in easily, Jeff obtained a third and it flew happily for many years alongside a Triple C flag made, I think, by Anne Langdon.

I once received a call on air from a Brendan Galliotti. I had been on air for years and had completed over 1,100 breakfast shows and hundreds of others by then. He said, 'you're pretty good mate. I reckon you'll make it.' Is nonplussed the word?

I was officially the Volunteers Coordinator and some took this to mean I was at their beck and call. One night at 10pm and I was in bed as I rose at 4.30am to do breakfast. The phone rang. Christine Evans explained that it was urgent and could I come in and help her record her two hour program for tomorrow? I won't tell you what I told her. Oh boy!

Brett Garsed was a local lad and a brilliant self-taught guitarist. I interviewed him once or twice and was delighted when he sent a tape of his work to Glenn Wheatley and was accepted to join the legendary John Farnham's band. Brett later went to the USA and toured with the Nelson Twins, made a number of records and, now back in Castlemaine, is making a good living as a musician. His current solo recordings sell all around the world. He is a friend of my son Glenn, having played with his band Darkcide on occasions and is a regular with his brother Andrew in the popular local band Black Dog.

Who doesn't like Santa Claus? Oh! okay. Anyway, my career as Santa Claus began the first Christmas at 3CCC when I hired a suit and went to work at the big Christmas party. We had lots of parties then. I must have done okay because from then on I had regular jobs with all sorts of groups. Mazza made me a beautiful Santa suit and neighbor Ian Foster gave me a pair of great motorcycle boots. I really looked the part and made a good Santa, even if I say so myself. I put my heart into it and really believed in Santa Claus for the kids' sake. This continued each year for the next twenty years until I finally quit officially in 2004. I rarely got paid, except maybe a bottle of red wine, but I did it for love, not money. I once got a job at Shepparton for hugely rich and generous Dick Pratt, owner of Visyboard. I was paid a staggering (for me) $200, given top class free motel accommodation for Mazza and me and had the biggest feast I have ever had. I even shared a dressing room with Julie Anthony who provided some of the night's tremendous entertainment. Dick Pratt was wonderfully generous and each and everyone present had a huge photograph of themselves with Santa as a memento of the evening. Even the great man himself had one taken. I still do the odd job as Santa because I love to dress up, being a ham actor – and I still have my photo with Dick Pratt.

* * *

Here are a few more samples of acts by 3CCC presenters: Kathryn Gibbons was on air on Christmas day at 4pm with a taped program preceding her. At 3.50 all fell silent as the tape ended early. Jack Miles was on duty and eventually rushed upstairs into the studio. He was greeted by Kathryn seated at the desk writing her script. Jack yelled her to get something on air to which she replied. 'But I don't start until four o'clock!'

'God help us,' cried Jack when he poked his head into my office!

Susan Green once interviewed a poet from Campbell's Creek who was renowned for drinking lots of whiskey; he also smoked like a chimney, enough to rival me. She suggested that he might like to read stories for kids to which he replied. 'I'm not reading stories for bloody kids. I hate kids.' And he meant it.

Calamity Clegg once had a request for a particular song and said. 'I won't play that, it's not country, it's rock and roll,' and proceeded to play instead Lucille by Chuck Berry!

I coached a young woman in the use of the Superscope recorders we used back then and she went off to The Brolga Hotel at Lake Eppalock to interview country music legend Chad Morgan. I was mortified when she gave me the interview to edit. She clearly demonstrated the need to learn about the person you are interviewing.

'Mr. Morgan, have you won many trophies?'

'No, not many,' Chad answered, obviously a bit taken aback by the question.

Later, 'Do you do any busking?'

'I have about ten gold records. I don't really need to do buskin',' a very patient Chad replied softly. He concluded the interview at that point.

Mazza and I went to the Strathdale Hall Bendigo to cover the visit of Bob Hawke P.M. He was greeted by a pack of Right to Life protesters. Banners and placards were everywhere as the mob was hurling abuse. In a quiet moment the voice of thirteen-year-old Melissa, Mazza's daughter rang out very, very loudly: 'Why don't you all f... off and go home.' They didn't, but the visit was a success and I had a good human interest story for our Listeners. Mazza had been more than a little shocked by her daughter's comment!

Chapter Thirteen

Hot dogs, Blue Heelers, a billy goat and a marriage

We were off the air! What the hell was it? It was about 10 o'clock on a Saturday night when 3CCC suddenly fell silent. Not so much as a bit of hiss. Jack Miles and Jeff searched frantically for the cause but found nothing. A trip up to the transmitter hut on Mount Alexander revealed nothing – until Jack realized that it was a problem with the cable reaching from transmitter to antenna away up the tower. At last, working by torchlight they found that some bastard had climbed onto the roof of the hut and cut the cable. It was tough and thick and whoever it was must have used bolt cutters – and at their peril. It took many hours to make a repair but finally by noon on Sunday we were back on air. Fortunately the damage didn't extend to the transmitter as it easily could have. We never found the culprit who must have planned it, as a ladder was needed to get on the roof. Somebody obviously had an axe to grind with 3CCC.

Mazza and I became used to poverty, a way of life for us committed to Community Radio. To bring in some cash we started to grow plants, thousands of them, which we carted off to Saturday and Sunday markets, making small profits for hard work. It meant very few weekends off and a constant job with daily watering.

My favourite fundraising endeavor was operating a hot dog stand at markets and shows. I became pretty famous locally as Hot Dog Harry, complete with aprons name-emblazoned by my 'assistant' Mazza. It was quite profitable, as were our super-fresh apple juice sales. Not organic by the way. We had permission from

Harcourt orchardist Warren Dowling to gather as many windfall apples as we liked. We did, and with two domestic juicers we churned out hundreds of paper cups of juice on site over a couple of years and at a hundred markets. Survival in Community radio wasn't easy.

In the mid 1980s Mazza scored a job as an extra on a movie being shot at Maldon. Also in the mix was Les Harding. The movie's working title, Marie Claire or similar, was demure enough but it turned out be R rated, not that it worried her or Rock too much. This job led to Mazza and me joining the union and becoming regular extras in a heap of TV shows and movies. We even appeared in a good number of TV ads, Marilyn far more and more prominent than me. Better looking no doubt! It's a long, long list that I won't elaborate on here. However, there was one notable experience. For eleven years we appeared in numerous episodes of the hugely popular series Blue Heelers which starred John Wood. Our friends Jack Paynting and wife Min from Bendigo alternated with us. Our principal role was as regulars in the Mount Thomas Imperial Hotel. The actual pub used in the exterior shots was the historic Imperial Hotel in Castlemaine. The bar however, was a mock-up in Studio 8 at Channel 7, South Melbourne. It seemed we always had a pot of beer or a glass of wine in hand. In the beginning the beer was real but one day a shearer, working as an extra, overdid the beer intake and from then on it was fake; undrinkable really, warm and awful to taste. The wine was grape juice.

Sometimes we worked on locations out and about the Melbourne suburbs or in one instance at Werribee. It was there, in a shearing shed scene, that I got my first speaking role. I had to say: 'That'll be a hundred dollars' as I collected a win on the result of a fight from the shed bookmaker. Apart from the several good jobs doing TV ads with speaking roles, that was the sum of my career as an actor who actually spoke! Mazza did similarly in most part but she scored a couple of really big and lucrative TV ad parts over a period.

Blue Heelers remains the best gig we had and we made a good number of friends among cast and crew over the eleven years, including John Wood, the Police Sergeant, and Julie Nihill the hotel keeper. It was a wonderful experience and of course it helped with our usually precarious finances. We still do the occasional job thirty years later.

I'll always remember the time I was taken from the 3CCC payroll. It was a Friday, 20th November, Christmas around the corner. Mazza and I were having lunch in the kitchen when Gerry came in. He expressed his sorrow but said the Board had decided to end my part-time paid employment on December 31st as a cost cutting measure.

Merry Christmas! Happy New Year! I was shocked, this was totally unexpected. Hadn't I recently been assured in writing by the Board that I would *always* have paid work at 3CCC?

Seated at the table with Gerry, Mazza cried and I could scarcely believe that this was happening. I was confused and didn't know what to do. Unemployed at aged fifty-two. It was a disaster; over fifties were not in demand for jobs. I loved what I did at 3CCC so what else could I do but stay with it and go on the dole and hope for a turnaround.

It did turn around four months later. I successfully applied for a part time, temporary job with 3CCC, producing programs publicising the activities of The University of the Third Age (U3A). A local chapter was being set up in Castlemaine at the time. This was the job I had already been promised when it came up, part of the deal when I took a pay cut earlier, when I was told that I would always have a job. That promise came in a letter from the President as thanks for voluntarily sacrificing my full time job and going part-time when we had been in crisis.

The U3A job was advertised in the press and I was shocked to have to formally apply and go through the process. The written promise apparently wasn't worth a damn! I was one of five short-listed applicants and had to suffer the entire interview process conducted by Gerry and three Board members. One of the female board members had no time for me and delighted in asking the most difficult questions. I don't know why she disliked me, as I had never harmed her in any way. I was embarrassed having to go through the full process but I knew that I had to put my best foot forward as the Board was fair dinkum, with no guaranteed outcome for me. I finally won the job on merit after sweating through a lengthy delayed decision.

I've said that Community Radio is all about people; people like Rosemary McKenzie, a volunteer and for a time the President of the organization. She was an extremely competent, fair and efficient person, one for whom I had considerable respect. I still have a letter she wrote to me thanking me for my contributions to 3CCC and giving the assurance of continuing paid work. Only Jeff Langdon has ever written to me similarly, and I still have that letter, too.

Rosemary was one of six children from a farming family from Boort in northern Victoria. She was well educated having gained her B.A. shortly before she joined our station.

Her first job was at Castlemaine Education Centre where Jeff Langdon was the Manager. He coerced or coaxed her into radio, as he did most he came in contact with.

It was there that she met her future husband, John Brumby, destined to become Premier of Victoria twenty five years later.

She was an unassuming person but also forceful and forthright. When she spoke everyone paid attention. John Brumby also became one of us at 3CCC and the Brumby family still occupies the secluded property near Harcourt which they purchased many years ago. We have a great photo of Mazza, dressed as Sassy Sue, sitting on John's knee.

Bev Stewart announced one morning that she was going to marry John Sutherland and she asked me if I would be prepared to give her away. At the time she and her father did not get along and I was truly honoured to accept the role. Jack Miles and Bev Ellis were invited to attend and, of course, Marilyn.

Mazza and I drove to the Sutherland's family farm at Teal Point. It was about ten kilometres out of Murrabit on the Murray River where we were to prepare for the wedding. It was a very hot Saturday and in the shimmering heat-haze distance we spied the farmhouse, set in the middle of a field of Sunflowers, wilting with the heat.

The entire wedding party was there, most of us sharing a stubby or two, preparatory to the ceremony. Bev was dressed beautifully for the occasion and her groom, John, was resplendent, if decidedly uncomfortable, in a new suit.

In due course the wedding party piled into two big sedans and took off toward Murrabit, hurtling along the dusty roads at breakneck speed. Mazza and I in our 1960 Volkswagen fastback battled to keep the cars ahead in sight, the speed was beyond the VW and all we could do was follow the slow-settling dust. Finally, after a scary ride in the old car we arrived at the church.

The ceremony went without a hitch and we, along with the other guests and the bridal party, headed back to Teal Point for the reception, Mazza and I again careering behind the rest at great speed.

It was a wonderful reception. Nowhere else but in the Australian bush would such a reception happen. There was a big marquee erected beneath some sparse trees at the rear of the farmhouse. We all sat on chairs and boxes around a number of tables and trestles and proceeded to eat, drink and be merry.

It was a hot day and the drinks flowed. Everyone was soon half full and the speeches were constantly interrupted with wise and ribald remarks from the assembled guests. A great time was had by us all. The best man, fully relaxed after his ordeal at the church, had lost his jacket and tie, kicked off his shoes and socks and donned a pair of thongs. His speech was interrupted by a group of squawking white cockatoos perched in a tree.

He stopped speaking and strode into the house returning with a loaded shotgun.

'Bastard things, they're pinching half me f...... crop.' He took aim and fired. There was a loud eruption of screeching, a flurry of feathers and the offending birds fled. There didn't appear to be any casualties. The best man placed the gun on the verandah and resumed his speech, totally unpurtubed, and the party continued.

Somebody wanted music so Bev backed her car up to the gathering with the hatchback open and put on a loud music CD. No fancy bands for us!

Soon the groom's Mum appeared on the verandah. 'The pudding is ready if any of you want it.' There was a rush to the verandah for a slice of Mum's marvelous pudding. I hadn't heard of sweets referred to as pudding since I was a kid when sweets were always 'Pudding', at least at our house! I don't know what Mum's pudding was as I was too slow and missed out!

Jack Miles and Bev left the party before Mazza and I and made their way home, hitting a kangaroo on the way and half demolishing Jack's Holden Kingswood, but they arrived safely.

Mazza and I opted to camp at a hotel at Barham, not far away and just across the Murray. It was the typical bush pub at the time; a spartan room upstairs, a bathroom and toilet down the passage and cook your own breakfast in the pub kitchen. It was however a magnificent two storey building.

We shared in a piece of Australia now almost lost; old fashioned pub accommodation and it was truly an unforgettable experience.

It was an extremely hot night as we settled into bed, tired after a hectic day. It was stifling in the small room and we opened wide the balcony window. It didn't help. The bed was old and the mattress likewise and Mazza and I rolled inward to the middle and at the same time the bed bent lengthwise like a banana. The heat became unbearable. First we dragged the bed close to the window; the result was unchanged. After a couple of hours of heat and sweat we dragged the mattress onto the floor. That was a bit hard for Mazza so she climbed into the spare child's bed near the balcony door. At least then there was no more sag in my bed but it didn't get any cooler. I can't recall experiencing a hotter, more uncomfortable night.

I was a smoker back then, thirty a day. At 4am I made my way along the dark passageway to the toilet. Half asleep, I stood at the toilet bowl and reached for a cigarette from my packet of Hallmark Dual Filters. It contained my last three cigarettes. Horror! It slipped from my right hand and went kerplunk into the bowl! My last cigarettes floated soaked in a most unsavory mixture, topping off a perfect night. I had to wait until the publican appeared at breakfast for my next cigarette. After a real country breakfast, hot and weary, we made it home safely in our magnificent VW.

The next day Bev Ellis was on air and invited me in for a yarn. Together we recounted the story of the other Bev's wedding. It was quite funny in the telling and drew a big response from the audience.

Sometime later, Bev and John had moved into an old farmhouse they rented at Newbridge. It was the typical old joint with a thunderbox down the back, a tin bath with a chip heater in the wash house and an ancient wood stove for cooking. It was onto this scene that Mazza and I arrived one Saturday night as dinner guests of The Sutherlands.

John had recently shot a wild duck and it was merrily roasting in the old oven as we set about destroying a few beers and cheap plonk and talking non-stop. From time to time Bev would peep into the oven muttering things like, 'It's nearly done' and 'It'll be ready soon' and 'I think the stove isn't very good.' The time ticked happily by and around ten o'clock Bev announced that the duck was cooked. By this time we were starving and three parts pissed. The roast was placed on our plates and Mazza sliced into her delectable duck. It was still raw! Still bloody raw! Ten o'clock and tea still not ready! We wept into our grog.

'No worries,' said Bev as she reached into a cupboard, producing with a flourish a can of Castlemaine ham.

So that's what we had for tea as the clock on the shelf chimed eleven.

Ah! Bev Ellis. Most of us loved her, but there were a few who didn't, especially one female who one day became a Board member. Bev was the centre of a public brawl when she accepted an invitation to the Bendigo Sportsmen's Dinner. It was in recognition of her work for football. There was outcry from some sporting members and others and poor Bev was the ham in the sandwich. Never one to shirk it she stuck to her guns and eventually was able to attend; but only after the Bendigo Advertiser had devoted several editions to the story. Yes folks, male chauvinism was still around in the 1980s.

Who could forget the 'Rock Hoppers Opera', a unique and a fabulous night's entertainment, part of the State Festival for its last year! Deep in the bush, about two kilometres up a rough dirt track, now the respectable Specimen Gully Road, was an abandoned slate quarry. It was cut into a hillside with towering walls that went up a sheer ten meters.

These magic nights that ran annually for three years, until the authorities forbade it due to the danger it represented. What a pity, because it was absolutely unique and not all that dangerous.

The several bands played and guests sang as a diesel generator, hidden a distance away, pumped out electricity. We even once had a didgeridoo player perched high on an embankment, in almost total darkness. This eerie experience has never left me. It was amazing. We danced and we drank; quite a few smoked some weed and it was all good fun.

Leaving the 'opera' on that last night, I having just got my drivers licence back after four long years, was driving from the concert to the main road. Rounding a bend we were confronted one hundred meters away by flashing blue lights and two police cars. Don't ask me how we did it but Mazza, in the passenger seat, and I swapped places in a flash. We could have saved ourselves the trouble. As we got close a policeman, spotting the heavily sign-written Kombi, yelled to another, 'It's okay. It's 3CCC, let them through,' as we were waved on. If I had been caught I would certainly have lost my licence again and for a long stretch as I was probably over the legal imit. Thanks Mazza (and the unwitting policemen).

Aussie music great John Williamson called to see us at the station one day. I had rung him and asked him for an interview and he happily accepted.

Mazza had visited the backyard toilet, past the well and the wash house. To her dismay when she went to leave the outhouse she found the way blocked by a very large and very smelly billy goat with long and dangerous looking horns.

She was terrified of the animal but somehow forced her way past the beast and bolted into the station office, hotly pursued by the goat.

'There's a huge monster animal thing out there and it tried to attack me,' she cried. 'I had to run for my life.'

There was a loud and prolonged thumping on the door. I peered though the small window adjoining the main entrance and sure enough there was this wild looking goat attacking the door. It seemed that it meant business and all present were mortified. Bev Ellis was having a 'hysterical fit', Mazza was trembling in fear, Bev Sutherland was clutching her sides with laughter and John Scarborough was as puzzled and fearful as me. This was a BIG animal. I had never had any dealings with a large male goat before – and he was an intact male for sure as demonstrated by the large, swaying sack suspended from his tummy.

The attack on the door continued and I felt I had to do something. Cautiously I opened the kitchen door that led into the yard and quietly made my way the short distance around the side of the building to the main doorway. Following at a safe distance were the rest of the crew. There he was, this giant billy goat earnestly butting the door with his huge set of horns.

Taking my life in my hands I approached the beast. As he turned to confront me I seized the large chain that hung around his neck and then grappled with him in a wrestling hold. The stench from his body was overpowering but I hung in there and somehow wrestled him out the gate onto the station platform, eventually securing him by his chain to the fence.

It was during this event that John Williamson arrived on the platform and witnessed a large part of the struggle.

'I've travelled around a lot but never have I come across anything like this.' He roared with laughter.

My struggle had me covered with the powerful Billy Goat odor and I had to head for home and a quick shower. John spent the time catching up with the folk present, sharing coffee and a laugh. He said that he'd have to write a song about the experience, but never did. I'll bet however that he never forgot that visit.

On reflection I am convinced that we misjudged Billy the goat. I reckon it's most likely that he was, in fact, simply trying to be friendly and was somebody's pet. A neighbor claimed him later in the day.

After a brief interview John Williamson made his way to Bendigo for the concert, first inviting us to the show, an offer readily accepted.

I had the privilege of interviewing John on a number of occasions and always found him a pleasant and unaffected person who so obviously missed his family when on the road.

Many of the visitors to 3CCC were entertainers. For example, Kevin Johnston, Lonnie Lee, Johnny Devlin, Rodney Vincent, Col Elliot, Old 55, Ian Wilson with the Delltones and I had the pleasure of interviewing most of them. I reckon the fact that we were unique in being located in a disused railway station away from any large town brought them in. They wanted to see for themselves.

We once met up with the Delltones where Mazza carried out an in depth interview with Ian Pee Wee Wilson, the long time group leader. The result was an excellent one hour Delltones Special that won an industry award for Mazza.

One day a young man called in, carrying a guitar over his shoulder. He gave me his name and said positively, without any nonsense, 'I'm here for the interview.' I had never heard of the bloke but figured that Calamity Clegg or one of the other country music presenters had asked him to come and be interviewed. I decided to tape the interview and hand it to the one who arranged it when I found them. Somehow I managed to make a reasonable job of my talk with him, having no background or knowledge of the man, which is generally regarded as an essential item. He thanked me profusely and went on his way.

I never did find the person who arranged the visit in spite of asking every possible presenter. None of the presenters had arranged an interview and the tape was never used. My only conclusion was that the man had come to the wrong radio station. That has happened before and is sure to happen again.

Chapter Fourteen

A Kombi van, Dachshunds, A Country Music festival and our Sopwith Camel

Community Radio is about local people and that's the way it was at 3CCC – all sorts of people from all sorts of backgrounds doing all sorts of things. Good people. Good country people. What I call real people. Hundreds of people over the years, mostly from the surrounding area were actively involved with 3CCC.

The saddest thing for me when I was eventually removed from 3CCC was the loss of so many friends that I had made in the organisation. This was probably caused by their lack of knowledge about the true circumstances of my departure and reluctance to 'take sides'.

My VW Kombi gets a quite a few mentions in this story. It was bought with a loan from Jeff Langdon. I had a desperate need for a decent vehicle and Jeff loaned me $1600 from his own pocket to buy this great machine. He was a very generous person and I thank him again for that. I asked one of my listeners, Roger McKellar a sign writer from Bendigo, if he would do a bit of a sign, contra, in exchange for advertising, a regular occurrence in radio. He readily agreed and wanted the Kombi for two days. When I collected it I was delighted. Wow! You should have seen it. It was fabulous and a vehicle the station could be proud of. It was a truly beautiful job and it cost the station nothing! Beautiful black, white and gold lettering, I loved it and it was a great ad for 3CCC as I drove it everywhere. The ad I recorded for Roger said he was 'The Busy Sign Writer' as indeed he was for the quality of his work. His brother Bill, a retired bank manager, lived on a hilltop at North Harcourt and was a regular Listener, a Morris Minor collector and a friend.

Roger Boehme presented a Saturday morning program for car racing enthusiasts for many years. He was still doing it thirty years later. Roger had high octane fuel in his blood and just loved being able to share his passion with others. Fittingly, he was a motor mechanic and when I first met him, he was a fellow Volkswagen enthusiast. That scored a lot of points with me!

Mazza and I often used to call at his home-based workshop in Golden Square and share coffee and a feed with him and his wife Lorraine. Their son Christian gains a mention elsewhere.

Dot and Paul Shapcott were a husband and wife team who presented a Baroque music program for a good number of years. They loved their music and, like so many in community radio, welcomed the chance to share their passion. They became good friends. In fact they presented Marilyn and I with our first Dachshund dog, Snoopy.

Dot and Paul bred Dachshunds. They also had a huge Wolfhound who took a particular dislike to Snoopy and attacked him at every opportunity. In despair they sought a home for Snoopy and handed him over to us. We were delighted and Snoopy became a wonderful friend. Sadly, when only eight years old we were compelled to have our lovely dog Snoopy put down. He became dreadfully ill and the Vet said he had been poisoned; accidentally or deliberately we will never know. We were very deeply saddened by this loss.

One Sunday morning we were on air at KLFM in Bendigo when Paul and Dot paid us a visit bearing a gift. In a small cardboard box was a very young and tiny miniature Dachshund pup. The Brereton kids next door suggested we name her Steffi after Steffi Graf the German tennis champion. Steffi was our loved companion for sixteen years.

The friends we made through radio! Ellie Seeley was a country music singer from nearby Daylesford. She performed under the name of 'Spot' and was managed by Mazza. Ellie made the journey to Harcourt once a week to present her program of country music with a bit of rock'n'roll. We got on very well with Ellie and soon came to meet her husband Alan and son Craig. Alan was a good, fair dinkum Aussie bloke, a hard working concreting contractor. We became good friends and often visited each other's homes. We even co-promoted a Country Music Festival set on Lake Neville, a private lake near Daylesford. It was the property of Big Jim Neville, a local earthmoving contractor. It was a magnificent site with the stage extended over the water and it looked a real winner. We promoted Daylesford as 'The Country Music Capital of Victoria'. Alas, it was not a raging success and we did not do it again. Daylesford never did become the Country Music Capital and returned to being 'The Spa Centre of Victoria' instead. Ellie, Alan and Craig eventually moved away to Queensland. We are still in contact with Ellie almost a quarter century later! We were deeply saddened to learn of the death of Alan from the dreadful Motor Neurone Disease. Alan passed away on April 1st 2014.

One of our success stories was Sheamus Haugh who was introduced to us by Catherine York-Moore. He did a few shows with us, including an occasional breakfast show after I vacated the spot. He eventually found a job with the ABC, a position only dreamed about by most in community radio. The ABC meant full pay, good conditions, superannuation, an audience – the works. Heavenly.

Ric Norris was a poet, as well as a part time journalist who worked for the Bendigo Gazette with Marilyn when she was there. He called his radio program Words and Music and that's what it was – a blend of poetry, most of it his, and soothing music. Ric had the smoothest and suavest of voices and was ideal for the job. He never drove a car and relied on a friend, former 3CV radio man, Ross Borchers for transport. They made a well matched duo. Often, Ric pre-recorded a program and posted it to us on cassette tape. I don't know what he recorded it on but the quality was absolutely awful and muddy (yep, tapes were still muddy!).

Ric presented a similar show on KLFM in later years and regrettably he passed away in 2008. Everybody loved Ric Norris.

Ross Borchers was the father of another 3CCC personality whom I mentioned earlier, Tim Borchers. Tim worked as a duo with Gavin McDougall, they were popular. They purchased Marilyn's company, The Entertainment Company in Mitchell Street Bendigo. They focused the business on discos rather than Mazza's focus on live bands and local musicians.

Gavin began at BTV8 TV in Bendigo as a news reporter. As explained elsewhere he eventually became Chief of Staff, News, Channel Nine in Melbourne, and now works in Asia. I have lost contact with Tim.

When Gavin first came to 3CCC as a student on work experience there was an 'incident'. Mazza and I went off on one of our numerous fake broadcasts, this time the Bendigo Cup. Accompanied by numerous sound effects records we did a tolerable job of describing the events, the crowds, Fashions on The Field and the general goings on. We interviewed a number of people 'attending' the cup including young Gav. The phone rang almost instantly. It was Gavin's mum Edna, very unhappy that her son was at the Bendigo Cup instead of being at work! That says a lot for our faking of it I reckon.

We sometimes took flights in our imagined Sopwith Camel aircraft, an ancient craft almost in tatters. Being radio, Listeners draw their own pictures, so we were able to fly at will, wherever our fancy took us. Our accompaniment was a sound effects recording of a sputtering T Model Ford engine. One time we went up on a nasty foggy, raining day. Sound effects that day included wild weather, thunder and heavy rain. The phone rang in the office. It was a lady in tears warning the people in the plane to come down as they were in terrible danger.

Another day we 'flew' across the Castlemaine Gaol where we knew the showers were open and unroofed in the yard. We described the blokes in the shower as Mazza called out that she knew now why they called one man we knew by the nick name Half Inch.

Out at Chewton we had people outdoors looking out for us to wave as we flew by. Really it was wonderful fun and as I've said before, radio is magic – truly the Theatre of the Mind.

Somewhere along the way I was appointed to the 3CCC Program Coordinating Committee (PCC) a unit I actually despised. I named it the Program *Control* Committee, shades of communist Russia, which upset some Board members and others. I considered it a load of bulldust and not conducive to consistency in programming. I believed that it was a job for one person, not a bloody committee. As you probably know it was a committee that designed the camel. In any event I went along with it and served on it until I was accused of disloyalty to the PCC and asked to resign by the Board. That decided me to run for the Board at the next election.

Live-to-air outside broadcasts were a regular feature of 3CCC in those days. The very first major effort came when Jeff decided to broadcast from the main street of Maryborough, forty-five kilometres distant. This was a bold step as we had no idea if we could line up the microwave link to Mount Alexander or even if we could get the distance.

We set up in High Street and fired up the link transmitter. Jeff was director, with Daryl Evans as Technician and Marilyn as Assistant. I was to be anchorman – again.

To our delight it actually worked and we had the job of concocting some sort of live broadcast from the street. We had no plan and had no 'talent' lined up for interview so I had to improvise. I raved about the wonderful features of Maryborough and God knows what else; it all came from my imagination! In desperation I began to 'interview' passersby, most of who shrunk away in horror, either of being interviewed on radio or in fear of the obviously deranged idiot with a microphone.

After a time of this, Jeff decided to move to a site behind Wattle Records a record store owned by one of our presenters, Peter Gray. We loaded everything into the back of the truck, first winding the tower down and removing the precious transmission antenna, or Yagi, from it. Jeff sped off to the parking lot behind Wattle Records where we commenced to prepare to start the broadcast.

'Where's the Yagi?' demanded Jeff.

Nobody knew.

'Shit. I left it behind,' cried Jeff as he leapt into the truck and roared off to retrieve the missing item, praying that nobody had snaffled it.

A few minutes later he returned, crestfallen clutching a mangled Yargi. He had put it on the road at the front of the truck and had run over the bloody thing. It was very badly bent and the myriad of prongs from the central rod were all twisted into a variety of shapes. Daryl and Jeff got busy with a pair of pliers and after a half hour of twisting, swearing and tugging the Yargi appeared somewhere near normal. We fitted it onto the tower, cranked it up to its maximum twenty meters and fired up again. To our astonishment it worked perfectly and we resumed our broadcast. After another half hour of 'in depth' coverage of Maryborough, mainly with me nattering to Jeff and Mazza, we packed and went home. Exhausted.

A memorable OB was one Easter in Bendigo. We had started doing live descriptions of the Easter Parade in about 1985 and it was now a regular event. On this occasion one of our presenters was assisting in erecting the linking tower, the dangerous, heavy twenty metre monstrosity.

I'll call him Bobby. Bobby was on the roof of the truck bending to struggle with moving the tower when his trousers split from rear waist to front.

Bobby apparently scorned the wearing of underpants and to everyone's horror there was revealed his family jewels and exhaust system in their entirety. It was a ghastly sight, also witnessed by a number in the crowd now gathering for the procession.

Bobby did not bat an eyelid but stayed in the bent over position until he had finally jockeyed the tower to where he wanted it.

There were gasps and whispers from those assembled, but mostly convulsed, suppressed laughter. Bobby then stood there on high with his withered equipment on display without the slightest hint of embarrassment, unlike those volunteers around him.

The Gas and Fuel float won first prize. It was however no match for Bobby's entertainment display, but he didn't get any official recognition or mention!

Bobby was aged about forty-five, a clear thinking man who spoke his mind on air and did not appreciate being told what to do. On one occasion he was ordered by Manager Gerry Pyne to clean up his desk. A board member had been in his office and was mortified at the untidy mess on the desk. Papers, notes, even food scraps, dirty cups and bits and pieces were piled high, covering every square centimeter of the desk surface. This was normal for Bobby who 'knew where everything was'.

When the Board members eventually filed in to inspect the tidied up job, they found that Bobby had set mouse traps in all the drawers. The Board members were not amused.

Sadly Bobby passed away at an early age and 3CCC lost one of its great characters.

We had so much fun at 3CCC! Mazza and I had two friends in Bendigo, a married couple with two kids. Les and Dawn were always in some sort of strife. Trouble followed them around.

We hit on an idea of creating a serial based (very loosely) on their lives. 'The Days of Our lives' was as popular then as now on daytime TV so we named our serial 'The Years of Their Lives – the heartrending story of Dawn and Les'.

Bev Sutherland took over the writing after I got it off to a start, but ran out of ideas after the first half dozen episodes. Bev used to collaborate with Mazza and occasionally me, but it was mostly her work.

We enlisted Daryl Evans to both produce the programs and to act as child number one, Dazza, in the show. Bev took the part of Dawn and Mazza became Mazza, child number two. I was Les and also the narrator. Macdonald Carey was the actual suave, smooth voiced narrator in the TV series so I became Carey McDonald.

We churned out about fifty episodes and all of them went to air in The Fabulous Fifties Show and it became a minor hit. Les and Dawn were tickled pink, especially as the fame of Dawn and Les grew to considerable proportions.

Jeff Langdon, still manager then, hated 'The Years of their Lives' with some passion and used get around the place grumbling loudly about 'non-productive time'. I'm sure he would have ordered that production cease if the show had not been so popular (not to mention the brilliant scriptwriting and acting).

We ignored Jeff's unhappiness and went on writing, acting and producing until the idea well was dry – over a year in all. Our little acting troupe got a real buzz out of it. Copies of 'The Years of their Lives' remain intact in my archive. It really was quite funny and certainly original and unique. And it was Australian made!

The Fabulous Fifties Radio Show was enormously popular and this led to 3CCC having a Fabulous Fifties Night. We optimistically booked the Library Hall in Castlemaine and started planning, unsure if anybody would turn up. We shouldn't have worried. It turned out to be a huge success. Our Listeners turned up in droves and many of our presenters came along. We served hot dogs, blue heaven milk shakes, lime spiders and icy poles. We played the great rock music of the 1950s (recorded) and every one had terrific fun. We put on a '50s Rock Opera that Mazza wrote which centred on a typical milk bar setting, featuring a jukebox, counter and stools. We had many of our presenters taking part, even Mazza's daughter Melissa. The leading cast was Jack Haynes, Doug Scobie, Justin Shortal, Bev Sutherland and Mazza. Not all of us drank Coke that night I hasten to add. One highlight was when Bev Sutherland, bopping around furiously in a 1950's dress borrowed from Mazza, split the rear zipper and her dress fell to her waist. Poor braless Bev nearly died of embarrassment but many hands soon had her back together again. The Fabulous Fifties night was one of 3CCC's best ever.

Chapter Fifteen

Writers, Rockers, Sky Pilots, sightless presenters and Poms

People, People and more People. That was 3CCC. How I wish I could remember them all and give accurate and adequate descriptions of them. Alas, I cannot, and anyway it would fill large volumes rather than this thin edition.

We had numerous visitors at 3CCC. Often they had had 3CCC recommended to them as a progressive radio station worthy of a visit, which was a feather in our cap. I recall one young man from Honiara in the Solomon Islands, who ran a community station there. Mazza and I took him to our home for a meal and he was so unbelievably thankful. He loved 3CCC and invited Mazza and I to go to live and work at his radio station! He was serious and the offer was very tempting but reality prevented it. Another I recall was a youngish man named Alan Josephs from the UK who was in Australia studying our community radio stations. I suppose everybody was busy and he was largely ignored, so Mazza and I took him under our wing for which he was most grateful. He went away impressed with our station a happy man.

One young man I recall clearly, not a visitor, was Brent Franklin who was totally blind from birth. Inspired by the 1960's blind DJ on 3AK, Grantley Dee, this lad approached me to train him in radio. Of course I accepted. Here was a real challenge but it ultimately proved to be exhausting.

I am delighted to say that Brent overcame his loss of sight brilliantly. He brought his Braille typewriter along on day one of training and suggested it would be helpful if he labeled all the knobs and levers with Braille. This we did and it was very successful. In a few short lessons he was ready to go to air. I was so proud of him, and just a little pleased with myself. He was a remarkable young man. Unfortunately his family moved away soon after he began and I have no idea what became of him. His Braille markings remained a fixture on the studio panel for many years after.

I hope he was able to find another community station that allowed him on air. He was amazing.

Phillip Edmonds joined the station as Writer in Residence on a government grant found by Jeff Langdon. Jeff also employed Geoff Hubbard as an Artist in Residence, Jack Haynes as a producer and he created a job for Paul Murphy as a Community Producer. Mazza also scored a job as part of the group. God knows where Jeff dug up these grants, but he was a real wiz at that. At one stage we had fourteen people employed at the tiny station; standing room only!

Phil Edmonds became an important part of 3CCC; staying around long after the six months grant money had expired. For a time he served as a Board member and in the end wrote a book about 3CCC, 'A station on Track'. He actually wrote several books, including one titled 'Locals' in which I had a chapter.

He was responsible for the editing of 'Radio Waves', 3CCC's monthly newsletter. Mazza and Geoff created the ads and did the lay-up. This was quite an elaborate production and Phil and his team did a wonderful job on it. In later years one time Board boss, Val Bland, took over as Editor and she eventually handed the job to Stephen McMahon who did a good job, but Radio Waves was never quite as good again..

Phil Edmonds and I did not see eye to eye on occasions and one time we had a particularly loud and aggressive 'discussion' at a Board meeting. I'm sure that Phil and those present recall it. However, we have remained friends. He returned for the 3CCC 21st Birthday Reunion which was organised in 2003 where it all began, the Harcourt Railway Station. This was the last time I saw him although he phoned me once seeking a copy of his book on 3CCC. I couldn't help him.

Phil lived with his wife deep in the bush around Golden Point. It was of necessity as his wife unfortunately suffered a seriously debilitating allergy to many things. Being isolated she wasn't exposed to so many hazards and didn't suffer so much in those conditions. She rarely, if ever left the house.

One day Phil was having a swim in the nearby Golden Point reservoir when he was rather surprised to see Melinda, one of our teenage volunteers, swimming alongside him completely naked. Phil, properly clothed, was a bit embarrassed, but he coped! The same girl was once detected at the station smoking some substance and in a strange condition along with one of our board members (not Phil). One other time he found a man dead in his car behind the reservoir, an apparent suicide.

Phil is a university lecturer these days and I believe it is Professor Edmonds now. I understand that he is in South Australia, probably Adelaide.

He was pretty rough and ready and always seemed to be broke, forever biting me for cigarettes; almost as bad as Jeff Langdon in that regard. He drove a beat up, dilapidated, neglected old Cortina that somehow clung together. He called into our home one night for a yarn, had a couple of drinks and stayed on to watch the footy with us on TV. It was an Essendon Bombers match. I forget who they played, and Phil turned out to be a very vocal Bombers supporter! He roared and yelled at every turn of the match and had a wonderful time. It showed us a different side of Phil as I am a Bomber supporter, too. One other night he came to our home to interview me for an article in the Bendigo Advertiser. He was supposed to be there at 7pm and finally arrived at 8.45; car trouble he said, parking the Cortina pointing down the hill outside our place so he could roll start it. He finally left at 12.30am and we went to bed. At 1.15 came a loud knock on the door. It was Phil, the car had refused to start and he was stuck on the road near the school in Market Street. It had failed to start on the roll so he pushed the bloody thing almost a kilometre, finally admitting defeat. I had to get up at 4.30am so Mazza took off in our VW and gave him a push with the bumper bar. The Cortina fired up, Phil went home and Mazza climbed back into bed.

Paul Mulqueen, who came from a prominent Bendigo family, presented a regular weekly program titled Trackin. It was very well presented and featured contemporary music of the time. I used to enjoy listening to Paul – he was a professional. Paul Murphy was another who was employed for a short time at 3CCC. He was a very intelligent and likeable young man, just out of college and made a valuable contribution to the station both on the air and off. He went on to a successful career, not in radio.

The Peter Harcourt Hour for intellectually handicapped folk was a regular feature on 3CCC. Kevin and Ann Lomas were the 'anchors' for this special program which featured several intellectually handicapped people. Kevin and Ann did a wonderful job in operating the panel for these wonderful folk and generally assisting them. Well done Kevin and Ann. It was a difficult job. The show ran every week for years and was extremely popular, with Victor Rothenburger and another worker from the centre, Maureen, as co-hosts. It was the most delightful program that I can recall on 3CCC. They played mostly fifties rock'n'roll.

Peter Sainsbury was another presenter who springs to mind. Peter was a big fan of 3CCC and he was regularly a co-presenter of rock'n'roll programs. He absolutely loved being on radio and he loved motorcycles. Saving hard for years he was eventually able to buy a brand new Harley Davidson, his pride and joy.

We had regular weekly Christian programs. One day Kath Mollitor had handed over to a youthful, inexperienced man of the cloth who proceeded to put two records to air at once. The mic was left open.

The preacher, called on our Saviour, 'Christ. What'll I do?'

Kath's broad pommy accent came next, 'The bloody mic's on.'

He. 'What?'

She. 'The bloody microphone is on.'

'Oh, God!' Then silence for about a minute before a hymn floated gently by.

We did the most marvelous and adventurous things at 3CCC. A couple of times we broadcast live-to-air concerts from the Big Room downstairs. The concerts were a regular thing, not always broadcast of course. We packed at least one hundred and fifty people into a room designed for thirty. The entertainers were drawn from our ranks and at times it was hilarious – a sort of poor mans 'A Prairie Home Companion' without Garrison Keillor! On one occasion a memorable highlight for me was a performance of Buttons and Bows by the wonderful Calamity (Edie) Clegg, with me as her straight man. It was side splitting fun. Mazza and I did our Frisky Slim and Sassy Sue act which always went over pretty well, but it did not compare to Calamity's effort. Bev Sutherland and Mazza took to the stage, appropriately dressed for the parts, with an animated presentation of the children's song, 'I'm a Little Teapot', which brought the house down. It was a magnificent night that went well into the early hours, with country bands Wendy Phyfers and the Sparnetts, Country and Piston and Open Road the main attractions. It was a concert worth paying a big sum to be part of but we did it free of charge.

A unique character was Dennis Zepnick. Originally he hailed from the USA where, he told me, he had dodged the Vietnam War draft and headed for Australia. Denny lived at Guildford, ten kilometres south of Castlemaine with his wife Janet and young family.

It was early days of 3CCC being on air and I was residing at Guildford for a time. I spent a lot of time at Delmenico's pub, as did much of the population. Denny used to come in quite regularly and I got to know him.

He was largely unemployed at the time, driving the most beat up Volkswagen imaginable. Soon after, he began training as a nurse and became a highly respected member of that profession – and yes – he bought a more respectable car.

He had a speech impediment and spoke in what can only be described as a hoarse whisper, a result of a childhood throat injury, he told me.

One evening he approached me in the pub, Delmenico's Guildford Family Hotel to give it it's full title, and asked if he could try out to present a rock'n'roll program. I was a little taken aback due to the noticeable problem with his voice, but invited him to come to the studio anyway.

Jeff Langdon was as skeptical as I was when introduced to Denny. In those early days we were not on air for half of the day and this made the empty studio vacant for training new people. Denny sat himself at the panel and let it rip, introducing himself as Guildford Gus. Both Jeff and I were astonished when we listened back to the tape. The microphone amplified Denny's voice and gave it a fantastic, exclusive and very appealing hoarseness. He sounded great and had an obvious aptitude for radio presentation. We couldn't get him on air quick enough.

'You're on the bus with Guildford Gus' became his catch cry and his Saturday night show was sensational, gaining a big audience who absolutely loved him.

He would arrive at the studio with case or box full of 45s in all sorts of condition, mostly badly worn and scratchy. I used to tell him and listeners that he cleaned them with steel wool! He would also bring an unknown quantity of stubbies of beer, unknown to the rest of us that is. This was strictly forbidden.

As time went by he also began bringing mates and their girls into the studio, also forbidden. His authorized helper, essential in running a request show, was 'Sunshine'. I never knew Sunshine's real name. It was to prove the undoing of Guildford Gus.

One night the lads had an on-air competition to see how far they could pee onto the rail track via an open window. One of the lads was later plainly heard to ask the whereabouts of one of the girls and Jimmy, one of the lads. A voice told us that they were 'screwing down in the car'. Then Gus delivered a joke that involved a man visiting his doctor complaining of a red ring surrounding a body part that he could not remove. The doctor advised him to try lipstick remover.

This was too much for even the most tolerant Board member and Denny was sent down the track. It brought to an end a terrific program at 3CCC and ended a wonderful community radio 'career'.

Sadly Denny passed away very suddenly when only in his early fifties. I have never forgotten Dennis Zepnick, Guildford Gus, and he is a legend among many 'oldies' in and around the town.

A young hippy type I'll call Moonshine unofficially 'boarded' in the station building for a while after Kathy and Narrah finally moved away. I believe he had nowhere to live.

He slept on a rough bed in a room adjacent to the entrance door. Jack Miles, a Board member was unaware of his presence. One Sunday morning Jack opened the bedroom door to enter, on the lookout for a piece of equipment. He was aghast to see Moonshine naked and being vigorously friendly with some visiting girl, also naked. That was the end of Moonshine at 3CCC.

Speaking of such things, a young man, I'll call him Trevor, once met up with a pretty eager and co-operative young lady at the pub who he invited to his car for a special purpose. Trevor had had a belly full of beer and whilst only half way through the job he fell asleep. The young lady was not impressed, left the car and went back to the pub, possibly looking for someone to finish the task.

Daryl (Dazza) Evans had been 'married' a few times and was father to several children. One Fathers Day Jeff called into my office. He grinned, 'Come and check this out.' Out at The Truck were the three women in his life, each with children in tow. It was a Fathers Day family visit with a difference and we wondered how Dazza was coping. We should have known that the unflappable

Dazza wouldn't turn a hair. I doubt that he saw anything unusual about it.

Jeff used to grumble a fair bit about Daryl's laid back manner and at times they had raging arguments. But Dazza's job was safe; Jeff recognised the talent of Dazza and deep down understood his ways well. For years Dazza drove a beat up old Toyota that finally and inevitably ground to a halt. Somehow he managed to buy a 1970 Valiant station wagon, his pride and joy. Two weeks after he got it he was driving along the tree-lined road to his home outside the township of Taradale when he noticed some mud on the seat. He was fastidious in looking after the new car and reached over to brush the mud away and crashed headlong into a tree. Fortunately he was going very slowly and was not hurt, but his beautiful Valiant was a mess. It was still drivable but badly bent, a shadow of its former self. Dazza was inconsolable.

Within a year the Valiant came to a halt, coming to its final rest in his yard. It is probably still there today. Daryl, his partner Julie and family then travelled in a tiny, bedraggled Datsun 1200 sedan of ancient vintage. We all loved Dazza.

We had a lot of fun. We needed to obtain a recording of a stuff-up from Calamity Clegg for use at our in-house Pere Awards night. She was on air in the upstairs studio and as she opened the mic to speak Doug Scobie, on the roof, dropped a stuffed toy (Herbert Collin, my fictitious panel operator) dangling from a string to outside the studio window. Calamity looked up but didn't crack boo. Next he tried a huge, ugly, grinning face painted on cardboard nailed to a wooden pole which he hoisted to the window from below. No response – so back to the roof with my doll. For probably the first time in her career, Calamity didn't miss a beat and we were foiled.

Herbert Collin, the stuffed toy, was my constant companion when I was on air. I derived his name from a professional voice-over friend, Col Herbert, who did lots of TV and radio commercial work. Herbert was my 'panel operator' for years, and I am certain many people believed that he existed. I never presented a show when he wasn't perched on the panel in front of me. Badly beaten up, he was about 30 centimetres tall, wearing a multi-striped jumper with blue pants and stuffed with polystyrene balls. I used to talk with him on air and sometimes he actually answered me in a squeaky little voice. Mostly, however, he was silent. I also appeared to have had a none-too-secret affair with his beautiful, blonde widowed Mum. Herbert and Mum lived at Wellington Flat on the north-east side of Mount Alexander, often in its deep shade, making it a slightly spooky place. I used to say on air, 'Where nobody goes.' Although I often did, apparently!

Mazza and I twice recorded shows deep in the Wombat forest at Blackwood where we had fabulous fun and I always finished up half drunk with a few of the locals. On one occasion we did a Saturday night recording and the next day moved to nearby Trentham to cover an important event, the inaugural Worm Race. This was said to be sponsored by Sustaworm Worm Feed, a brand name cooked up by the promoter. Ron was the man's name but I cannot recall it all and the race was held at the Pandora Ponds. We even had T-shirts printed for the occasion. Mazza and I did a reasonable job at the microphone of describing the imaginary heats, not an easy task. The day culminated in the final won by our entry, the giant worm Mandingo, bred at our property at Harcourt. It was great fun and showed what you can do with imagination and the images created in one's mind through the magic of radio.

Peter McAndrew was a great character who played the Irish drums. I don't know what he did but I believe he may have worked for Telstra. I do know that he helped Mazza write a song named Country Tips. It was recorded by Frisky Slim and Sassy Sue for the album they launched at the Castlemaine tip.

Peter lived at Guildford where it was said witches gathered to dance naked around a circle of stones in the moonlight. Peter fell foul of them and to his distress they informed him that they had placed a hex on him for some comment he made. To his relief nothing happened.

Some characters and events stand out in memory. One such involved Kevin Alexander, a not too bright weekend presenter. He complained to me about his bank having painted the front of their building. He was deeply distressed as he had written his PIN number on the wall in black marking pen and they had painted over it. Now, he could not remember his number. Fair dinkum!

Chapter Sixteen

Surveys, songwriters and radiothons

We received a leaked copy of the McNair Anderson Listener Survey for November 1987. I'm not telling how. These surveys were expensive and the results jealously guarded by those who paid for them, usually the commercials and the ABC shared. The results were horrific for us. 3BO 66.4%; 3CV 11.2%; ABC 11.6%; Other Commercial Stations 12.9%; Others 1.9%. Others! Hey! That's us! How bloody depressing. We were obviously going backwards at a great rate.

Christmas 1988 came and things were no better. Our sponsorship income was down to $1350 for the first week in December and to $1000 for the last week. The future looked bleak and the responsibility fell on me (Sponsorship Manager, remember). What could I do? Our rep said nobody seemed to want to sponsor us anymore. I prayed; but it didn't help!

KD had called for letters to his Christmas Day special program, a recorded announcement and on heavy rotation for ten days. Not one letter came, except two written by Mazza and me.

Showtime. KD stood at the top of the stairs bellowing as only he could. 'No Letters. Not one f.....g letter! Not one! Nobody listens. What a waste of f.....g time. I'm finished. Christmas Day, goodbye.' But he did the show anyway.

Looking at the disastrous survey result, we few concerned staff members became increasingly worried, especially when the board meeting set for the 17 December 1987 was delayed until the 20th, then put off again until 2 January 1988. This had never happened before, Christmas or not, the meetings always went ahead. It seemed that something was definitely amiss. Bev Ellis promptly wrote to the President, Val Bland, expressing concern and seeking answers but no response whatever came. Eventually nothing at all came of this worrying episode but there remained considerable unease in the air. I found it a constant worry and I wished I had taken a role as a board member when I had the chance in the early days.

Raising money was always difficult in the early days of 3CCC. Survey results like we had seen didn't help at all. If we had seen it, likely our sponsors had, too.

You'll recall that Community Radio was not permitted to sell advertising, restricted by regulation to running forty word sponsorship acknowledgements. These were to carry no inducement for a listener to buy or support the sponsor. It made the job of selling the station very difficult. We had to appeal to the business person's sense of community and beg for their support. To supplement the meagre income from sponsorship we had a system of subscription where Listeners paid us $10 a year as a gesture of support. At one time we had about four hundred of these, a fantastic result, in the finish we had less than one hundred.

We also ran fundraising dances and concerts which, more often than not, actually cost us money!

A good money spinner was the Radiothon, where we got all of our volunteers together in shifts on air over an entire weekend and begged for money. The first year or two it worked well. Regrettably, Listeners grew tired of this and the income from Radiothon's all but ceased. By the sixth Radiothon I began a week ahead of the weekend event. On the Monday I got $50 in pledges, Tuesday $130, and it didn't get much better all week. The Monday 4–5pm drive time raised a miserable $2. When it was all over a total of around $2400 was raised for the entire seven days; that for a massive effort involving about eighty people for a poor result. Over $600 came with Glenn Heyne between 6am and

8.30 Saturday breakfast. The songwriting competition organized by Marilyn had raised around $300 in entry fees. That meant the rest of the time had brought in a miserable $290 to that point!

The songwriting competition raised funds but more importantly it raised the station profile. It gave us the opportunity to get free press and even TV publicity. People like Peter Saltmarsh, John Beavis, Kerry McDonald, Rod Willaton and Glenn Braybrook were among the many winners along the way and this also raised awareness of the station with more publicity. All very important.

From then on Radiothons were a failure – certainly not worth all the work and organization involved. I don't believe anyone in their right mind would try Radiothons in small regional Victorian stations again.

For the very first birthday Radiothon in April 1983 Mazza and I stayed on deck all weekend, camped in the yard in our 1955 VW Kombi Safari. (I soon after sold it for $100 and how I wish I had kept it. Safari models are scarce and very valuable today.) We were exhausted at the end but it was all worthwhile when we added up the takings. Surprisingly, most of those who rang and promised money actually posted or otherwise delivered it! I was on air when a young man walked into the studio. He was sweating having ridden his old pushbike from Castlemaine. He handed me a donation of $50, a significant sum back then. He was shabbily dressed and maybe on the dole. 'It's great. I listen all the time. I love it.' Later in the day Clyde and Herb, from commercial station 3GL Geelong, called in to make a donation. They had been two days in Bendigo at a conference, tuned in because they had heard of this radio station at a railway station, and liked what they heard. I do not recall the precise amount raised by that Radiothon, but it was several thousand dollars. Jack Miles, Vic McGowan, Calamity Clegg and Paul Mason had raised about $700 of the total on the nostalgic and Country music Sunday afternoon. It showed clearly where our major support lay.

The interest and response to Radiothons began to slide quickly into deadly decline. By 1988 when Gerry Pyne began as Manager the bottom had fallen right out of it (nothing to do with Gerry) but that year's radiothon was a memorable event, but for the wrong reasons.

It was on the Friday late afternoon when Gerry Pyne and Mick Ahearne had a huge yelling match. Gerry had told Mick he objected to some comments from a musician who Mick had on air and he did not want the man near the place again.

Mick did the block. 'Nor me either,' he yelled. 'I resign.' He stormed from the office as I looked on in amazement. I later tried to talk Mick out of it but he was determined and made it official at an *in camera* Board meeting.

How well I recall the offer of the donation of a wardrobe from a Bendigo Listener for a radiothon auction we held. A handful of us had the job of collecting all the one hundred and fifty items donated in a large trailer attached to any available car. This wardrobe was huge! Two meters high and three and a half meters wide, fitted with drawers and shelves, it was a monster! It was made of thick chipboard and Doug Scobie and I had to lug it from within the house fifty metres to the trailer in the street. It was one of the heaviest lifting jobs I ever did – and I had had some beauties. To top it off the thing did not sell and we had to take it to the tip! In fact very little of the donated junk sold and we did not try that again.

The songwriting competition for 1988 also sticks in my memory – for one good reason. Mazza had gone to endless bother to select judges for each section from her contacts in the music world. She had an impressive line-up including a man named Red Symons mentioned earlier. The list of secret section winners lay for all to see on Gerry's desk for a day and a half before Mazza spotted it. She was pretty upset and told Gerry so. One section however had not yet been judged, that of Red Symons who, at that time, was quite a big name on TV's Hey, Hey, It's Saturday.

Mazza had made several phone calls to chase up the results, but by the Thursday evening Red had still not sent his winner's name. By then Mazza was in a bit of a panic. The announcements were to be made on Saturday at about 10am. Time was running out.

I was on air for breakfast when she came to the studio at 7am saying she was driving to Red's home in the city to collect the winner's name and the taped entries. She asked me to ring Red to expect her and she dashed off in the old VW. I dutifully rang the man. It was probably about 8am by then – a bit early and I was very conscious of this. However, I was not prepared for his response. The wretched man abused the shit out of me for ringing him so early. My pleas for understanding fell on deaf ears as he hung up on me. He was particularly obnoxious and offensive. From that time on my respect and regard for the bloke vanished. He did apologise to Mazza for his tardiness in getting his judgment to her which had caused her unnecessary stress and a trip to and from Melbourne in her old car.

May 1988 was particularly memorable for a good number of events. The Bendigo Advertiser ran a story that said that the Bendigo Council claimed that 3CCC had only five hundred listeners. This caused a lot of anger and resentment around the station. It was of course untrue. In fact I believed that we had more like five thousand. We lodged a complaint with the Council which was ignored and there were several strong letters sent to the Bendigo Advertiser. But the damage had been done.

Also in May, Neil Cowan crashed his car on the way to do Friday breakfast and Bev Ellis was called in to fill the space. She arrived an hour and a half late so we had ninety minutes of dead air.

Jeff Langdon, by now departed to a job at a Bendigo Health Centre, had his fortieth birthday in May and was quite depressed when I caught up with him.

In May 1988 Mazza and I took over the management of talented Country singer Wendy Phyfers from Daylesford. She was brilliant and we felt that she had a big future. It all ended in bitter disappointment after a few months, with us having put in a huge effort behind the scenes. We were certain she was set for a huge career. Alas, Wendy was just not the type to focus as intently as is necessary to make the really big time and she elected to go her own way. Mazza and I were disappointed and we still come near to tears when we hear her sing. With her band she won a major award at Tamworth in the late 80s and was voted group of the year in 1990. However I believe that she never has achieved her full potential. Wendy remains a very talented Country singer, working with her band The Cartwheelers, mostly around the Ballarat district.

Then, in a real shock, on 8 May 1988 Bev Ellis announced her resignation as Sales Rep as she had landed a job as CEO of the Bendigo Capital Theatre. Oddly enough Jeff had also applied for that job having tired of being at the Health Centre. I think it irked him somewhat to be beaten by Bev Ellis, a previous subordinate!

Said Jeff, 'I knew I couldn't win when I saw the interviewing panel of middle aged men. She's got nothing that I haven't except cunning!' He forgot to mention how attractive Bev was!

Later, Jeff, backed by the Labor Party, ran for Bendigo Council but was defeated there, alas. He would have been a good councilor for sure.

* * *

In a blink of an eye we had lost Mick Ahearne and Bev Ellis. I didn't always see eye to eye with Bev but she was a great asset as Sales Rep. Her going left a huge hole at 3CCC. Her job was a difficult one.

By the time she started we had purchased a new Ford Laser for the rep and other station use. It improved our image significantly, especially with the intelligent and attractive Bev in the job. Bev was not all that fussed about the new car saying she thought it made us 'Look too affluent'.

One incident I recall involving Bev is funny from this distance. She was driving to Bendigo in the Laser when crossing the railway overpass Porcupine Hill she was astonished see in her mirror a giant trail of papers scattering to the four points of the compass. The hatchback had flown wide open and her briefcase, full of important and often confidential papers, had sped out the rear. Every piece had to be retrieved and this she eventually did, perhaps missing a few, in a task that took an hour. Bev was very good at her difficult job and was a big asset to 3CCC. I knew from experience how hard her job was and as Sponsorship Manager, I was very happy to have her out selling.

Alas, her eventual reward from the Board was a sound condemnation of her at a meeting in February 1989, some time after she had departed. There was a claim that she had brought in only $800 to $1200 a week in sales. That was totally incorrect. I could not recall a single instance where she brought in only $800. I did recall a good number of weeks when she brought in $3000 or more. A particularly nasty comment, attributed in the minutes to a nasty female board member, that the board had 'propped up' Bev for some time was outrageous. I wrote to the President and told him so.

With the departure of Bev I felt I was pretty much alone. Of the originals, only Jack Miles remained on the Board and he was not particularly active or forceful. In one bright spot Jeff made a comeback, being elected to the Board. I believed that he wanted the Presidency but was denied that in a close vote of fellow Board Members. Bev now lives at Alice Springs where she owned a Dymock's Book Shop until she retired, and she loves it there.

Very soon after this Phil Edmonds resigned from the Board causing some to perhaps unkindly say that he had only stayed on to keep Jeff out of the top job. Some thought it was a little suspicious however. Why run for election and a week or two later quit for no good reason?

So the Board was now Val Bland, who I always felt had little time for me, Paul Spooner, Bill Borrie, Ken Gilmour, who rocked our Monday evenings, Jack Miles and Jeff Langdon. Paul Spooner won the Presidency. There were now five Bendigo people and two from Castlemaine.

Jack was removed from his position as Staff to Board liaison person and the position abolished. Staff was no longer permitted to make any direct contact with Board members and all inquiries and comments had to go through the manager, Gerry Pyne.

At 5.30am the next day after the vote as I prepared for the breakfast show I wrote in my diary. 'In view of the make-up of the Board my time at 3CCC must now be limited.'

By that time I realized that Gerry was not exactly warm toward me and I was certain that Val Bland had no liking for me. I think I still had respect from most volunteers and shareholders. Certainly I was popular with our audience.

What nagged at me was that I was, apart from Jack, the last remaining 'Langdon man'. Jeff's influence at the station had been such that he still dominated the place in spirit. Some people disliked working in his shadow and the place appeared to me to be in the process of being 'de-Langdonised'.

But while Jeff remained involved I felt that my position was safe.

Chapter Seventeen

Morning shows, presenters, Footy, Dad and Dave

Everyone hated doing Sunday breakfast 6 to 8am; few were listening and the effort was not worthwhile. Over the years dozens of people were roped into it. It was the bottom of the announcing barrel.

Often the chosen ones were youngsters, keen to get on the air and become famous, people like Phil Campbell, Brad Geier and John Hunter. How well I remember John Hunter one morning saying at least fifteen times in a most plaintiff tone. 'Good morning. I'm John Hunter and I've been here since six o'clock.'

Many times nobody turned up at all and I had to drag myself from bed to fill in. Most of the time, nobody at the station knew that I did this. As I said, nobody listened.

It happened so often that I had eventually prepared an hour and a half tape. From then on I would go to the studio by 6.30, put the tape to air and go back to bed. I used the same tape at least twenty times and nobody knew any different. If we had one hundred listeners we would have been lucky.

Some of the young presenters went on but most fell by the wayside. These young blokes were often painful to listen to as they attempted to sound grown up like their favorite commercial announcer. Only a handful ever made it to commercial radio or the ABC. Some that did were very disappointed as it turned out not to be as glamorous as they imagined.

Brad Geier and Phil Campbell, so they told me, both returned to Bendigo after short stints at some faraway unnamed place. Brad decided that Community Radio was the best and set about gaining a license for his own station in Bendigo. By 1989 he had formed Bendigo Education Broadcasters Inc. and went after a license for an Education based radio station – an E Class license as they were known. Phil Campbell joined Brad in his Bendigo venture for a while but fell away. Maybe his small taste of commercial radio had proved enough for him.

Brad could have returned to 3CCC but he had a dream of conducting a Community Radio station that sounded professional and was acceptable to a mass audience. He said 3CCC was too amateurish, nor did he like their Manager. He told me he felt uncomfortable with him. For a short time he had a job as Producer for the local ABC on Saturday mornings but that led to nothing.

Mazza and I increasingly shared Brad's ideas and ideals. We were very close friends by then and remained so for many years. At one time Mazza and I were given plane tickets and three nights accommodation package in Hobart by a friend that could not use it. I refused to fly so Marilyn and Brad flew off to Tasmania for a weekend, sharing the same room and exploring Hobart together. They passed for mother and son and indeed that was not far from the truth.

Many of the programs and presenters on 3CCC by 1989 had been there since the beginning or soon after. Notable was Daryl Evans and Ian Jorgenson's excellent Southern Star Show, Frank Stowe's 'Jazz on Saturday' survives on another station to this day. Estelle (Edith) Bunn presented 'My Kind of Country' for many years. She began as a panel operator for the blind Fred Paynting but it wasn't long before she had her own program. She continued to present her kind of country on KLFM of Bendigo, even following a serious stroke, almost until she died in 2015. Kerry McDonald, a Solicitor, was 'The Organic Swagman' who presented an excellent folk music program. Barry Gillen rode his bike eighteen kilometres each way from Guildford to present his folk music, with a dash of Blues. Cassie Thorburn was quite young and she was a modern music presenter who did well. Malcolm

Fyffe, Mal Peters, Phillip Rice, Phil Scott, Paul Straughn and Alistair White. The list is long. Trevor Thomas, Peter Fairthorne, Helen McGechan, Ian Huxley, Ken Tester, Graeme Furlong are names that come readily to mind.

Bernie Denher burst onto the scene in 1987 and was given a Top of The Morning slot. We understood that he had worked at 3AK in Melbourne and he was brimful of confidence. His performance, disappointingly, didn't actually come up to expectations. In fact he was dreadful. Along with everything else he had the annoying habit of referring constantly to *Hardcourt*, not Harcourt, and I am sure he believed his version was the correct one. Bernard moved on in October that year – maybe back to 3AK? They should be so lucky! But admittedly he did very good work in promoting Men's Health in the district.

Who could forget Doug Scobie and Craig Deed with their series Farmer to Farmer; it was really great fun, featuring Doug as the Editor of the Bagshot Times and Craig as The Earl of Bagshot. With the slow drawl of the narrator and the general hick sound, some felt it a little insulting to farmers, but it was done with good humour and no intent to offend. Husband and wife team Dot and Paul Shapcott presented Mainly Baroque, Paul Mason and Tony Cook, both from Melbourne, presented Stepping out with a Memory, a great nostalgic music show. A wonderful kids' program presented by kids was Kids Stuff with ten-year-olds Danielle Grumont and Jaala McDonald. Jaala went on to be elected to state parliament and, as Jaala Pulford, she was promoted Minister for Agriculture in the Dan Andrews Victorian Government in 2014.

Speaking of parliament, David Kennedy, a veteran Labor Party politician and a friend of mine, presented his regular two hour weekly program of Classical music without fail. To this day he continues to do so with a station in Bendigo.

Graeme Taylor joined the staff for six months as a community producer and Jeff Hubbard as an Artist in Residence under a grant from the state government. Phillip Edmonds similarly as a Writer in Residence. All these appointments came as a result of Jeff Langdon's submissions to the state government for grants. Marilyn Bennet and Peter McAndrew joined the paid staff for six months under the government community Employment Initiative Program (EIP) . Paul Murphy was engaged as a Community Producer and all these people became important cogs in the Jeff Langdon 3CCC machine. Collectively we called these employees EIPS. At one time we had a staggering fourteen people working in the cramped conditions of the old railway station building. All made very worthwhile contributions to the success of 3CCC.

Kath Mollitor was a classic personality. Hailing from England she had a very broad accent which many people loved. Kath was a delightful person but her talent for radio was rather limited, especially when it came to operating the studio equipment. It was often a disaster but, like Calamity (Edith) Clegg, listeners loved her many stuff-ups. Kath's heart was in the right place and I had long conversations with her, often about her life in England during the war when Germany bombed the hell out of her London. Ironically she was married to a German, Mathew, a great bloke. Val Victor-Gordon, a polished presenter, turned her hand to book reading with her presentation of Crooks, Chooks and Bloody Ratbags, written by Kerry Cue of Kyneton. The ever reliable Daryl Evans produced it.

Our footy broadcasters; Jock Clark and Bill Ashby (later joined by Anthony Hudson of TV fame) were a very talented team, completely devoted to the game. They had a vast knowledge of football and handled this most difficult job very well. They attracted a sizeable audience and brought in many thousands of dollars a year in sponsorship. Footy is an important part of rural communities and radio stations ignore it at their peril.

John Keuhn used the identity 'Johnny from Dunolly', although he didn't come from there at all but from Tarnagulla, another town nearby. For a long time he presented an overnight show and one daytime program each week. I believe his background may have been Dutch; in any event he was a good friend to me.

In later times Wallace Teasdale came on the scene and went on to carve himself a career in community radio. Wallace eventually became manager of 3CCC in Bendigo until its demise and he then went to The Fresh where he remains as Manager, a position he has held for some years. Bill Borrie comes to mind as does Noel Tamblyn and Paul Spooner, the latter to be the Board President when I was dismissed.

I didn't like all of our volunteers of course but overall the people who made up 3CCC were marvelous. I learnt a lot about life and living from them.

Top of the Morning, the mid morning show conceived by Jeff, continued for a long time and Morning Music, the baby of Jack Miles and me, went on for years and was very popular.

This show, combined with the breakfast show, convinced me of the necessity for consistency in programming to attract a good size audience. Sure, people will tolerate and find amusement in sloppy presentation and stuff-ups, but the novelty fades quickly. The Morning Music presenters were principally Kevin Daw, Jack Miles, Vic McGowan, Lorraine Foley and Noel Tamblyn, Kay Baker and Trevor Penno. They were competent panel operators and understood the special needs of communicating on radio. Their music was consistent in style and quality.

I felt frustrated by the often poor presentation and extreme diversity at times in some daytime programs. I had to live with it but it annoyed me immensely and I sometimes had disagreements with management who believed in the Phil Edmunds philosophy of 'unity in diversity'.

From that time on I was a firm believer in providing consistency across at least the 6am to 6pm slots, a policy I adhered to in later experiences. I also learnt that you do not change a format that is working. It takes several years to attract an audience but only a few days to lose them all. There are plenty of stations for Listeners to choose from.

There were rumblings from some volunteers who did not like the style of Morning Music's music and by various means applied pressure to the Program Control Committee and it ordered that the show expand its music from '40s to '70s to include music in majority of the current '80s. Much of the '60s and '70s was retained but the program veered wildly off course as a result. Then the committee ordered that a fifteen minute talk segment, 'Yarn Spinners', comprising recollections of the old days, in interview form, but usually boring, be included. We presenters jacked up and refused to play it so the board was called in and they ordered us to comply. We had to obey and our original winning concept went completely out the window. We lost interest and enthusiasm; Jack Miles and Vic McGowan were furious and penned a hostile letter to the Program Control Committee and the board, to no avail. Morning Music struggled on for another year under a new title, 'Spectrum', but finally we gave up. In retrospect I think it was my involvement in that particular episode that sowed the seeds of my destruction.

Several of us worried constantly about the direction 3CCC had taken but were not in a position to beat the numbers. We watched what we considered the decline of 3CCC. I often disagreed, privately and usually openly, with the decisions of Management and Board.

In 1986 I introduced the serial Dad and Dave which continued successfully for years. I had to wait for four years to get it from Grace Gibson as 3BO was running it currently and it was therefore not available to another district station. It proved very popular. KLFM of Bendigo eventually took it when 3CCC (by then The Fresh) let it go. It was still running every weekday on KLFM Bendigo in 2014.

Every day at 3CCC was exciting and challenging for me and it put me in touch with all sorts of people. I think that this is what I enjoyed the most – being in a position to meet and talk with people. It was a privilege I thoroughly enjoyed and one that I valued. I was lucky enough to have a gift that enabled me to communicate easily with most people. This was probably because I had a lot of previous experience in living in the 'real world'. My experience as a door to door commission salesman (the world's toughest job other than being a cat salesman!) for several years gave me an understanding of people that many do not have. And my working life ranged from farm laborer, shearing shed hand, wool presser, spud digger, bricklayer's laborer, salesman, to truck driver and conducting my own retail business. Whatever job I did I always had a good relationship and good rapport with those I worked with.

I enjoyed the same relationship with my radio Listeners. They were my friends and many of them were to come to demonstrate it in the not too distant future.

I know I wasn't everybody's cup of tea on air. That's not possible. We received a number of letters over the years accusing me of everything from racism and homophobia to sexism – I stoutly deny any of those traits – the opposite is the fact, but I accepted the criticism as part of the job. It also proved that people were listening! The most scathing and hurtful remarks came from within. One female presenter, hiding behind a nom de plume, wrote to Radio Waves stating I was 'a pain in the arse, always complaining about how poor I was.' She demanded that I have my time on air cut back or better still, I should be removed entirely. I knew who it was and that hurt a bit, it also showed she lacked courage.

Another incident that was reported to me hurt badly. A recently elected Board member confided to a small group enjoying a drink and a smoke, *in the studio mind you,* that 'If there's one thing I'd love to do it's get rid of Ian Braybrook.' He was soon to get the position of power to carry out his wish.

The resentment of me was added to when the time of my 1000th Breakfast Show came around. I was proud of this achievement and let my listeners know. I had never been paid and there had been lots of days of sickness, hangovers and generally bad days along the way. All this was more than compensated for by the respect and friendship of our Listeners.

Two days before number one thousand, I was visited by a reporter and a photographer from The Sun newspaper and on the big day a page three article featured a photo of me on the railway station platform nursing the station cat. I confess that I was delighted. I do not know who arranged this with The Sun but suspect it may have been my friend Kevin Daw or maybe even Mazza.

That morning on the breakfast show the phones began ringing and did not stop. Somebody had even teed up our member of Federal Parliament, Neil O'Keefe, who asked to be put to air. He really wrapped me up, which was great. Former Manager Jeff Langdon also rang and congratulated me as did Kevin Daw, Roger Boehme and Bev Ellis. In all I took over fifty Listeners' calls that morning and I admit that I was very pleased with myself. Noticeably the new Manager, Gerry, didn't ring or even mention the event when I saw him later. Channel 8 TV Bendigo came down to interview me too, and in response to a question I said I was aiming to do two thousand before I retired. 'I hope I can see the distance.' As it turned out, I didn't.

It was a genuinely exciting milestone for me but my joy was disrupted when at 8.30 I crossed to the Bendigo studio for Top of the Morning presenter, Alf Hooley. Alf was an environmentalist Englishman who hated our reliance on corporate sponsorship and pursued green issues with passion. I got on pretty well with Alf but his opening words shocked me; 'Thanks Ian for the breakfast show. I've got a message for you mate. You don't have to keep a dog when you bark yourself.' Pretty nasty and uncalled for, I thought, no matter what he thought of me, I had made a lot of sacrifices for 3CCC.

Alf was responsible for one of the worst broadcasts from the Old Fire Station studio in Bendigo that I ever heard at 3CCC and I heard plenty! He conducted a ten minute interview with a person who we did not hear utter a word – the guest mic was not turned on – there were further long gaps later of dead air and records were miscued and cued on air. It was appalling. At the same time elderly Kath Mollitor was taken off air for her mistakes. She was very angry when she heard Alf's broadcast attempt as she was nowhere near as bad.

The signs of resentment toward me largely went over my head. Marilyn tried to warn me of the rumblings she heard of the tall poppy syndrome, but I took no notice. I should have read the signs. We had a comprehensive 'Rogues Gallery' on the staircase walls – dozens of photos that encapsulated the history of 3CCC. I ignored the fact that many displayed photographs of significant (and other!) events which included my image were being drawn on and disfigured, mostly moustaches and blacked out teeth. Because I was involved in almost every event I appeared somewhere in many of the photos. Obviously somebody or some people didn't care for me and my prominent role but the attacks' significance didn't dawn on me.

One morning KD said 'Don't know what you've done to Gerry mate, but take care. He's out to get you.' That did trouble me.

Chapter Eighteen

Buy Australian, accusations, advertisement, suspension, pain and skullduggery

The end of a love affair can be a very painful and shattering experience, especially when one is betrayed.

There had been all sorts of ups and downs at Triple C for me since Jeff Langdon, Bev Sutherland, Bev Ellis and other friends had moved on. I felt more and more isolated, cut off from the Board and out of favour with manager Gerry Pyne. Coming soon was one of the worst periods of my radio life.

Neil O'Keefe, MHR, had always been a supporter of mine. At this time I was not employed at 3CCC and pretty desperate for money, Neil heard of this, and through his recommendation, I was awarded a contract with the Advance Australia Foundation (AAF) promoting 'Buy Australian' on community radio Australia-wide.

Marilyn and I met with AAF Director, Norm Spencer on several occasions at his office in St Kilda Road, Melbourne. Norm was famous in the media industry for his work as a senior producer for GTV9, including the famed In Melbourne Tonight with Graham Kennedy.

I was to produce community radio material which urged people to 'Buy Australian'. The content, distribution and production was left in our hands, but suitable contacts for interview, spread across Victoria, were supplied by Norm.

The job involved considerable travel and face to face interviews with a number of Australian people who had manufactured or invented items of significance to our export and local market.

Marilyn and I met a raft of fascinating people with wonderful stories to tell. Once the interviews were completed we then had to write scripts and edit the interviews appropriately or vice versa. The final product would be produced for distribution in a series of six half hour programs. It was a big project, with a big responsibility for me.

I arranged through the CBAA that each station that agreed to broadcast the resulting material would be paid a fee of $300 by the AAF, a good deal. I had based my price for the job on a quote from Gerry Pyne of $15 per hour for the use of the production studio, a total I carefully calculated at $1050. It was a handshake 'gentleman's agreement' with Gerry. I estimated that, with careful management, the project would gross me around $2500 over three months; not a fortune but an income nevertheless.

Before we even began our first preparations I was stunned when Director Norm Spencer rang me.

'Ian, I don't think we can go ahead with this arrangement. We have had threats from the manager of some radio station, 2 double C (sic) or something. (3CCC) The Manager said if we went ahead they would contemplate legal action against us. We won't get involved in that.' This was shocking news and I was thunderstruck.

Mazza took the phone and pleaded with Norm, who finally agreed that if Neil O'Keefe could clear it up he would proceed. Neil readily agreed to phone Gerry Pyne and to write to the Board to explain that it was all above board. He did so immediately.

My friend on the Board, Jack Miles, told me that there was strong talk about that I had misrepresented myself to the AAF, acting under the 3CCC banner for my own benefit. It was being said that I had got the deal in the station's name and then switched it to myself! He said that the figure being circulated was an astonishing $35,000 which, it was being said, should have gone to 3CCC. Nobody ever said this to me directly but serious harm was being done. If this were true it would surely amount to fraud.

I learnt from Jack Miles who told me that there had been *in camera* Board discussions, not recorded in the minutes, which had debated my alleged dastardly deeds. Jack kept me as well informed as he dared.

Eventually Mazza went to confront Gerry Pyne. He denied all knowledge of contact with Norm Spencer and the stories being told about me and then dropped a massive bomb shell. He said that the Board had increased the studio hire fee to $5000, take it or leave it.

The inference of course was that I had ripped thousands from 3CCC and could afford to pay. In fact I now stood to lose over $2500 and to work for weeks for nothing. I had signed a contract with the AAF and I was obliged to proceed. Mazza and I were devastated, not knowing where to turn. But you can't give up without a fight.

With help from some good friends and Marilyn's father, Gordon Boyd, I erected a 'studio' in our yard. It was constructed basically from two plywood car cases placed together, with openings cut for a door and two windows. It was fitted out with a tiny second-hand mixer, a turntable, microphone and an old Rola reel to reel recorder. Total cost was about $300 but it served the purpose and allowed me to complete the contract with the AAF. Daryl Evans came around to help me on occasions. On reflection, the quality we managed to put out was quite amazing. I made the programs available through the CBAA to stations across Australia. I know for sure that on 3CCC it did not see the light of day.

Despite the shabby treatment from board and management I continued to present my great love, the breakfast shows, four days a week. But the stress clearly showed in my presentation. I lost my zip and made small mistakes, several people rang to ask how I was, 'You don't sound yourself.'

From day one of the dispute I resolved to attend the next board meeting and clear the matter up. I was very angry and hurt by the allegations.

Meanwhile there had been some bother and controversy surrounding an alleged act by our number one football broadcaster, Jock Clark. The story was that he had had a serious altercation with a representative of a big footy sponsor and unless he quit they would withdraw their dollars. I rang Jock and he was deeply distressed. He loved broadcasting the football and his unhappiness showed as he told me he had no alternative but to resign.

I felt sorrow and anger for him and recklessly (in hindsight) decided to place a tongue in cheek ad in the Situations Vacant column in the Bendigo Advertiser seeking a replacement for Jock. It was not malicious and it was well intentioned, intended only to show support for Jock. I thought that was obvious and I suspect that Jock was happy to have the recognition.

The ad read: *'Football Broadcaster. Qualifications: ability to organise experienced broadcasters, knowledge of all aspects of football, approx 40 hrs p w including weekends. Broadcast all matches and coordinate sports panel, obtain sponsorship of approx $15,000 per annum, other duties as directed. Pay own expenses. Salary: Nil. Apply 3CCC or Bendigo Football League.'*

A few days later the new board President, Paul Spooner, rang me. We joked about the ad and I was quite comfortable with him. He then invited me to come to the board meeting two days hence to explain the ad, 'A couple of people are not happy.' I didn't see any problem with that and I readily agreed as I fully intended to go anyway to complain about my treatment over the studio hire and the appalling stories being spread.

Mazza and I arrived for the meeting on time and were surprised that only Jack Miles was in the room. Jack was my trusted friend.

'The rest are inside having a meeting in the office. I wasn't invited.' An alarm bell rang loudly in my head.

Eventually the Board members filed in, giving no recognition to Marilyn and me. The meeting formally opened and I immediately asked to speak.

Given permission, I went angrily into my belief that Gerry had acted improperly in contacting the AAF and jeopardising my job. I was certain that any misunderstanding would melt away when they read the letter from Neil O'Keefe MP.

'What letter?' the President asked. They had not seen it! I was astonished.

Gerry was flustered. 'It arrived too late,' he said.

I had a copy in my hand dated three weeks previously so obviously it was well in time for distribution and inclusion. 'Bullshit,' I said angrily.

'Okay. I confess. I forgot it,' said Gerry.

'Forgot it! How could you forget such an important letter?'

I handed my copy of Neil's letter to the President and he read it aloud. I was confident that my name would now be cleared.

However, the assembly appeared totally unimpressed. Their faces showed that they had already made a decision about me.

There were more protesting, unfriendly words between Gerry and me before Mazza and I rose to leave.

'Hang on', said the President. 'There's still the other matter.' Oh yes, the ad in the paper.

I explained my actions and my motive as recognizing the great work done by Jock Clark for football and 3CCC. As I spoke I observed the faces of the board members. They all stared impassively straight ahead. I was alarmed. I apologized without reservation for any offence I may have inadvertently caused.

I should have saved my breath.

A female Board member, who had never concealed her dislike of me, took a document from a folder and read from it. Obviously this had been prepared well in advance, probably at the earlier meeting. I cannot recall the full text of her motion she read out, only the words – 'placing an unauthorized advertisement

– smoking in the studio – suspended for the balance of the program period plus a further three months to be reviewed at the end of that time.'

I was shocked beyond belief. I was devastated. Such a severe penalty had never before been imposed; the only other suspension had been two weeks in our earliest days for a woman using the 'F' word.

The regular three month program period had only just begun so in effect I was suspended for a massive six months. I knew at once that this was the finish for me. It was not a suspension but a sacking.

I recall the President intoning, 'If it had not been for your good service we would have been much harder on you.' The bit about smoking came as a complete surprise. Admittedly I did smoke in the studio on a number of occasions, at the window with it thrown wide open and early morning with nobody else around. I had received a written warning from Gerry Pyne a week or two before and I worked hard since to obey. I was a very heavy smoker and couldn't resist the occasional puff at the window. I had been admonished for it two years before by Jeff Langdon. I had been ambushed.

Marilyn and I went home in a state of shock and distress. My life was in tatters and Mazza shared that with me.

Of course I would fight with every means available to me but the numbers against me made it impossible to win.

The next morning the Bendigo Advertiser front page carried the story of my sacking. The board and management cried that I had gone 'running to the press'. I had not. I know who it was, an old and loyal friend, but I will not reveal his name here.

What followed was absolute furor. People were very angry over my sacking and dozens of letters appeared in the Bendigo and Castlemaine papers. The prison inmates lodged a petition for my return signed by all ninety-four of them.

Don Gunn the editor of the Castlemaine Mail was a friend of mine. He pursued the matter and wouldn't let it go. We went back to the days at Williamstown, the Melbourne suburb on the bay. I lived there too for a good number of years. He lived with his parents and siblings in College Street, two doors away from my girlfriend, later my wife, Joan Hayes. Don was of the typical working class stock of the people of 'Willy', much like the people of old Castlemaine. Like Castlemaine, Williamstown has been claimed by people from 'the other side', as we Willy people used to call those who lived across the bay. Pages of names in my support came through by various means.

Here are brief extracts from a lengthy letter that colleague Bev Stewart (Sutherland) wrote to the board on 26 September 1989.

'There seems to have been resentment toward Ian because of his popularity. ... (it is) felt by Triple C's Board that Ian was stealing funding from the station. Anyone looking at the facts would find this is not the case ... the only conclusion I can come to is that Ian was suspended because of personal dislike by some key staff and Board members.'

Bev was awake to what had really caused my demise and it took a lot of courage for her to write to her employers in my defense.

A particularly gratifying and supportive letter came from professional counselor, the late Geoff Morris, a regular Listener. He concluded that I had been removed because of pure jealousy and deep resentment of me. 'You stuck your head up above the rest and they had to cut it off.'

Geoff, although blind, later became a presenter of bluegrass music on a station in Bendigo where he was elected President.

Castlemaine Mail Editor Don Gunn angrily pursued the story and he got stuck into the board and management. 'JACKBOOT TACTICS at 3CCC' yelled the bold page one headline. The controversy went on for weeks in The Mail and The Advertiser, but to no avail. The board dug in with the knowledge that they had the numbers. The only comment they made was a statement from Gerry Pyne, 'Braybrook should have known better.' One solitary letter of support for the board and that was critical of me came from Ruth Feiler, who at the time worked as a volunteer in Gerry's office. She said that my main interest was in my inflated ego and not the well-being of 3CCC. Inflated ego? I don't deny that ego had a role to play but 'inflated' I deny. Everybody who presents a radio show is driven by ego; it's a fact of life.

I continued to fight for my position in any way I could. In doing so I riled the Board considerably, but I always told the truth. Then the Board demanded an apology to them and to Gerry Pyne and they even had lawyer Kerry McDonald draw up what he thought was appropriate. Again I told them to place it where the sun doesn't shine.

After the expiration of five miserable months of my sentence and my constant requests to be reinstated, I was advised that I could indeed return. I was delighted but with some reservations about how I would get along with the bosses. My joy was short lived however when told my return was to be 6 to 8am Sunday. I was flabbergasted. This was a time-slot that nobody wanted and nobody listened to. A Board member told me: 'You won't get a breakfast program. We don't want personalities. There'll be no stars at 3CCC.' I'd been handed the ultimate insult and humiliation and I angrily told Gerry to shove it.

I knew that my reputation had suffered dreadful damage by the accusations, innuendo and false rumors and I was very angry and hurt. It was even being said (seriously) that I had broadcast illegal coded messages for my Listener friends incarcerated in the Castlemaine Gaol.

I saw a solicitor who recommended action against the Board so I applied for Legal Aid but it was denied. If I had had the money I would certainly have proceeded.

I then received a letter from Bendigo lawyers, Petersen Westbrook stating that I was saying things detrimental to 3CCC's reputation and if I persisted they would take action against me.

Through my solicitor I attempted to call a conciliatory meeting, but the Board declined stating that 'internal procedures were more than adequate'. They weren't. I lodged a complaint with Corporate Affairs but that was ignored.

Eventually I had had enough, realising I could not win, and pulled my head in. Through it all I had sought only to be treated fairly and with justice.

I learned that if you have the numbers you cannot be beaten, a lesson I never forgot.

Three weeks after my sacking I had formed a loose alliance with Tony Jerome and Jock Clarke to run for the soon to be held board elections. I believed that we shared a belief in a professional approach to broadcasting. The expected support from Tony and Jock did not eventuate however. Jock had been asked to withdraw his resignation as footy broadcast leader so he was happy with that result. In September 1987, Roger Boehme, Trevor Thomas and I in loose alliance and 'Moonlight Knight' Chris Spencer had run for Board election and were defeated. Elected were Phil Edmonds, Bill Borrie, Jack Miles and Paul Spooner. It should have been no surprise when Paul Spooner moved to keep the Bendigo studio open. Tony actually turned around and attacked me in his election speech. Surprisingly, my 'ally' Jock, ripped into me after the vote protesting I was one of the group wanting to close the Bendigo studio.

I certainly did, seeing it as the beginning of the end for Harcourt, correctly as it turned out. In fact I had prepared a motion to put to the Board meeting of October to that effect. I was thwarted when Paul Spooner (Bendigo) got in first with a motion to establish a committee to investigate the studio matter. It passed and effectively stopped my motion. I did my block and told the board to stick their committees up their collective bottoms and left the meeting, followed by Jack Miles who shared my anger.

A serious disturbance erupted in November 1991. I was by then well outside the station. The Board issued statements to members and the media that the Department of Transport and Communications had ordered a change in the station frequency from 103.9 to 89.5 with little or no notice. The statement said it would require an expensive new transmitter and antenna. The cost would be $60,000 and a public appeal to 'save the station' was launched. The community responded sympathetically and a number of people like musician Peter Saltmarsh ran special benefit nights and events to raise money. In fact the community response was inspirational.

However, I seriously doubted the facts as presented by the committee and felt that the station was seeking public money under questionable circumstances. I stuck my head up to challenge the claims in a letter to the press. In this, I questioned the amount quoted and the claim that the order had come as a bolt from the blue. I knew from experience that we had known since day one, and were specifically advised in 1988, that we would have to change frequency in the future. I suggested that 3CCC was asking the community for money under debatable pretences, both in the short notice claim and the massive cost they claimed.

The Board responded publicly to my claims, with accusations that I was not being honest and they stuck to the $60,000 figure, asking the public to contribute more and thus 'save the station'.

I firmly believed this to be wrong and was strongly supported in this in letters in January 1992 from the Transport and Communications Department's Michael Saloom and from the federal Minister for Communications, Warren Snowden.

Michael Saloom wrote '- at no time has 3CCC been threatened with closure – the claim of the cost – appears exaggerated.' He questioned their claim that there had been no government support saying that the Department had been assisting 3CCC in locating a second-hand transmitter from the Commonwealth for $1000 and 'was doing all it could to assist 3CCC'.

Minister Warren Snowden indicated similarly, saying, 'The cost of $60,000 to effect a frequency change also appears to be misleading' and 'claims that frequency change would cost $60,000 therefore seem to be exaggerated.'

A fiery battle raged in the district press with the focus again on me. In an uncommon event the Bendigo Advertiser was moved to write a prominent, but kindly, editorial saying 'there seems little doubt now that this (the $60,000) was an overreaction.'

Of course I could have, and maybe should have, let the entire affair go with a shrug of the shoulders, but such was my animosity toward the Board for their treatment of me that I went in head first. I could not stand aside and see this claim unchallenged, feeding off a concerned community. It proved to rival my sacking as the most highly publicised occasion in 3CCC's history.

In time the matter disappeared from the headlines, the changes were made at a cost that was never revealed. The last figure of the amount raised from donations that I heard was $35,000.

Soon after this, the push to relocate the station to Bendigo gathered strength. From the outside I did all I could to raise the awareness of Castlemaine people and to do all I could to to prevent this, again strongly supported by The Mail Editor, Don Gunn. Alas, Bendigo had the numbers and the station was dismantled at Harcourt and set up in Bendigo. There was general excitement among the Bendigo move backers who claimed the station would grow and prosper by moving from what Gerry Pyne described as the 'backwater' of Harcourt.

In a particularly disturbing act, all of the hundreds of photos decorating the stairwell wall were destroyed in the move. With them went the pictorial history of the station. I always believe that a group or person that does not respect their history has no future. That was to be the case with 3CCC. Ultimately 3CCC failed and eventually lost their Broadcasting Licence completely. Our beloved 3CCC vanished from the face of the earth.

The pioneer FM and community radio station in rural and regional Australia that began in Castlemaine in 1978, no longer exists. Twenty years later, Gerry Pyne who was Manager at the time, told me that he was probably wrong in supporting the move to Bendigo. Broadcasting from an abandoned railway station in a tiny bush town had made 3CCC unique.

Chapter Nineteen

New beginnings, Education, testing, a dreadful transmission, KLFM, huge wins

Back in 1990, when 3CCC began folding its tent to leave Harcourt, I heard that Brad Geier, the youngster that I had helped train in radio, was in the process of setting up a community style station in Bendigo, one that would rival 3CCC should it ever move to that city. He was in the process of applying for an 'E' class (education based) licence and had received the okay to conduct a test transmission. At that time this class of licence was still available, but this was to soon change.

I contacted Brad and told him of my interest in joining him. He was enthusiastic. However, his response in a letter to me in February was negative. He felt that my well publicized dispute with 3CCC may draw his group in and cause problems they could do without. I was disappointed but fair enough I suppose. In a later letter to Brad I asked him if I could attend a meeting of his Board and put my case. By reply on 21 March he agreed and I attended their next meeting. My explanations and assurances did the trick and I was invited into the fold. However, in the upcoming test transmission I would not be allowed on air but permitted only to operate the broadcast panel, my presence not acknowledged. Of course I agreed, happy to be involved at any level.

The broadcast was from a room at the Community Health Centre in Havilah Road Bendigo where the group's Treasurer, David Kippen was employed. We had only the most basic equipment and the small transmitter was set up in the toilet.

On day two there was a small explosion in the toilet as the transmitter demanded a rest. Mike Tobin, engineer and ex-Telstra communications whiz, hastily restored it to working order and the test resumed. We all judged it an overall success.

Progress from then on was pitifully slow as the wheels of bureaucracy turned. Then, a setback with the changes to the broadcasting Services Act in 1992. The E class licences were abolished and we went back to square one, competing now for a then non-existent Community Radio Licence.

By this time I had joined the inner circle of the group and was warmly welcomed, especially by Brad. The group consisted principally of Brad Geir, David Kippen, Catherine Yorke-Moore, Mike Tobin, Graeme Knight, Tracey Jeffrey, Bill Kent, Alan Williams, Mazza and me. We were a very happy, close group all focused on the hoped-for future success. God knows why, because the chances of us ever getting a licence were remote!

Brad called it Bendigo FM Education Radio and we conducted a number of test transmissions over an extended period, just enough to keep up our enthusiasm. We did this from a dilapidated goods shed on the west platform of the disused railway station at suburban Golden Square. The conditions were dreadful but we didn't mind. There was no water connected and no toilets. The row of peppercorn trees backing the platform served the purpose quite well.

On one occasion we conducted a test broadcast weekend and at the conclusion Marilyn and I made our way home to Harcourt. The radio was tuned to our frequency and to our dismay we heard the voices of Brad and Mike in the studio. They still had the transmitter on and the microphones were open! The duo was involved in very earnest and frank discussion about the attributes (or lack of) of one of our female members. What they were saying was obviously slanderous and libelous, no mistake about that. I won't detail it here but believe me it was far from complimentary.

It was in the days before mobile phones and Mazza and I desperately sought a telephone box, finally locating one at Kangaroo Flat. Bugger! We had no coins!

Mazza ran into a nearby shop, got some change and made the call. There was a shocked silence on the other end when the duo realised what they had been saying to all who cared to listen. What would happen next?

The person concerned had indeed been listening and guess what? She had inserted a cassette tape into her recorder. Armed with this she stormed into the 'studio' and began a quite justified tirade. Embarrassed, groveling apologies were extended and to her credit the person took no legal action. If she had, the new radio station could have ended then and there.

I have to acknowledge the dedication and commitment of our President Brad Geier to this community radio project. He created a good impression with the powers in Canberra through his determination and, I suspect, because of his youth. He was about seventeen at the time and it was unusual, to say the least, for one so young to be in his position and to display such a will to achieve a dream. His parents, Neil and Cynthia must also be recognised for the help and encouragement they always gave him along the way. Cynthia never went on air but for a long time acted as principal office person. Neil turned out to be a very good presenter but stayed out of the business end. Graeme Knight was always there as well. He was a good friend and we had good times together.

We ran our second test transmission in November 1990, twenty-four hours over a weekend. Bendigo Education Broadcasters were on the air.

Katherine York-Moore even arranged for Liberal MLA the late Michael John to officially launch the broadcast. We worked hard for two weeks before to prepare for the event. To impress the Tribunal and the doubters, it had to be good. As we were applying for an Education Class licence the broadcast varied from words for pre-schoolers to popular music (musical education!) and religious education, pretty boring stuff. But it was a success, at least technically.

The annual Easter Fair Parade in Bendigo is a huge event, and one year we decided we should do as the 'real' radio stations do and enter a float in the procession. We knocked together a very basic display, some big speakers and signs, on the back of a borrowed truck and away we went. I was the one with a heavy vehicle licence so I was the driver. When the procession ended we were driving back to the station to unload when we saw in front of us the float of our rival, 3CCC. They had gone to a lot of trouble to build a mock studio building with lots of signs and stuff to impress the audience. Their truck was immediately in front of us as we approached the railway bridge in Thistle Street. To our astonishment the plywood 'building' in front of us, caught by the wind, suddenly lifted and crashed to the road. We were almost on top of it. The mock-up sat there, wobbling badly. I should have braked hard but instead I planted my foot. We struck the display and it disintegrated into a hundred pieces. Brad, sitting beside me was amazed and fell about laughing; we both did. Brad was astonished at my action, thinking that I would have tried to avoid the float, but he loved it just the same. We sped off and were quickly out of sight and until now, nobody knew exactly who destroyed the 3CCC float.

By July 1991 we were given a permit for our third test broadcast. Among the newer announcers was John Croxford, a computer whiz who proved a huge asset to the station. By this time Brad had negotiated a lease of the B side of the railway station platform and we had worked hard to set it up as Office and Studio, a huge improvement on the A side. We now even had a toilet, a 'kitchen' and running water.

By March 1992 the Broadcasting Act had changed and we were now number two in a queue for a community radio licence for Bendigo. A hearing was scheduled for July and we had to be well prepared. In a 'white paper' to the Board, I said that they should pursue the seniors of Bendigo and put the Listener into everything we did and every decision we made. I said that we needed to work hard and actively seek supporters and 'Action, not words will win us the right to the licence.'

When we later adopted the policy of catering for seniors it was a remarkable success.

Brad Geier's ambition and determination was admirable and 1994 looked like being good. He told the Bendigo Advertiser that we would have our C class licence by years end. He was twenty five years old by now and had spent his teen years preparing for the time when a licence came his way. His first effort was with his mate Graeme Knight. The two lads set up an illegal pirate radio station centred in Brad's bedroom. It had a range of half a kilometer and ran for several months until shut down by Radio Inspector, Vic Pleuger. Vic could have hit the boys with the law but instead, without fuss, simply told them to shut it down.

Around June 1994 I went back on the air with quite a fanfare from some press – 'Braybrook Returns'. It made me feel great to be in the swim again. At this time we planned to (somehow) open a studio in Castlemaine and in July, Brad announced in 'The Mail' that we would be building a studio in the old School of Mines next to the town hall, with support of the Shire Council. He added that plans were afoot to transmit from the Old Gaol at a future date, contradictory maybe, but he was uncertain which way to go. Eventually we began at the Old Gaol with a test from there in January 1995, and we started construction of a studio there. We lasted there only a week when we took the opportunity to move to the former nurses' home in Myring Street. It wasn't until January 1996 that we officially opened decent studios there. The ceremony was conducted by Mostyn Thompson the Chief Commissioner and included the raising of the KLFM flag, specially designed and made by Milly Palmer. We were then able to present a limited service from Castlemaine via a link to the

Golf Club atop Wimble Street, but needed more equipment to do it properly.

In February 1995, the Hawke government announced that in August the country would commemorate the fiftieth anniversary of the end of World War II with 'Australia Remembers'. I saw an opportunity for our station to be involved. I had a brainstorm that we should apply to make a special broadcast over two weeks to commemorate, aiming at the age group concerned. We would broadcast nothing but appropriate music, old radio shows and serials, interviews with returned service men and women and so on. Brad thought it a good idea and immediately and successfully applied for a special test licence.

We began gathering material. I contacted Con Sciacca the Minister for Veterans Affairs and asked to be granted the status of the 'Australia Remembers Station' for the region. Within a week I received a written reply. The minister had signed the letter personally and had readily agreed. We were on our way as the official 'Australia Remembers station for Central Victoria'; a real coup for our fledgling station, one that would soon put us firmly on the map.

Mazza and I decided it would be good to contact and interview as many returned servicemen and women, wartime nurses and females in the wartime workforce and so on as we could. We set out to do so.

Meanwhile, I had applied for a grant from Department of Veterans Affairs to finance the cost of locating and visiting suitable folk. Nothing appeared to be forthcoming so we went ahead hoping to cover the costs ourselves somehow.

Mazza and I attended a RSL conference at the Flemington racecourse around June of that year. There, among other important people, like fiery Bruce Ruxton, the RSL State President, I interviewed Con Sciacca, the Minister. Now, here was a really good, fair dinkum bloke. Of Italian descent, he had a great love of Australia and what it had done for him and his post-war migrant parents. He gave me a brilliant and passionate interview.

I thought, what the hell, I've nothing to lose, so at interview's end I told him of my funding application to his department had met with no response.

'How much do you want?' I told him the figure.

He walked a short distance away and got on his mobile phone.

He came back to me. 'That's all set Ian. It's on the way. When you come to Canberra I want you to call and see me and let me know how it's going.' He gave me his card. 'Just call this number, they'll be expecting you. Okay?'

Blow me down! What a great bloke! There is more about Con Sciacca later.

We decided it may be a good idea to put on a big Australia Remembers night and approached the Bendigo RSL with the idea. They were quite enthusiastic and allowed us free use of their magnificent venue and dining room. We charged a minimum entry of six dollars and people ordered from the menu. The small profit went to defray the expenses – almost. It was a fabulous night and a greater success than we dreamed of. The venue was packed with people of all ages, including of course a good number of returned servicemen and women. We played the great music of WWII, and danced, ate, joked and laughed our way through the night. It was absolutely marvelous. Some people dressed in the old service uniforms and looked great, even if some uniforms were a little tight. It must have shrunk said one! Mazza looked really terrific dressed in a dark skirt with her father's Air Force uniform jacket and hat. She was lovely and her parents were so proud of her, not just for her dress, but for the big effort she put into organizing the night. We even had the front half of a WWII fighter plane set up on the stage, provided by an RSL member.

Mazza and I soon drove to Canberra to gather material from the Sound Archives and the War Memorial for the coming Australia Remembers broadcast. The cooperation and help we received was outstanding. We had previously made an appointment to visit Minister Con Sciacca and were ushered into his spacious office, somewhere in the vast Parliament House. We were given coffee and made to feel welcome and relaxed. After a formal interview, Mazza and I had a lengthy talk with Minister Sciacca during which I mentioned that my half brother Ron had died age nineteen, on the Burma Railway.

As we made to leave, Con went to a shelf, taking down a polished board on which was mounted a railway line spike given to him by the Ex-POW Association as a memento of his visit to the Death Railway site. He said 'You take this, Ian; it has more important significance for you than for me.' He handed me the board. I was astonished at this caring act from a government minister and my respect and regard for him grew even more. I display the item in my home with great pride. I was never more impressed with a politician and I had met quite a few.

The Australia Remembers broadcast was a huge success. The audience response was amazing, particularly as we were a station not on air yet but operating on a two week permit! We not only attracted a huge response but went on to win two major national awards for our effort: 'The Black Diggers' and 'Australia Remembers', the programs that Mazza and I had put our hearts into.

The announcements at the annual Community Broadcasting Association of Australia (CBAA) conference in Melbourne that November shocked everyone, especially when a further award came for the broadcast of an international cricket match held in Bendigo, organised principally by Brad. Those assembled from all over Australia had never heard of this upstart small aspirant station and were astonished as the compere read out our name three times! We were thrilled to bits as Brad accepted the awards. Mazza hadn't registered for that conference due to our lack of money but she was able to attend as the guest of Simon, who was a representative of a company that sold a lot of gear to Community Radio stations.

The wins at the Awards were a massive boost to the group. Importantly, they finally convinced everyone that we should apply for a licence to serve seniors. When the time came, we applied and guess what? We received the licence. KLFM has never looked back, soon gathering a large and loyal audience. It is a community radio success story and I am proud of my role in it.

Brad Geier and I were best friends, and he told me one day talking over drinks on my veranda, that he would never make a decision without first running it past me. He had always done this and we spent much time together planning. He appeared to respect my input and opinions and I became involved with the centre of management. He also included Marilyn, respecting her advice. Indeed we became more like second parents to Brad than colleagues.

Best Aboriginal radio program in Australia.

Congratulations from Jeff Langdon at CBAA Awards Night in Melbourne.

Mike Saloom (ABA) me, Brad Geier and Graeme Knight at HQ of ABA, Canberra.

Mazza, Brad Geier and Mike Tobin at CBAA Conference Albury.

Mazza, Graeme Knight, Brad Geier and me at a CBAA conference, Albury.

The street parade, Harcourt Applefest. Our VW Beetle.

Chris Goodall, Stan Munro, Barry Palmer and Steve Virtue at Northern Hotel, fundraiser for KLFM. Stan and the crew raised $1,000.

In 1940s gear, with Mazza, for the Castlemaine Show Parade. Mazza's wearing her father's WWII Air Force jacket and cap.

With Paul Thieman and Faye Barker showing our brand new Castlemaine KLFM licence.

With Mazza conducting an interview for KLFM with a Mirridong resident.

O.B. at Maxi IGA store. Me, Mazza, Ian Nicholls and Barry Palmer. Maxi, great supporters of the station.

Barry Palmer and Jeannie Norris at OB from the Castlemaine Market steps.

With Troy Cassar-Daley outside KLFM Castlemaine studio.

Mazza and Brad Geier on holiday in Hobart.

The day after the closure of KLFM Castlemaine. The faces tell it all. MLA Bob Cameron to my left, was a wonderful supporter.

The devastating mess that remained of the KLFM Castlemaine studio the day after the closure.

With Jeannie Norris and Mazza at the launch of Jeannie's book. Rev Ken Parker in background.

Interviewing Premier John Brumby at Don Smallgoods factory.

The late Len Cockerill and Faye Barker at Radio 88

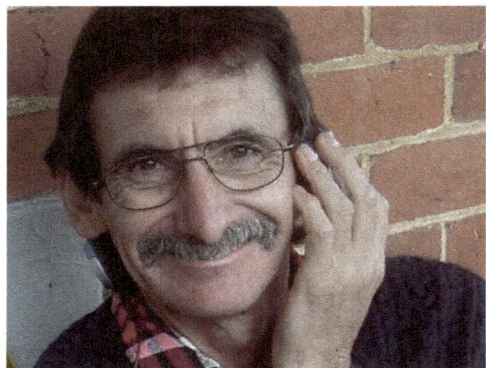

John Jenkins. The heart of the technical system of WMAfm and later, Radio 88fm.

At the mic at an Outside Broadcast.

One of our first Footy Broadcasts. Brian Moon, Stuart Dunn, Brett Cole and Jackson Saunders.

WMAfm Board members, Roger Shillitoe, Bill Stephens, Me, Beverley Latham-Stephens, Josephine Shillitoe and Mazza.

Glenn Braybrook and Bettie Exon in WMAfm studio.

'Fifty and Over' broadcast from RSL Castlemaine. Neil Woodfine, me and Mazza.

WMAfm sticker.

The Radio88fm little man.

Gene Fisk, Mazza and me at Gene's newest CD launch at Kyneton.

With Paul Reed, Vin Cappy and James Morrison at James's concert at the Theatre Royal.

Sharyn, Marcia & Mazza at Gene Fisk's newest CD launch.

With Our dear friend Gwennie Coupland.

The WMAfm O.B. trailer, the metal roof cover was made by Bill Stephens.

The original team of WMAfm when it was Radio88. Me, Mazza, Wilson Bunton, Beverley Latham-Stephens, Glenn Braybrook, Julie Higginbottom, Faye Barker and Len Cockerill.

Winners of the award as 'The Most Outstanding Small Station In Australia' at Hobart. A proud occasion for Castlemaine's radio station of the time.

A deeply unhappy occasion, the WMAfm wake. K.D., Robyn Thomas, Ken Ford, Rod Hadfield, John Jenkins, Ken White, me and Mazza.

From 2010 WMAfm Annual Report.

Chapter Twenty

*KLFM to Castlemaine, conferences, from Old
Gaol to nurses'home, a flag raising*

There were many people involved at KLFM but, in fact, nowhere near the number we had had at 3CCC. Many were forgettable but some stand out, Brian Coghlin for example. Brian was a bright and enthusiastic person, young and fit. He was a bit of an entrepreneur and among other things ran an indoor cricket centre in Bendigo. However, his heart was in radio and he was determined to get into a local commercial station, preferably 3BO. He respected my opinions and the knowledge I had gained and sometimes asked me for advice or to assess his performances. He was a natural talent and I was not surprised when he eventually landed a job with 3BO. He never looked back and became the heart and soul of that station, very popular around Central Victoria as 'Cogho'. To his credit he never became big-headed, in fact remaining pretty ordinary. He'd mix with all of his mates, drink at the pub and rarely if ever wore a suit. Mostly it was old jeans and sneakers when he wasn't representing 3BO. I really liked Brian and was very pleased to see him do so well.

Another good broadcasting talent was Peter Lesuey who, through hard work, came to own a very comfortable and popular hostel for aged people in Bendigo. This meant he became too busy to continue in radio, but he still does the occasional show on KLFM. Mike Weeks was another great asset to KLFM, presenting the 9am to noon program Monday to Friday for several years – a huge commitment for a volunteer. He was easy to listen to and quite accomplished. He has now retired from radio as far as I know. Ian Nicholls was the breakfast presenter five days a week for several years and became a bit of a household name in Bendigo before handing the show to Brad Geier. Ian was a major contributor to the success of KLFM and I respected him and regarded him as a mate. Mazza and I once went with him and his wife Ruth to the trots in Bendigo. He loved a gamble and we barely got a glimpse of Ian all evening as he spent most of his time at the Tote. The last time I saw him during the confusing period to come, was at an EGM venue in Bendigo where he assured me that everything was on track, and the problem with Brad would be happily resolved very soon. He was station manager at the time, so I accepted that as gospel.

An important step in the success of KLFM was to get a licence to translate (relay) into Castlemaine where our signal was almost non-existent. Set in a large valley, Castlemaine was not able to receive other than the most powerful radio signals from outside. Since 3CCC had left, there was, of course, no station in the town. I was determined that we would have one and went to work on it, helped of course by Brad who supported the idea. He set out to gain a licence to have a separate transmitter and frequency for Castlemaine although the likelihood of us winning was pretty remote.

But it's surprising what determination with a good dash of bulldust can achieve. Brad mastered in both, and he was liked and respected at ACMA headquarters in Canberra and Sydney.

We were attending an annual community broadcasters' conference in Sydney. Brad, Mazza, Mike, and I sat in the audience as we were addressed by a big chief from the Australian Communications and Broadcasting Authority (ACMA). Blow me down if he did not casually remark that KLFM had been granted a translator licence for Castlemaine! We could scarcely believe it. This was amazing and we were as thrilled to pieces as we were shocked. What a way for us to be told. It was wonderful. The ACMA has human traits after all!

We attended a number of CBAA annual conferences; Albury, Sydney, Canberra, Melbourne and generally had good times. One year, Brad and Graeme Knight set off in Brad's old Holden and Mazza and I in our equally aging Holden, to far off Canberra. As usual we were all pretty broke, although Graeme had a regular job with the state government and had money, we three others did not. We camped in a pre-fab unit at Black Hill Caravan Park, all four in the tiny space, a double bed for Mazza and me and two bunks. To stretch the money we four ate each night at the Ainslie Football Club, stuffing ourselves at the 'All you can Eat' deal smorgasbord whilst paying only for two, and loading heaps of fruit and bread into Mazza's large carry bag for 'later'. At the unit much fun was made of Mazza wearing her old leopard skin dressing gown which the boys dubbed as 'Mildred's' after the female personality in TV's 'George and Mildred'. Mazza wore one almost a replica. We had loads of fun, playing the pokies, getting sloshed, with Mazza as our drink-free driver. One night we spotted a huge reflective street sign, two metres long, which had been knocked down and we stopped, bent it double and stowed it in the car boot. I had that sign for many years, prominently displayed in my back yard.

At the Albury conference there was Mike Tobin, Brad, Mazza and me and again we had a lot of fun, visiting clubs, sightseeing and the odd drink or two. More than equal time was spent at that rather than participating in the conference. At Sydney, where the conference was held at the University, we found cheap digs at Glebe, an old inner suburb, upstairs in a clean but old hotel named The Rooftop. Blow me down, you wouldn't believe it; also camped there was Gerry Pyne my old adversary from 3CCC and one who Brad had little time for. Late the first night, both in 'sedated' condition, the two sat on the stairs with some stubbies talking for hours and emerged as friends, well sort of.

On the second day we men left early (walking) and Mazza, always a slow starter, had to walk the two kilometres to the conference later. The heat and humidity was awful. Her feet swelled enormously and she got blisters so bad she could barely stand. Next day she found an op shop and bought a pair of used Dr. Scholl's sandals, spending the day on the bed counting the bricks in the wall that our 'room with a view' looked out on.

Another night we walked a good distance to the Glebe yacht club down on the harbour seafront, where we ate well and played the pokies. On this occasion our treasurer Pastor David Kippen, a rather conservative man, was with us and to our enjoyment and surprise he put a ten cent coin in a poker machine! He played his two shots, lost, and walked away, disappointed and disgusted with the machine.

The Melbourne conference I mentioned previously was a great event, with KLFM winning so many awards. One of the people attending that we went out on the town with was Maurie (not his real name) one of the senior staff from the ACMA. We made our way to the temporary Casino, spent a lot of money, got half cut and generally covered the town. Maurie was very much the worse for wear and insisted that Mazza, our driver again, drop him off where he could catch a tram. We were then in Fitzroy Street St Kilda, so we let him off there. Maurie was to be a guest speaker the next morning at the conference; we all arrived late but Maurie was much later. He finally arrived sixty minutes late, holding up proceedings, looking very much the worse for his night out. We didn't question him about his activities when we left him on notorious Fitzroy Street.

I didn't attend the conference in 1996, the tyranny of distance, but Brad did and collected an Award for Shirley Ballardi's excellent program, 'Australia Remembers Vietnam'. Earlier we had been awarded the State Government Award for excellence in community service. We were pretty good, you know!

* * *

KLFM Bendigo was running beautifully. Now we needed to focus on a studio and offices in Castlemaine, plus all the equipment that goes along with a separate radio station, for that's what it was to be. In June 1995 we arranged with Kaye and Kevin Duncan, owners of a business operating from the Old Castlemaine Gaol, for KLFM to set up there. The late Barry Lakey, a man of considerable experience in climbing transmission towers and an all round good bloke, risked his life to climb with ladders to the mighty roof top. His job was to install our dipole on an existing pole about five metres high which soared to the heavens. This pole had previously been used by the jail for its radio communication system, now obsolete. It was held upright with guy wires but still moved about seriously in the wind. It was very dangerous; not only extremely high, but perched on a rooftop about two metres in diameter. To add to the danger it was a day of persistent misty rain and we, safely on the ground, watched anxiously, hoping Barry didn't put a foot wrong. To do so would almost certainly mean death. As usual Barry Lakey made no charge.

Unfortunately it didn't work out. The lady owner seemed to regard the radio station as her property and began directing us what we should do. Alarm bells rang and we promptly made a decision to look elsewhere.

We asked the Mount Alexander Golf Club if we could locate our transmitter on the roof of their machinery shed. They readily agreed. We then asked the Castlemaine Hospital for space at the abandoned Nurses Home in Myring Street and were successful with that too. We were given excellent rooms free of charge; sheer luxury compared to Bendigo KLFM's Golden Square set up! (Although I must say that Bendigo had now graduated to the up side platform building and accommodation was pretty good.)

Old Castlemaine people and businesses couldn't give us enough help and support, respecting us for bringing a radio station back to town. Brad and I approached the Chief Commissioner of the City of Castlemaine, Mostyn Thompson for help. He and the other two Commissioners didn't hesitate and even agreed for Council to pay for a brand new transmitter. Various other bits and pieces were obtained, again much of it from Alan Williams and installed by him, Barry Palmer and Bill Kent. Alan, Barry and Bill set up a complicated linking system that enabled us to broadcast from the studio to the tower at the golf club thence by microwave link to the KLFM main transmitter on Big Hill and through that to Bendigo as well as back to Castlemaine. Whatever originated in Castlemaine was broadcast across Bendigo and across Castlemaine simultaneously and vice versa. It was a moderate success, albeit flying by the seat of our pants at times.

The Mt Alexander Golf Club committee was very cooperative and for a small rental, allowed us to install our tower and dipole as we asked on the shed roof and set up a receiver and computer inside. The day for the dipole installation came and Brad, Barry and I fell to the task. It wasn't significant to start, but it turned out that this important event for KLFM coincided with one for the hospital. It was the opening day of the sparkling new Castlemaine Hospital, set on a big hill overlooking the town, to be part of the Alexander Home for the Aged.

Bill Kent supplied us with a metal extendable tower, operated by a crank handle and ratchet. It extended to about five metres and this we had to juggle and struggle to get onto the roof. We bolted it down, fixing stabilising guy wires in each direction and it was time to extend the tower to full height.

Barry and Brad grappled with the tower atop the roof and I had the job of cranking the handle as needed. The tower went up in stages of about a half meter as it was necessary to adjust cables and wires as it rose, Barry had jammed a hammer into the works to hold the tower in place as adjustments were made. He called to me, 'Okay, crank it up.' I turned the handle and next instant I copped an almighty whack on the head that sent me sprawling, half conscious. I had no idea what had happened. I blacked out for a minute or so and awoke to anxious Barry and Brad peering down on me. I was covered in blood which poured from a huge wound to the top of my head. The damned hammer, freed from propping the tower, had fallen five meters and struck me full force on the scone. The blood was everywhere. Barry grabbed a rag from somewhere and tried to stem the flow as they half carried me to the car.

I have the distinction forever more of being the first patient treated by the new Castlemaine Hospital. The doctor on duty came in and put my head back together with fifteen stitches, a nurse cleaned up most of the blood, and they told me to go home and rest. I didn't of course, but went back and finished the job.

I know now that I was extremely lucky that I wasn't killed or suffered brain damage. It was a mighty blow. Some say the latter did happen which explains a lot of things about me.

Part of the deal with the golf club was that we did a live broadcast from the clubrooms, which we did as soon as we could. It definitely was not the best effort yet for an OB as we had little to talk about for the six hour broadcast. Once you have interviewed the President, the Secretary and one of the lady kitchen volunteers and with all the golfers out on the course what can you do? Talk among yourselves – and that's what we did. Radio can be awfully boring at times!

As always Barry Palmer was there to help set up the equipment and with the on-air stuff. He was one of the silent workers behind KLFM (and later Radio88 and WMAfm), always willing to help out. He was good on air too, with a professional approach to the job, so often lacking in community radio.

In April 1997, we moved out of the Nurses Home into the Castlemaine train station building, the lease organised by Brad. Alan Williams had discovered that the railways had a perfectly good landline that was unused and available that ran all the way to Bendigo, right past our Golden Square studio. It had been replaced by radio communication some years before but the copper line was in perfect condition, able to carry full stereo.

It was to prove a boon to us. Everything we produced in the Castlemaine studio went directly from our panel into the line. At the Golden Square end the line was tapped into by Bill Kent and Alan. They fed it into the studio panel there and voila!

We had a fantastic connection that enabled us to switch between Castlemaine and Golden Square with the flick of a switch. We were so fortunate to have this available to us as a Telstra landline would have cost thousands of dollars a year and been way out of reach.

We had a massive scare when we were in the process of setting up in the railway building. It looked like we were doomed again! ACMA announced its proposal to alter the licence area plan again. It looked very much like we would lose our Castlemaine frequency and, after all our efforts, our radio station. Once more we called on our loyal Castlemaine community for letters of support and received over a hundred in a week. Brad and I begged our masters at ACMA for mercy and once again they came good with another temporary frequency. God bless 'em! It's often said in the industry that ACMA is difficult to deal with, but I have always found them most cooperative, understanding and helpful.

Although the accommodation at the train station was pretty basic it served us well for a long time. One large and dilapidated room, with twelve foot ceilings, became a very good studio. We put in a false ceiling and lined it throughout with acoustic tiles donated by the owner of a factory being demolished in Bendigo. He was a regular listener to Mazza and I on Bush Wireless and he rang us with the wonderful offer. Barry Palmer helped us dismantle the lining in an old building being demolished at Golden Square and we moved it all by trailer, in car boots and a borrowed utility truck. Barry Palmer was our chief builder and designer and with his help we built a first class studio; technically, but maybe not aesthetically! We painted the studio a soft French Grey colour, provided free by Lindsay Dale's Paint

Store. The large passageway housed our reception desk and the second room a storage area.

We were making good progress but still operated only on the very limited Saturday and Sunday hours imposed by the ACMA.

We still had a long way to go and it was not until 23 January 1998 that I was able to announce via the Castlemaine Mail that at last Castlemaine would begin full time broadcasting, simultaneously with Bendigo. The date was set for 6am on 26 January, Australia Day. It was a happy time for all of us and Brad, Barry, Mazza and I had several drinks on the Sunday in respect of our extraordinary achievements. We actually fired up at midnight to make sure all was in order for the early start. At the time our frequency was 100.5MHz, which was scheduled to be changed when ACMA reviewed the Licence Area Plan some time after. It was very much later that we were granted 106.3 MHz, the current KLFM Castlemaine frequency.

We went to air from Castlemaine by an unusual method. From the panel our programs travelled by landline to Golden Square. From there they were sent by the regular link transmitter for transmission from KLFM Mount Herbert site at Big Hill. That signal was picked up by a receiving unit at the golf club in Castlemaine and fed into the transmitter. Therefore, our Castlemaine originating programs travelled thirty-eight kilometres north to Big Hill and returned the thirty-eight kilometres to the golf club; seventy-six kilometres before it went to air in our town. It was complicated, but it worked beautifully.

Chapter Twenty One

*Census, heritage, gardening, promotions,
outside broadcasts, generosity*

Mazza and I were always on the lookout for ways of earning extra money. One year we signed up to work for the Australian Bureau of Statistics Census. Our job was to distribute census forms and then collect them when completed. We swore on oath to keep any information we received strictly to ourselves, given a crash course in the old fire station at Elphinstone and we were Census Collectors! It was a brief but glorious career.

What a job it was! It was early August, the middle of winter. It was cold and many days it was wet and windy. Mud abounded in some of the areas we were assigned; a large area on the periphery of Chewton, Harcourt and Elphinstone, a mostly rural area. Houses were often scattered far and wide and difficult to find, but our charter was to leave no stone unturned. We didn't. We did our job diligently as we made our way up hills and down gullies in our aged HT Holden in search of everyone that existed and some that no longer did. It was really an awful job and the pay was not good but we stuck it out and successfully completed the allotted zone within the time allowed, about a month all up. Mazza did a lot of footwork, but mostly she did the driving. During that time we found people in the Chewton Bushlands settlement that we were sure had not seen a fellow human in decades! This part of the shire was inhabited in part by hippies who had fled to the bush back in the 1970s. They were good people but 'different'. Some wore lap laps and some nothing at all. Some lived in bush huts and some in old railway carriages, others in mud humpies.

But we found them all, sometimes venturing on foot up bush tracks to where we had been told by neighbors a person lived.

At Golden Point I was chased by an enraged German Shepherd, I would have suffered serious injury if I hadn't suddenly developed wings and beat him to the front gate! In the terrified rush, my spectacles fell off and smashed as I slammed the gate. For the rest of the time as a Census Collector I was half blind. At a house in Barkers Creek I stepped onto a back verandah and from out of nowhere an angry Blue Heeler leapt from his couch and seized my right hand in a vice grip. I managed to free myself and bolt out the gate, blood dripping from a deep wound. I trotted off to the doctor in Castlemaine and got a Tetanus shot and a couple of stitches. I was very wary wherever I went from then on.

In our constant endeavour to bring in some money we also did gardening jobs for locals. Two of our clients stand out. In the first instance a widow named Sybil James who lived in a tiny cottage near the Harcourt Bowling Club. We became good friends and I would often get calls from her for one reason or another. Mazza and I frequently shared cups of tea and coffee with Sybil. This friendship indirectly led later to the establishment of the Harcourt Valley Tourist and Heritage Centre and the famed Applefest. Sybil told us of her late husband's collection of historical information which had been stored in a derelict caravan in their backyard for many years. It was a massive collection detailing just about every event in the valley since it began in the gold rush. In the 1850s, Harcourt men began growing vegetables to sell to the diggers. This led to the setting up of the major apple growing industry that still existed at the time we were there. Before long the industry went into decline until only a handful of small, family orchardists were left by 2015. A couple of bigger growers also survive.

In a period when I was no longer at 3CCC and I had some time on my hands, Mazza and I started the process of establishing the Heritage Centre in the old ANA hall on High Street, Harcourt. Assisted by a small committee, which included long time local

Rex McKinley, we had managed to obtain from the now defunct Metcalfe Shire Council, free possession of the old hall, previously earmarked by the council for sale. We then successfully applied for a grant from Arts Victoria and received a whopping $30,000. This enabled us to refurbish the hall to a pretty good standard. The Rotary Club of Castlemaine hopped in and painted the exterior with paint supplied free by retailer Lindsay Dale. Brian Seimering, a local builder was hired to do the extensive remedial work and a retired plasterer from Castlemaine generously relined the kitchen and dining room at low cost. My friend the late Tom Curtis, who lived with wife Nancy nearby, and I spent almost every day for three months painting all the indoors and external trim, helping with plastering, laying paving and a hundred other jobs. As a fundraiser we sold pavers at $10 each, permanently engraved with the donor's name; my grandsons, Jake and Jesse, among them. Major contributors have their names engraved on brass plates mounted on a lump of local granite beneath the old Monkey Puzzle tree. The completed building was excellent and an asset to the town.

Sybil James was impressed by the project and offered to donate her late husband, Hedley's, collection to kick the Heritage Centre off. It proved that Hedley had actually willed his collection to the Castlemaine Art Gallery, whose committee didn't hesitate in assigning the bequest of any Harcourt related material to us. So we had a good start, complemented by various donations of items from orchardists and other residents of the valley.

Some time after the Heritage Centre was up and running, Barry Johansen, the popular and progressive local publican, spoke to the group about incorporating a Tourism Committee in the group and this was done. It became The Harcourt Valley Tourism and Heritage Centre and the land on which the building stood became James Park, after Sybil and Hedley James. Then in a conversation between Mazza, Don Gunn, Editor of the Castlemaine Mail and me, Don suggested we look at an apple based festival for the valley. From that conversation grew the immensely popular and successful Harcourt Applefest. So in a way the valley owes its Festival to the late Don Gunn. These days Mazza and I get a lot of satisfaction seeing the old building in regular use, the annual Applefest thriving, and the trees we planted now almost fully grown and casting shade.

Another gardening job with local people who became good friends occurred when we answered an ad posted on the Post Office notice board. This led us to 'Atherstone' historic homestead in Thompson's Road, recently acquired by world renowned artist, our neighbours, Robert Jacks and his wife Julienne. We began to work for Robert and Julienne, clearing the long neglected garden, and this relationship soon developed into a good and lasting friendship. They had a young daughter Ellie living at home and two teenagers, Angie and Nick living in the city. I spent many happy hours with Robert in his studio, consuming considerable quantities of his excellent wines. We would yarn away for hours on end, seated on whatever was at hand, surrounded by thousands of dollars worth, if not millions of dollars worth, of Robert's paintings and sculptures. Sometimes we would listen to his fabulous collection of country music albums; most quite rare and collected by him from his times in the U.S. – Texas in particular. I think we were rather unlikely companions, me with no real appreciation of Art, a Philistine, and Robert one of the world's best artists in his field. But we were very good friends. Sadly, Robert passed away in October 2014.

* * *

Our KLFM service in Castlemaine was a great success. Mazza and I worked hard to promote it. We were guest speakers at every gathering that would have us, thought up all sorts of publicity stunts, entered in the show parades, had a double sided KLFM sign affixed to the roof of our VW Beetle and drove it around and around the town each day for a month. We did live broadcasts from the street and there was rarely a week when we didn't get a story in the local paper. Before too long KLFM became a household name in Castlemaine.

We had a small crew of volunteers, principally Paul Thieman, Barry Palmer, Faye Barker, Daryl O'Brien, Tess Buzolich, Marilyn (Mazza), Peter Seward and me. But we were pretty good, I reckon. Sadly Tess, who became our group's secretary, was killed in a car smash about a year later. Faye Barker was truly dedicated and presented a great show named 'Sentimental Journey' every Sunday afternoon. She was a skilled broadcaster who did her homework and had a large audience. We all loved Faye and were horrified to hear of her early death, aged sixty. She had just returned from a sea cruise in celebration of that birthday when stricken by a brain hemorrhage and she died soon after. Marilyn and I received the news in a phone call from her daughter Kelly whilst waiting to board the ferry at Devonport, Tasmania. It was a sad end to a great holiday in beautiful Tasmania, a place we had grown to love.

Between us all at Castlemaine, we were on air for thirty prime hours a week plus incidentals from our studio at the railway station. We got a fantastic response from the station's local and widespread audience. I was rewarded by my mate Brad with the position of Castlemaine Branch Manager. The business people in the town rallied around and we were able to generate considerable revenue for the station. The Lions Club dug deep and donated a couple of thousand dollars and the Rotary Club donated a beaut new computer, presented by stalwart supporter, Vin Cappy.

We had some good presenters and a good blend of styles and music. Barry Palmer was into '50s, '60s and '70s music, Faye Barker loved the golden oldies, Peter Seward likewise, Daryl O'Brien enjoyed just about any music so long as it was not rowdy, Paul Thieman loved the '60s and '70s stuff, I liked almost all popular music from the '40s to the '80s, and Mazza likewise.

Tess Buzolich liked more upbeat modern sounds. As a result we had a listenable mix and importantly we all had fun and this transferred to the Listeners.

Mazza and I had co-presented 'The Fabulous Fifties' for a decade or so and we converted it to 'Bush Wireless' from Castlemaine. It started out as a light-hearted program on Sunday mornings with the intention of letting people know what was happening in the district. That never happened as we sidetracked into just about anything that came to mind. The result was probably the most popular show on radio in the region. It was all fun and nonsense, ideas Mazza and I dreamed up at home over breakfast. It was all spontaneous and never rehearsed. I have never enjoyed radio so much. We had a swag of listeners and took a staggering number of phone calls. Every week we gave away a posy of flowers from our sponsors, Ian and Barbara Potter. It was amazingly popular. Sometimes we had to get Paul Thieman in to help us answer the calls; he once took sixty calls in under three hours, not all for the flowers of course, but general inquiries and comments. It was terrific, but people really loved the show. We had listeners from all over central Victoria, people many and varied. Typical were the blokes from the Vietnam Veterans Association in Bendigo. Maurie Betts, their Secretary, regularly had Mazza and me as guests at their fabulous Cabaret nights. Several women used to invite us to their homes for afternoon teas and talk; one dear lady once slipped me an envelope with instructions not to open until we got home. It contained a fifty dollar note! That was certainly a first! We saw the dear lady many times over the years and although we tried to hand back the money she absolutely refused it. We felt a bit guilty but accepted the gift in the spirit it was given.

Paul Thieman was always ready to help and enjoyed his radio shows immensely. His presentation style was well suited to the era of the music he preferred to play; not a perfect presenter by any means, but enjoyable to listen to. Regrettably Paul decided to leave Castlemaine in about 2010 and his contributions to the community, which were many, were greatly missed. I called him The Local Hero, in fun but he really was a local hero. A stalwart of the Lions Club he worked extremely hard on many Lions Club community projects and events. He used to refer to me as The Great Pretender, due to my frequent telling of tall stories, pretending to fly and pretending many other things whilst on air. Radio is The Theatre of the Mind, remember.

As mentioned, we frequently 'flew' my imaginary battered old Sopwith Camel, to the delight of many. Marilyn was the person who swung the propeller to start the old girl and I was the chauvinistic pilot shouting instructions. Sometimes the dope, the glue that held the paper covering of the plane together, began to disintegrate and more than once we had to put down in an emergency landing to paste it together. We made up all sorts of yarns and created all sorts of scenarios. It was a fabulous time.

We also conducted 'outside broadcasts' from all sorts of imaginable, and unimaginable, places. One time we were delighted to be invited to the opening of the new toilet block at Harcourt Heritage Centre. The Chief Commissioner of the shire at the time, Mostyn Thompson, was to conduct the ceremony. We saw an opportunity for a unique broadcast and (in the studio) we conducted the first ever broadcast of a dunny opening ceremony, complete with crowd's cheering, speeches by dignitaries and some dreadful sound effects recorded in our toilet. We even heard the Commissioner 'christening' the bowl. It was all positively hilarious and our Listeners could scarcely believe what they heard.

We once did a direct broadcast of the arrival of the very first steam train from Maldon that signaled the opening of this wonderful tourist attraction. We used the simple device of a wireless microphone. The studio actually adjoined the railway platform so it was quite practical. I stayed in the studio crossing to Mazza who was describing events outside. I left all the panel settings in place and joined her. We spoke to many of the passengers who made this historical inaugural journey, including Bob Cameron MP, Felix Cappy and his brother Vincent.

We never missed an opportunity to promote KLFM and one year we won a first prize for our entry in the Agricultural Show procession. Our group all dressed in 1940's and 1950's clothes, me in a gabardine overcoat and felt hat, carrying a Gladstone bag complete with a long neck bottle of beer, and Mazza in her father's WWII RAAF uniform. Barry Palmer and a dozen other fifties rockers, all dressed appropriately, joined in and we had a line up of classic 1940's and 1950's cars as well. It was a great effort and we deserved the award, and our pictures in the local paper!

To carry out our numerous legitimate outside broadcasts we required pretty good gear. Much was built and supplied by Alan Williams but other we had to provide ourselves. Alan was an absolute marvel and I doubt KLFM would ever have properly got off the ground without him. In Castlemaine the Rotary Club and The Lions Club were always very helpful. They donated various pieces of equipment with the understanding it was for use in Castlemaine. This was to prove a bone of contention in future developments.

There was always something exciting happening at KLFM Castlemaine. There was always lots of fun and laughter. We also had plenty of interesting people to talk to on air. One day country music great Troy Cassar-Daly was in town to perform at the old theatre so I rang him and invited him into the studio for an interview. He readily agreed and turned up at the appointed time, carrying his guitar. We yarned on air for a while and he then picked up his guitar. 'I've written this new song and I'd like to give it a try. Is that okay?' He then sang the song named 'Trains', which before long became a major Country hit for him. But the first time ever performed publicly or broadcast was on KLFM in Castlemaine. Troy explained that he had an affinity with trains because his mother worked as an attendant on trains at home. He was a lovely bloke and went on to become one of Australia's best.

One regular visitor to the studio was retired local railway man Les Denton. Les wrote mountains of excellent bush verse and he would rather shyly bring pieces in for me to read on air. People loved Les's work and we went on with this for all of our time at KLFM. Don Gresham recorded some of Les's verse in song form and we played those as well. Les, his wife Anne and their entire families became lasting friends. Some Listeners were amazing and stand out in memory. One was Keith Reid who lived with his brother in a former general store in the tiny township of Jarklin. He was constantly in touch with us at 3CCC and later KLFM. Keith loved listening to our older music and frequently sent us tapes of songs from his huge collection of rare CDs and vinyl. His favourite presenter was the late Faye Barker, who had many similar fans.

Barbara and Mal Hales were outstanding and we became good friends. Mal once sent me a cheque for $1 million in response to my grumbling about being broke. I still have it, uncashed.

Noel Hanrahan from Kerang was another aging loner. He used to frequently phone me and write lots of letters; an ardent Listener. We called on him a couple of times as we went through Kerang.

Terry Moss from the Shepparton district, a retired policeman, was a real fan and rang us many times. Terry also called in to see us several times at our Swap Meeting broadcasts bringing his son, a great golfer, with him.

The late Jim Lewis was a friend and a huge fan of Bing Crosby, an actual member of the Bing Crosby Fan Club. Jim used to love the programs of old music.

Unforgettable was Wayne Hirst, a retired mounted policeman, who lived with his charming wife Kath at Lockwood. He joined in the fabulous fun we had on Bush Wireless. He delivered to us a home made flag of the Muckleford Surf Life Saving Club, located at the Muckleford Beach, the latter of course a figment of my imagination. Wayne once did a phantom race call by phone of the Muckleford Cup from my imaginary Muckleford Racecourse; his horse Radish being the winner. Another time he invited us into his home for Kath's birthday party.

Muckleford is a minute settlement just west of Castlemaine and certainly had no beach, surf, Surf Club or racecourse, except in our minds!

A less welcome guest in the studio at Castlemaine was another lone person, a bearded, aging man who lived in a shack behind a shop in the north of town. He was a well known figure as he pedaled his bicycle around town. I never knew his name. The studio door was always open to visitors, who were almost always welcome. Not so this bloke, who all too frequently used to come in and simply stand watching me on air. My attempts at conversation were ignored as he chattered on and on, about what I have no idea. He simply would not shut up, even when I opened the microphone, his yabbering a background sound. He would do this for an hour or more and it was quite disconcerting to say the least. He was one of the strangest people I have ever met.

Chapter Twenty Two

Autonomy, suspension, haircuts, broken bones, prison, optic fibre

Such was Castlemaine's contribution to KLFM that we local volunteers decided to ask the head office for a little autonomy; things like arranging our own accommodation sites, opening a bank account, sending out accounts to our sponsors and signing them up on our own letterhead. Nothing too drastic, but we thought it enough to justify our claim to be truly local. There was a feeling among some important people that we were not local enough, the ghost of the loss of 3CCC to Bendigo was always present. We figured that this would show that we were local indeed and here to stay and somewhat independent from Bendigo. Castlemaine people were extremely parochial in those days and treated any outsiders with suspicion, something we had trouble communicating to Brad. He and we had always assured our sponsors that all money generated in Castlemaine was for improvements and maintenance of the Castlemaine station.

Our group also decided that, to accompany this change in relationship with head office, we should form our own organisation. So Castlemaine District Radio Inc. was born, intended to operate within the overall organisation, a subsidiary of KLFM. We had absolutely no intention of declaring ourselves independent; realistically we believed that Castlemaine could not hope to maintain a competitive, fully functional and quality radio station without Bendigo. That's a view I still hold and even more so in view of much later events.

I talked the idea over with Brad and he readily agreed, with the proviso that all accounting and banking remain with the Bendigo office. 'No worries Brad,' I agreed.

Shortly after this, Brad decided to take a complete break from KLFM and made his move temporarily to Charlton, one hundred kilometres north. David Kippen the station's dedicated Finance Manager assumed the managerial role until Brad's future return. This coincided with our decision to go through with the change approved by Brad and I submitted our proposal for approval of the Board, along with a request for a $50 petty cash float.

To our dismay our request was knocked back cold by David Kippen. Not even the $50 petty cash was approved. We protested loudly and David called us to a special meeting held in the Castlemaine Lions Club rooms. As spokesman I expressed our concern, especially in the light that Brad, the President, had already approved the proposal and we had proceeded on that basis. I argued that we owed it to our sponsors to have an actual locally controlled group in view of the claim on brochures that 'The money you spend stays in Castlemaine.' I pointed out our disappointment that the committee had overridden the approval given by the President. I said that we of Castlemaine were proud and happy to be a part of KLFM and would continue to be so. However, I did differentiate between the two centres, Bendigo was Bendigo and Castlemaine was Castlemaine. I said I was conveying the views of all Castlemaine presenters who endorsed my remarks, David countered that it was KLFM Central Victoria and not either Castlemaine or Bendigo. A valid point that I had no argument with. We simply wanted more recognition of Castlemaine contributions and the ability to act with limited independence. We would always remain a part of KLFM

David would not shift and so we reluctantly accepted his decision and set aside any and all ambition in that direction. He made it very plain that night that if we rocked the boat he would have no hesitation in shutting us down. However it remained fact that the concept of KLFM Castlemaine was always a Castlemaine initiative and was always intended to be heavily Castlemaine oriented

I presented several weekday shows from Castlemaine as well as Saturday breakfast and Bush Wireless on Sunday with Mazza. I also had to work part time at different things, so I was pretty busy. Early in 2001, we had made a decision to relocate our transmitter and dipole from the golf club to the old Castlemaine Gaol, our original site, but much lower down. It was a big job involving hire of a very expensive crane for a day, with an elevation of 33 metres to lift our workers and the gear to the roof top. Col Herbert, Rod McLeod, Barry Palmer and Brad Geier did the dangerous work while I watched from the safety of the ground. I was terrified of heights.

With the dipole perched high on the roof we expected our signal to travel much further. Alas, it was a real disappointment and within a week we put it all back at the golf club.

In May 2001, I was astounded to receive a letter from Col Herbert who Brad had recently appointed Program Manager. It appeared that I had made a comment about Optus being greedy swines for their rush to take over a failed communications company. I had also criticized moves for clubs over the border in NSW to ban smoking in their venues. (I was still a smoker then.) As a result I was suspended from being on air for six long weeks, but I had to wear it, albeit being more than distressed. I appealed to Brad, unable to understand why this had happened. Brad expressed his astonishment and dismay; he said he had had nothing to do with the decision. Apparently it was entirely Col's idea. I had doubts about that, a doubt proved correct some years later in a talk with Col.

In September I copped another massive spray in a letter from Col. He said I had ignored his earlier orders and admonished me for my 'sloppy presentation', 'parochialism', 'inane drivel', and my inability to match the performance expected of a Manager plus my 'amateurish statements' and 'self-centred, egotistical attitude'. But wait. There's more! Col told me I was responsible for 'some of the worst radio' he had ever heard! He also reminded me that we were not KLFM Castlemaine but KLFM Central Victoria. I'd heard that before somewhere!

I couldn't comprehend why Col had unleashed such fury on me. I simply did not deserve it. I was quite distressed by the ferocity of the words, especially as he told me to obey the rules or be suspended again without further notice. Col appeared to take great exception to me and my various on-air comments and antics. I don't believe I was any of the things he mentioned.

The 'egotistical attitude' bit probably came from my words to him that I was the voice for Castlemaine. I truly believed that I spoke for Castlemaine, and thus gave the town a voice.

That's what our branch and translator in Castlemaine was all about, and I was determined to continue to speak for my town. Brad again firmly denied any involvement in this nasty attempt to be rid of me, permanently I suspected.

In a much later conversation Col told me that, far from not knowing anything, Brad had been included and he indicated that Ian Nicholls was also involved. I suspected that there was a strong move on to be rid of me but couldn't understand why. It's good to have friends you can trust!

It seemed I had come down a long way in the six years since 1994 when Brad nominated me as the Community Broadcasting Association of Australia 'Volunteer of the Year'!

We had some good presenters and good friends at KLFM in Bendigo. Names that come readily to mind are Tony Fittock, an old-school rocker who began at 3MA Mildura and who Mazza and I convinced to make a come-back, Mark Coombes an employee at Centrelink alongside Jim Garden, Ron Mitchell travelled from Malmsbury. There was Dean Besley, Randell Jones, experienced and capable broadcaster Grant McMaster, John Croxford our I.T. expert, Brett Dunlop a Christian broadcaster and Neil

Geier the father of Brad, all Bendigo people. There was a good number of ex-3CCC people; Derek Gibson, Barry Palmer, Daryl O'Brien, Julius Porlai, Calamity Clegg and Mazza. In the office were Cynthia Geier and Heidi Tobin. A good, close-knit team; all enthusiastic and dedicated to KLFM. Calamity even put money into the station in the form of a significant loan. Later, on her death bed, she confided that she never pressed to get it back.

I've lost track of the number of outside broadcasts we did at KLFM Castlemaine. Just about every cat and dog show in town found Mazza and I there; events like the annual shows, horse shows, swap meetings, Buda historic home open days, a historic house open day at Fryerstown, the IGA supermarket, a table set up in Barker Street, the market at Wesley Hill, from the platform of the train station, Australia day and Anzac day commemorations, even (pre-recorded) from a steam train from Maldon; the list is long. Mazza and I always enjoyed this type of broadcast, getting out there and meeting people. We involved KLFM in so many things; we sponsored a section of the annual business awards in 2002 and were delighted when Donna and John Walter from the Theatre Royal, one of our sponsors, won. I got to present the award at a gala function at the town hall.

We visited Mirridong Home for the Blind in Bendigo and recorded interviews with aged residents, to use with many others, in a 'KLFM Remembers' week-long broadcast. That week was a great, successful idea that brought back so many memories to older Listeners. At the time I wrote to Penguin Books and obtained permission to record, for his personal use, a reading of the excellent book 'Keep Moving' written by blind resident Frank Huelin. He had by then lost his sight. He was thrilled to bits when Mazza and I presented it to him and, although it took me many hours, I was feeling good about the opportunity it gave me.

'The Show Must Go On', is a show business tradition. We were not quite in show biz, but in 2005 Mazza went on with the show in spite of a broken foot. That year marked the 150th anniversary of gold discovery at Forest Creek. To mark the occasion a re-enactment of many gold seekers' long walk to the gold fields was put on. Mazza entered to fly the KLFM flag, intending to walk only part of the distance from Chewton to Castlemaine. She got carried away and walked the entire distance. The result was a stress fracture in her left ankle. With her leg in plaster and unable to do more than hobble on crutches, we put her in a wheelchair, gave her a long lead microphone and she continued to broadcast Bush Wireless with me. She did this from in front of a big step, not wheel chair friendly, outside the entrance door. I operated the panel in the studio and could not see Mazza. It was difficult and different but it was great fun; and Mazza showed true spirit.

In 2002, when the idea was new and novel, Paul Thieman and I both had our heads shaved on air to raise money for the Leukemia Foundation. Hairdresser and sponsor Terry Evans came to the studio and did the job on our Bush Wireless show. The effort served two purposes: money for a great cause and publicity for KLFM. We had the important picture and article in the paper which featured Paul, hairdresser Terry and me. Our listeners sent in $570, a mighty good result for a two hour show in Castlemaine.

While all this was going on Mazza and I still had to earn a living. We put in a lot of work and devised a teaching schedule to present to state prison authorities. We managed to convince them that we could conduct a worthwhile rehabilitation and personal improvement program for inmates that centred on radio.

It proved to be a very successful program and resulted in amazing improvements in communication skills and self esteem in a lot of men. We took the lessons very seriously and were pleased that the men felt the same. Without exception they knuckled down and worked hard to absorb the lessons and pick up the skills we showed them. In particular we had wonderful success with aboriginal men at Fulham Prison near Sale in Gippsland.

This item was challenging and it was different to anything we had done before. Like most of us, we had no knowledge of Aboriginal customs and ways and had had little contact with them. But we soon learnt; and we learnt to respect them and their heritage.

For a start though we had to get used to working on 'Aboriginal time'. These blokes had no regard for the clock and our 9am starts rarely began before ten. However, at the conclusion of the week-long course most of the ten trainees were able to stand before the Governor and other assembled staff to tell them about the course and talk in general terms. This was actual public speaking, difficult for most people at the best of times, but for shy Aboriginal men with low self esteem it was considered astonishing. The officers and managers were frequently amazed at the change the training made in one short week. We aimed to instill confidence in the men and raise their self-esteem and we succeeded with most.

As well as teaching them how radio works, and the fundamentals of presentation and voice production, we always had the blokes put together an actual radio show of half an hour duration. In this they were given a free hand in content and sometimes the results were brilliant. Mazza and I were respected by the aboriginal men and were accepted almost as 'brothers', and that was an achievement we are proud of; one that many white people do not accomplish. We taught them how to prepare and present a radio show but concentrated, without making it obvious, on building their confidence and improving their speech

We taught at Fulham on a number of occasions and similarly at Ararat and Langi Kal Kal prisons. We made many good friends among the prisoners and staff, including Kaye, the Fulham Prison program director. She invited us to visit her home as her guests at Lakes Entrance and elsewhere on several occasions.

These times in the Correction System were some of the most rewarding Mazza and I ever experienced and we were disappointed when funding for the programs was stopped by the authorities. The money we earned was only a part of it, but it was very handy! Some of the programs the men produced we actually broadcast, they were that good.

At Ararat Prison there was a different class of prisoner to Fulham and Langi Kal Kal, many were sex offenders, and we did work with a few undesirables. For example one notorious paedophile actually repeated the course. He was incarcerated for ten years and had a further ten years added under a new Act of Parliament, the Serious Sex Offenders Monitoring Act. It was designed for him and a few others. Under the Act offenders finish their jail term and are then transferred to units outside the jail where they wear electronic ankle bracelets at all times. We had no bother with him but he was freaky. On the whole, though, we found the blokes good to work with, trustworthy, reliable and genuinely interested in what we were teaching. Our weeks at both Langi Kal Kal and Fulham concluded with the production of a complete thirty minute radio show, with content decided and produced by themselves and occasionally broadcast on KLFM.

We always had a 'graduation ceremony', with cakes, sandwiches and soft drinks. It included a presentation to the Governor and senior staff of the finished program and speeches from a couple of the graduates. At no time in the prisons did we ever feel unsafe, or threatened. This particularly applied to Mazza, a woman amongst hundreds of incarcerated men. I believe that the overall success of the prison training program was extraordinary and I know the prison hierarchy was quite impressed. It was so successful that we were invited to Melbourne to demonstrate to a large group of educators within the prison system exactly how we did it.

It was at Ararat on 29 March 2005 that we received troubling news. As mentioned earlier, Brad had moved to Charlton, one hundred kilometres north of Bendigo. His friend Tony Jordan had also moved to Charlton. We had arranged for Brad to come to the prison and address the prisoners about his role as station

Manager and community radio in general. We were paying him a small fee from our earnings to provide something different for the blokes, a different perspective perhaps. He drove down from Charlton and we met him at KFC where we had lunch and went over the next day's program. He stayed the night in our unit.

After we had finished the next day Brad received a call from Ian Nicholls, who was at this time Studio Manager. It was bad news. The long awaited removal of the old landline connecting Castlemaine with Bendigo was going to happen on 13 April. It was costing the owners too much to maintain. We had expected this for years and had been well warned, but it was still a shock. I had been pestering Brad for almost three years to make arrangements for an alternative.

He dashed back to Bendigo saying he was going to talk urgently with Telstra to see if they would contra a broadband deal for us. Maybe we could link that way. A deal with Telstra! Experience said it was not likely, but Brad said it was worth a try.

Nothing came of that so Brad then decided to ask the State Government Transport Department if we could tap into the brand new optical fibre line installed for the new Melbourne to Bendigo fast train service. The cable passed our door on its way. Peter Batchelor, the Transport Minister, responded that we could connect but it would cost a heavily discounted $25,000! That was an impossible figure for our little community radio station. Obviously, another method of connecting had to be found and to this end Brad had then purchased three Tieline units for the job. These Tielines used a standard telephone line, encoding material at one end and decoding at the other, full stereo and the works. Expensive to buy, but cheap to use and magic! Brad told me that one of the units was for the base reception in the Bendigo studio, one for Brad so he could broadcast from Charlton and the other for us at Castlemaine. Happily, the connection problem was solved.

We soon began to use the units and although we had some problems with drop outs due to poor quality phone lines, overall it worked brilliantly.

With Brad living at Charlton and still apparently acting as a sort of long distance manager in spite of his 'taking a break', it became difficult to maintain the close contact we had always had previously. However, we managed to contact him fairly regularly by phone. Mazza and I were close to Brad and we were horrified when he rang us and informed us that he had been having treatment at Peter McCallum Cancer Hospital in Melbourne for a brain tumor. It was dreadful news; Brad struck down by a brain tumor; it was almost unbelievable and it shook us up pretty badly. At the time the outlook for those with this was not good.

We soon piled in the Toyota Crown and drove to Charlton to see the lad. When we arrived there we were pleasantly surprised to see that Brad looked pretty good considering his circumstances. He said he had an appointment with the local doctor later that day but had some time to spare. He showed us his home studio, took us for a stroll around town where he and Tony Jordan now ran a video hire store. He showed us the supermarket where he was going to set up a branch of KLFM and took us to the pub where we had a couple of beers. He told us that he was coping really well with the tumor, was being treated locally with antibiotics and was due for a shot that afternoon. However, he later decided that he really didn't need to see the doctor that day.

I was concerned that Brad was losing control of KLFM living one hundred kilometres away and with only occasional visits to the station. I told him it was not sustainable and he must return to Bendigo and take the helm or lose the station. Brad agreed that he would consider it seriously and let me know.

We said goodbye, wishing him a quick recovery and we drove home, more than a little puzzled but relieved.

Brad told me that he 'had heard' that Work Care was going to inspect our studios at Castlemaine. If that was correct it spelt a possibility of closure as they were not up to standard. Mazza and I began again to cast about for a new home but it was a task almost certain to fail. Commercial rental rates were out of the question and spare space for groups like ours nonexistent. This was troubling but, we at least had the Tieline, which allowed for broadcasting from almost anywhere where there was electricity and a phone line. Eventually we would find somewhere. Happily we still had our Tieline. Or did we?

In a shock development I then received a memo from Brad advising that the third Tieline was 'never intended for Castlemaine' but was for the occasional outside broadcast (OB) in Bendigo. In another memo he stated that if we wanted to do any OB's in Castlemaine the price we had to charge was to increase ten fold! He made it absolutely clear that no Tieline would be permanently allocated to our studio. It seemed that the rare OB or two and his broadcasts from Charlton took precedence over the city of Castlemaine. It made no sense whatever.

It was an astonishing decision. Charlton, where we had few if any listeners and no advertisers, got a Tieline, whilst the flourishing Castlemaine service would be put off the air. It seemed obvious that our closure was Brad's purpose. But why?

I sent a memo to David Kippen who was still acting General Manager, at least in title, expressing concern over the refusal of Brad to let Castlemaine have the use of a Tieline. It meant that all of us at Castlemaine would have to drive to Bendigo if we wished to present a show.

I told David that weeks had passed and nothing else had been done to replace the lost Vic Track landline and asked why. He didn't offer an explanation.

On 26 April 2005 I rang Brad. To my astonishment he said he had decided to let us have a Tieline in Castlemaine after all. The only problem he said was that the spare unit was in Perth being fixed as it had been damaged in an OB. He expected it back by the 29th, 'so don't panic'. Brad rang me on the 29th and said the unit had indeed come back to Bendigo and all that remained was for Alan Williams to give it a test run and it was ours!

I hadn't heard in a couple of days so rang Alan who told me that he had never been told that the unit needed repair and it was stored under a bench. Ian Nicholls had told me the same thing earlier but I dismissed it as a joke. It was no joke! It seemed that the unit had sat there for weeks. Whether in need of repair we were never sure but Alan didn't think so and he should have known.

As the Manager at Castlemaine it was my responsibility to keep our volunteer announcers informed. I tried to explain what had been happening but I think they thought I was having some sort of mental problem. What I was telling them made little sense although they were concerned about Brad's health. Whilst we had fretted and worried and had driven hundreds of kilometers, the solution to our lack of connection sat under a bench in Bendigo? Come on! This debacle defied belief and we still had no connection to Bendigo. Hopefully the unit had now been sent to Perth for repair, assuming it actually needed it, but we had to rely on Brad's reports.

Meanwhile the Castlemaine crew continued to journey to Golden Square to present their shows.

In mid-May we had a meeting of our group (Castlemaine District Radio Inc). As a result I sent off a scathing letter to the KLFM board in the form of my Castlemaine Manager's Report.

While all this was happening Mazza and I continued our hunt for better accommodation for our studio/office. We had already scoured the town for months, leaving no stone unturned. We had looked at everything from a van in the hospital grounds to a room at the Continuing Education building; an empty shop and even a disused morgue! Our frequent attempts to obtain the former Tourist Information Centre in Forest Street (known locally as The Octopus because of its unusual octagonal shape) we eventually had had to abandon. We had fought hard for The

Octopus because, although tiny, it was highly visible at the town entrance. We had applied to the council for its use several times but they finally advised us that the U3A had decided they wanted to continue to use it and it was theirs for as long as they needed it.

We were aware that our rooms at the train station were not up to scratch, but they served the purpose and, at $100 per annum rental, it was dirt cheap. Our group was quite happy and comfortable there but we felt a higher profile spot would be an advantage. But I have always believed, and we had proved, that it is what comes out of the speakers that is important, not how luxuriously up-market is the studio!

Time passed and finally, weeks later, the repaired Tieline unit arrived in Castlemaine and we resumed as before. It was terrific and the unit worked very well with only minor dropouts. These were caused, I was told, by the poor quality Telstra line. The 'Castlemaine Eight' rejoiced.

And so we continued on our merry way, but my relationship with Brad had become strained by the Tieline incident. I no longer felt I could depend on him. I believe that this feeling was well founded.

By early July 2005, heeding my advice, Brad returned from Charlton to run the station full time. I felt comfortable and relations with Brad resumed as before. We had been friends for so long and I was happy to have him back. Mazza and I were still concerned about the treatment he received for a brain tumor. Would that cure him?

We continued to broadcast all of our shows from Castlemaine with only the occasional hiccup from the TieLine. It was not enough to bother us as we were confident that it would be fixed in due course by Telstra installing a decent line to the studio. (On 15 October 2005, in a letter to MLA Bob Cameron, Brad claimed that the service dropped out five–ten times every hour, absolute rubbish of course.)

Meanwhile Brad had continued to hound local Bob Cameron MP for use of the railway optical fibre line from Castlemaine to the Bendigo studio. Bob tried all he could but could not get the Minister Peter Bachelor to bend. It was $25,000 full stop.

Brad would not accept this. He continued to press the government publicly for free use of the line, indicating that the refusal put the Castlemaine service in doubt. He made it clear that if it was forced to close it would be the fault of the government, especially the local member Bob Cameron. All good stuff for the publicity mill but not well founded. His action put Bob offside and any chance of government help was dead on the vine. As far as I was concerned, as the Branch Manager, I was quite happy with the Tieline connection. It wasn't perfect of course, but beggars can't be choosers. All of us at Castlemaine were satisfied.

Chapter Twenty Three

A shock, a missing link, empty studio, new deal, a pub meeting, confusion

Eight weeks after his return from Charlton, I received a phone call from Brad that devastated me.

It was a Friday night, 5 August 2005, and as usual I had gone to bed early in preparation for a 6am start on the breakfast show. It was nine o'clock when the phone rang. It was Brad. What he had to say left me speechless and distraught.

I made notes of what he said: 'You wanted me back and I'm back. And I'm closing Castlemaine.' He added that out of respect for me he told me first. He said he was sick of us being 'Castlemaine centric'.

I was at a loss. What he now said was completely at odds with a conversation I had with him days before. He had agreed enthusiastically with our Castlemaine focus. 'F...k Nicko, that's why we have the studio there.' From that I gathered that Ian Nicholls was the one behind the objections. I have since thought maybe he was a strong influence on Brad in his decisions concerning Castlemaine and possibly me as well.

Brad rambled on. Toning it down a bit, he said that Paul Thieman was 'useless' and he was 'sacking him' and when Paul went we may have a chance of staying open, but I had to agree to drop the focus on Castlemaine. He then said he would give me time to show him why Castlemaine should continue. He said, 'We share the dream and I know you busted a gut for a Castlemaine service but that is my decision.' The rest of my night was sleepless.

I rang Brad first thing next day. He immediately apologized for his statements the night before and invited me to Bendigo for a meeting to discuss a couple of changes. I happily agreed. Included in the meeting would be Ian Nicholls.

In fact Ian came into the meeting only briefly and only after the arrangements had been finalised. The meeting went well and we agreed on some very minor changes. We met briefly with Ian after the meeting where the agreed terms were presented to him. At the time he basked in the title of Station Manager whilst Brad was the General Manager.

Brad then surprised me with a promise that he would meet with the entire Castlemaine crew in two weeks where he would sign an agreement that guaranteed us that KLFM Castlemaine would remain open forever. I was elated. We shook hands and it left me wondering what the hell had it all been about!

On the appointed day I received a message from Brad that he was delayed in Melbourne and would now sign the agreement in a further two weeks. He did not keep that appointment either. There was a distinct odor in the air.

On air on Sunday 11 September, I told listeners that they should ignore the claims in the press that the studio was inoperable, that it was working well, that the speculation about its closure was damaging the station. It proved to be my final show.

Brad apparently took exception to my on-air remarks and told me he thought I was saying he was not telling the truth. 'You said I was a liar!' I assured him that it was not the case.

Brad posted an article in The Mail that indicated that without government help we were in great difficulty, still flogging the claim that MLA Bob Cameron was to blame for our impending disaster.

On Tuesday 14 September 2005, Mazza went to the studio for some reason. She was shocked when she found the Tieline gone and a note from Daryl O'Brien saying that Brad had ordered the unit to Bendigo for repairs as it was faulty. That was very, very odd as it had worked perfectly for the news connections that very morning. To get the news to air we picked up the service off-air from 3BA Ballarat at the Castlemaine studio. From there it went up the line to Bendigo. Therefore it was definitely functioning well that morning. When I was told I rang Brad protesting as loudly as I could. He was firm, the unit was faulty! I believed it was bullshit and angrily told him so. Castlemaine was off the air. He had apparently made arrangements to take the news off-air from a station in Shepparton.

Two days later I went again to the studio and was horrified by what greeted me. I almost collapsed with anger and grief. Our beautiful studio had been stripped of all equipment and all that remained was an empty desk, a microphone stand and a pile of debris. It was heartbreaking and I could scarcely believe the scene. However, by then I put nothing beyond Brad in his determination to be rid of Castlemaine and in particular, I believed, his old friend and ally, me.

Castlemaine had been a brilliant success, brought in a lot of money and attracted a good audience; a couple of our programs were the biggest attraction KLFM had. For example 'Bush Wireless' was extremely popular and on one occasion attracted over sixty phone calls in two hours. We had run a small, inexpensive competition and had to have Paul Thieman assist by taking the calls. Amazing! Nothing like that had ever happened in my radio experience before or since.

Paul was a pommy from Manchester and a good person, very keen and dedicated in his contribution to KLFM. He had come down from Sydney to live in Castlemaine where he got a job driving a cab. Later he worked for the IGA Supermarket where he rose to be manager of the freezer department. We got on very well and he was always the first to help out. For some reason Brad had a set against him.

I went to see Antonia, the reporter at the Castlemaine Mail, and she was mortified when I told her of the studio being stripped. She dismissed the stories from Brad, coming out strongly in support of the locals. She led a huge battle in the press in Castlemaine which spread to Bendigo and onto TV news; to no avail of course as Brad dug in, continuing to claim it was a temporary closure and all the fault of MLA Bob Cameron and the State Government. Then he went on air lambasting Castlemaine people as 'idiots'. He accused Bob of ranting and raving – of complete nonsense and uttering mistruths and untruths. 'Some people in Castlemaine seem more intent on rubbishing us instead of helping us get new premises.' His obvious intention was to switch attention from KLFM removing our gear and shutting us down to a suddenly urgent need for new premises.

My friend and council member Felix Cappy attempted to talk with David Kippen on our behalf and tried in vain to achieve a settlement. There was obviously a determination at KLFM to see Castlemaine closed forever.

I rang Ian Nicholls and we spoke at length. He told me they had received no response from the State Government to the publicity. He said there was little chance of Castlemaine ever opening again and offered me Saturday breakfast and Bush Wireless on Sunday from the Bendigo studio. On principal I had to refuse.

Mazza and I then began talking to local sponsors about supporting a move for our very own station and several thousand dollars were pledged in two days. Such was the anti-KLFM feeling and the support for our group.

A meeting between Brad Geier, Mazza and I with MLA Bob Cameron was arranged in a further effort to reach a settlement. We observed a person that looked like Brad having a smoke in the car park at Bob's office. Brad did not attend the meeting.

Bob was not impressed and having taken strong exception to Brad's on-air remarks about him, now demanded a logged recording of the statement. Brad hung out and refused to supply it, using dubious stalling tactics that stretched to the horizon. Eventually Bob let the matter slide, having been insulted by more accomplished in the art than Brad and no doubt having better things to waste time on.

However Brad did not get off unscathed. A parliamentary colleague of Bob's, Rob Mitchell MLC, unleashed a merciless attack, soundly condemning Brad Geier under parliamentary privilege. There was nothing a fuming Brad could do about it.

A couple of days after the raid I received an evening phone call from David Kippen. He told me to have all materials and equipment remaining in the building removed within the next three days as they were coming down with a skip to take everything remaining to the tip. They were handing the building back to owners VicTracks on Friday. No discussion, no apology, no comment. It was obviously final, not a 'temporary closure' as claimed by Brad in letters and press releases. I told David that Brad had no balls and he had got him to do his dirty work. He did not comment.

We had thousands of vinyl albums to remove among numerous pieces of furniture and assorted bits and pieces and we had two days to do it or see it in the tip. Noel Flanagan from the Agricultural Society offered us their shed for storage and, not only that, Noel hopped in and helped the removal. A woman who lived across the road from the station, Julie Higginbottom, was also a willing helper. Julie was disgusted with the Bendigo action. (Later Julie joined us in the early days of our next station.)

It was a stressful and sad occasion and hard work, but we got everything out by 9am on the deadline day. Before we shut the door we had a meeting on site with Bob Cameron. Antonia from The Mail came to write a story and about fifteen locals attended in support. I recall Gwen Coupland arriving dressed in a white T-shirt covered in her own hand-drawn Texta colour which proclaimed her disgust with the KLFM hierarchy. Gwen was in her mid-seventies and the most ardent fan the station had. We all loved Gwennie. I also recall as attending Salvos volunteer Mary Claire, Simon Muntz and Julie Higginbottom, all wonderful local people and avid Listeners. Antonia's article in The Mail described the closure and the method used as 'contempt, not only for Ian and Marilyn, but for the people of Castlemaine and district.'

Noel, the railway station manager, was sympathetic and helped us where he could, allowing us to store a couple of items in the railways shed. He was annoyed at Brad's claim that the old cellar area beneath the station had been flooded with sewage. This was incorrect of course and designed to switch the focus from KLFM misdeeds to the undoubtedly poor condition of the part of the building we shared. The truth is that on one occasion a block in the sewer caused an overflow that entered a part of the cellar. This had been quickly repaired and cleaned. The claim could have proved damaging to the railway business and it reflected badly on their management.

There are so many more misdeeds to this story, but I'll spare readers much of them. You probably would find them hard to believe anyway. I'm not sparing you this next bit though!

One day I was shocked to get a call from Brad Geier. I was even more shocked by what he had to say. After umpteen failed approaches from me to hand over the frequency or share it he now offered to hand over the entire Castlemaine 106.3 MHz frequency and service to Castlemaine. I was absolutely astonished but also delighted.

He assured me that the arrangement had the full approval of the ACMA, even quoting a couple of names he had spoken with. This was wonderful news and we arranged to meet to seal the deal at the Ravenswood Hotel. This old pub was about midway Bendigo–Castlemaine. We made up our differences, had a couple of beers (he shouted), shook hands and the deal was done. All that remained was the paperwork to sign and Castlemaine had its very own radio station.

I excitedly rang all of our local volunteers and anyone else I could think of, including The Mail reporter Antonia and Bob Cameron. Oh such joy! Mazza didn't share the joy but said she didn't believe a word of it.

Progress was slow with the promised draft agreement and I rang Brad numerous times, unable to talk except to his answering machine, which I regularly did. Finally, seven weeks later, in mid March a draft arrived. All seemed in order but we thought it was sloppy work for the city lawyer Brad had engaged, the suspicion was it may in fact have been written by an amateur in Bendigo.

We made a couple of minor changes and waited for the final document to be issued by KLFM board at their meeting on March 23rd as promised.

Strangely, no communication was received from Brad at the due time and my efforts to contact him were fruitless. By 6 April I had left a dozen messages for him to call me. No response. I asked Bob Cameron and our Mayor Dave Gittus to see if they could raise him. No response. I continued to phone with no result and then sent three faxes over two days. Finally I rang Brad on Good Friday, suspecting that he may not expect me on that holiday. Success! I got him!

He apologized profusely for the delay as he 'had been moving house' and promised me that all was on track and he would call me back. He didn't. I subsequently faxed Ian Nicholls to get him to ask Brad to call me. Nothing happened. It was now mid April.

In mid May WIN TV rang and asked for an interview. I declined as I believed I had to honour the confidential nature of our agreement, as rapidly fading though it was.

Later on Bob Cameron rang me, he had apparently spoken with Brad and he was told to tell me that it was all going ahead. What?! I felt relief and excitement, but was puzzled to say the least.

Bob was then interviewed by WIN TV and the Bendigo Advertiser about the situation. I do not know exactly what he said but I am sure it was positive. I declined a follow up interview with WIN as I believed the agreement we had negotiated remained confidential.

Then, out of the blue, Brad Geier announced publicly that he and Nicholls were unhappy with (presumably) Bob Cameron's comments on WIN TV news and that 'they would be conducting no further negotiations' with Castlemaine District Radio. Nichols stated that we had used every dirty trick in the book' to get the 106.3 frequency. That surprised me as until now he had not had a lot to say. It looked like the end of the story, but it was only the end of another chapter.

It was Friday 19 May 2005. The phone rang. It's my mate Brad. He spoke as if nothing had ever happened and said without hesitation that he would be transferring the frequency to CDR Inc. without delay. In fact he had already organised it with the ACMA and gained full approval from his board, David Kippen and Ian Nicholls.

There was no doubt in my mind that this time it was for real. It was inconceivable that this could be false hope. I was elated and rang everyone I could think of including Maree Edwards who was thrilled and said she'd tell her boss Bob Cameron. I arranged to meet Brad the following Friday for the handover and all was sweet.

I asked Brad about the article in the Bendigo Advertiser with both Nicholls and him bucketing Castlemaine District Radio Inc. He said he had had a change of heart since the comment was made and he had asked the Editor not to print it. It had appeared despite this.

Confused? You bet I was! Mazza then rang a woman named Laura in Steve Atkin's office at the ACMA and asked for the forms 25 and 12 to complete the transfer, Laura said she would fax them immediately. Minutes later the phone rang. It was Steve Atkins, the ACMA officer who Brad said had approved the transfer.

'What!' He exclaimed when Mazza explained to him why she was calling. 'There is no way we will carry out such a transfer. It cannot be done.' He was flabbergasted. I rang Brad and he was astonished, stating it was all above board and both he and David

Kippen had obtained full approval from someone named Ann in Atkin's office. Brad said he would willingly put that in writing.

In the afternoon Brad rang me back. He said he had spoken with Atkins and he had agreed that the apparatus could be transferred. I was pretty raw then as far as ACMA terms went and assumed that the broadcasting licence went along with the apparatus.

'Send in the transfer forms. It's all okay.' I asked him about the bucketing article in the Advertiser and he said it was a press release sent earlier that he had regretted and he had phoned the Editor to have it stopped. There were no problems; the deal would proceed as agreed! We obtained the forms suggested from the internet and posted them to the ACMA.

On May 30 Mazza rang Steve Atkins to check on the progress of the application. He said it was not that easy and he had explained that to us earlier. Mazza said that Brad had spoken with him since and it was now all okay. He denied all knowledge of this talk, said he had still never spoken with this person. He said he would ring Brad and 'sort it out'.

In a further conversation with Brad he assured me that the deal had been approved by Giles Tanner himself, an ACMA big boss. Brad claimed that in a phone discussion on seeking the okay for transfer Tanner had said, 'Do you want a ruling now? Okay, you've got it.' Had he really given approval? It seems that he had not.

And that's the way it finally ended. It was all beyond belief and this latest episode was definitely the last straw in our relationship with our former close friend, Brad Geier. What on earth had prompted him to go through this charade? We couldn't understand then, cannot now and never will. It had been a long and painful exercise with many false starts, but KLFM Castlemaine branch was finally and definitely finished for good.

When I re-read some of the letters and fax messages that Brad sent me over my time at KLFM I become angry. He says how much he owes me and things like, 'Thanks for the support you have given me and continue to give.' 'Thank you heaps. You are very dear to me,' etc. etc. It was all very sad and disappointing; probably worst it ended a long and happy friendship.

Chapter Twenty Four

Building a new station, a community rallies, helpers, LPONs, Old Gaol again, good news at last

So began the task of building a community radio station for Castlemaine. I contacted the ACMA and was advised by them that no licence was available for Castlemaine nor would it ever be likely. It appeared to be a hopeless task, given that no FM frequencies were available and, as far as the ACMA was concerned, Castlemaine was well served with radio stations, including 3CCC which still existed in Bendigo at that time and KLFM which retained a licence to serve Castlemaine and district. As well, there were several commercial stations and three ABC stations. How many does a town of seven thousand need?

But we kept going, determined to find a way, determined to get a community radio station for Castlemaine.

After our talks with local business people, we decided our next move was to demonstrate to the ACMA strong community support. On Friday 7th October 2005, we began the fight with a stall inside the IGA supermarket. One of our strong supporters was Mark Howie, the store manager, and he happily gave us a small space near the checkout exits.

Mazza and I set up a card table. Sandra Grant, the store ticket writer, drew up two posters proclaiming our purpose and we asked every passerby whose attention we could get to sign a prepared individual 'letter' to the ACMA. It was hard work but the response was overwhelming! In two days we received over five hundred signed documents in a town of seven thousand men, women and children. Added to the support of local business people, it was obvious that the town was with us.

I immediately wrote to the ACMA again, formally requesting a frequency, more in hope than anything. I received a stock answer that my inquiry would be examined etc.

Later in October I contacted the ACMA to lodge my interest in obtaining a Low Powered Open Narrowcast Licence. These licences are issued for specific purposes and operate on one watt.

The idea was to use that licence as a fill-in and training ground whilst we pursued an elusive Community class licence. Alas, the 88MHz frequency we required, and many others, it eventuated, was already owned by John Jost a former ABC TV anchorman. He held a good number of the licences, probably with the hope to turn a profit on them.

I investigated and found that the 88MHz frequency was available in Maldon so I bid at an ACMA auction and was able to buy that. Again the idea was to have a training ground for new presenters and to stay in touch. Barry Palmer searched the internet and found a one watt transmitter for sale in Israel for $100 so we bought it. It came unassembled but I was able to call on help from Phil Rice, from my 3CCC days, to assemble it and house it in a metal case. We bought a used computer, loaded a purchased Reduga automated radio program on it, applied for a licence from APRA and AMCOS allowing us to load a heap of songs burnt from CDs. We were ready to fly but from where? I borrowed a device which measured elevation and cruised around Maldon looking for a suitable site. First up it seemed that a building at the Bill Woodfull Reserve, better known as the footy ground, would suit. It turned out to be a government owned building and not available. Finally, I landed at the Derby Hill Blue Light Children's Camp and arranged with Michael and Jeanette, who managed the place, to install the newly purchased Dipole, computer, the one watt transmitter and some other equipment there. Michael and Jeanette were most helpful allowing us to take space in their storeroom. Radio 88 Maldon went on air and the coverage of the town was excellent considering the low power. It was a step forward. Several small business people of Maldon were very supportive and contributed enough in regular advertising revenue to cover our operating costs. A problem for me was that it was a sixteen kilometer drive to load items onto the program or if things needed adjustment or repair. We had a radio station but we still needed one for Castlemaine.

Early in January 2006, I sent an official application for a community radio frequency for Castlemaine. It was a bulky document loaded with every argument I could think of. I added a massive bulk of the five hundred and three letters of support from Castlemaine people. All I could do was wait and hope.

In mid January I rang John Jost and he agreed to lease us the 88MHZ frequency for a smallish fee plus a 25% share of any advertising revenue. I didn't believe it a good deal and knocked him back. I identified the holder of the other LPON frequency in Castlemaine 87.6 MHz as United Christian Broadcasters, with their transmitter located in Lewis Drive. The site they claimed was owned by the McClure family. I tried in vain to listen to any signal from 87.6MHz and went to inspect the transmitter site. It turned out that the McClure family had no knowledge of anybody using their radio tower in their works yard. In fact nobody had any idea what we were talking about and still not a sound came from 87.6MHz. The location listed was false and no transmitter was operating on 87.6MHz. I decided to complain to the ACMA and ask that the licence be sold to me. I now had two vaguely possible avenues for an LPON licence. I immediately lodged a request for the United Christian Broadcasters (UCB) licence to be cancelled under the 'Use it or Lose It' rule and it be sold to us.

After an ACMA investigation the LPON licence of UCB was cancelled. We were delighted and we looked set to move forward. I officially applied for the licence. Alas, the powerful UCB lodged an appeal and somehow, flying in the face of the regulation, they were successful! It didn't seem fair and we now had to find another way. It was an unhelpful setback. Our Committee agonised over our situation, but decided to fight on. At the time we had Paul Thieman, Marilyn Bennet, Barry Palmer, Judith Muntz and me as committee. Later we gained new people like Wilson Bunton and Debbie Hamilton. Debbie is one of the hardest community volunteers in Castlemaine. She has been Secretary of the Agricultural Society for over a quarter of a century, a member of the Lions Club and much, much more. Debbie is one of the unsung community contributors and is highly respected. She happily gave up more time to serve on our Board in the early days. Wilson Bunton, a retired school instructor, did a great job as our Treasurer in our early days and remains a worker for the community. All of our people contributed in many ways.

Our inquiries and request to ACMA for the UCB licence cancellation must have stirred John Jost into action because he promptly sent two of his men to Castlemaine to actually fire up the 88MHz service. He was not impressed by the possible enforcement of the 'use it within six months or lose it' rule for LPON services. He operated from Bill and John Sekora's shed south of the CBD, probably paying them a small fee. His equipment consisted of a home-made dipole, a computer and small transmitter.

The committee decided to lodge an application for that licence claiming (correctly) that the service had previously been idle for years. ACMA sent their investigators to look firsthand and eventually John Jost's licence was cancelled. No appeal was lodged. Success at last! We were then able to apply for the licence. All LPON licences are sold by auction and to our delight our bid was accepted. John Jost was probably not happy but we looked set to go. However we still needed some equipment; a transmitter for instance!

Our need for that essential item was answered by my former adversary at 3CCC, Gerry Pyne. I phoned Gerry, now a Queenslander and still in radio, looking for help. He didn't hesitate and sent me a used transmitter on permanent loan. I'm pleased to say that Gerry and I had mended the bridge previously when he had called at my home. We discussed our differences and agreed to put it behind us for good. Later, when the loaned transmitter chucked it in he sent me another. He also sent me a second hand computer which we put to good use. It was most generous of him and was a major contributor to us getting off the ground.

It had been a tough battle but 'Radio 88 Castlemaine for Seniors' finally hit the airwaves. For a time we broadcast on automation from a caravan in McClure's yard in Lewis Drive via the tower that UCB claimed they had used. Poetic justice perhaps? However we obviously needed to find a place to set up the gear and build a studio.

Central Victoria Group Training (CVGT) was in the process of leasing the Old Gaol to use it as a training centre for unemployed youngsters. In early December 2005 Maz and I were, after many meetings, able to obtain a sub-lease through Bob Evans of CVGT and General Manager Paul Green for a small area at generous rates at the south end of the former guards' quarters. It proved to be a good home for our radio station. It was particularly good for me as Mazza and I lived in an old cottage diagonally below the Old Gaol on the corner of Charles and Bowden Street. This made it easier for me to access the station in the years that followed

Our studio was built at the south wing of the building, where we divided the room we rented in half with a timber and plaster wall. CVGT occupied the north wing. As always Barry Palmer was there to help and he did much of the work involved. My friend Nigel Lill was a plasterer and he did all the plaster work – all free of charge. Jason Mills who owned Tonk's Timber and Hardware store supplied all the timber free of charge and Lindsay Dale, the paint. Barry scrounged a window from somewhere and Jean Wyldebore donated a large desk to accommodate the studio mixer, computer, CD players and the like. Not that we had much of anything. All the equipment belonged to Mazza and me. Barry and I collected the desk from Jean's upstairs office at the old school of mines. It was a monster; so big and so heavy. We had a terrific struggle getting it down the stairs and onto the street where Barry had a trailer waiting. We finally got the monster into the jail and manipulated it down the narrow passage. When we came to the door into our room at the passage end we found that, no matter how hard we tried, the desk would not go through it. Barry solved that problem by grabbing his power saw and cutting seventy five millimeters from the legs. *Then* we got it through, but it was gut-busting all the way.

The new CVGT Castlemaine boss Randall Blakemore was very good to us, even helping us with a great spread catering for our official launch celebrations in mid December. As time went by we gradually took over more and more space at our end of the building. Every time Randall came in he found us occupying yet another room. Finally we had taken the lot and an exasperated Randall said, 'Next thing you'll be in my office!' But he didn't try to stop us. Later Fran Cox succeeded Randall and she was equally generous. Locals were very good to us too, and helped considerably. Denis Cox the manager of the Castlemaine Mail agreed to a contra advertising arrangement which gained us publicity we desperately needed. Denis kept the arrangement going for the duration and I believe it still may be there to benefit the radio station. At this time we operated LPON stations in Castlemaine and Maldon, both going well.

We were on our way but how on earth would we get a Community Radio licence?

I sought help in that task from MHR Steve Gibbons but his response was not at all helpful. Likewise, a plea to our Senate representative, Michael Ronaldson, was totally ignored with no response whatsoever. On the other hand state MLA Bob Cameron could not have been more helpful or supportive, aided in this by his right hand, Maree Edwards. Bob and his electorate officer, Maree were terrific. If only their federal counterparts had helped us in the same way! Bob even gave me a personal $200 cash donation to help us along.

Speaking of cash donations I was in the street one day when retired small businessman, the late Jack Stuart, approached me. From his wallet he took a $100 bill. 'That's a little to help you on your way,' he said. You don't forget generous and thoughtful people like Jack.

Local business people rallied around us and we gathered a group of very loyal and generous sponsors and supporters. One person in particular deserves a special mention. Mick Hall ran the Commercial Hotel and one day he rang me. 'I want to support you guys so I am running a special pool comp night to raise money.' Typical of Mick he didn't expand a lot more on that. A week later he rang and asked us to call in. Mazza and I went to the old pub where he presented us with $500 in cash; money he said was raised on the night. I have to say, I suspect that he pitched in much of the total from his own pocket. It was a great boost for us, the display of support as much as anything, and when we finally got on air Mick continued as a regular sponsor. Good on you, Mick! Another great helper was entertainer Stan Munro, a former part of the famed Les Girls. He put on a free concert at The Northern Hotel in Castlemaine which raised over one thousand dollars for us in KLFM's early days.

Many of those supporters remain in support in our continuing radio efforts.

While all this was happening Mazza and I decided to investigate linking up with Highlands FM from nearby Kyneton, with a view to boosting their power to get into Castlemaine. We met with Dave Delle-Vergin their Manager and the late Charles Gaal who were quite enthusiastic. Unfortunately, in spite of several meetings, it never came to anything when Highlands FM moved from Kyneton to Woodend. Charles later moved to Castlemaine and found his way into community radio there. Sadly he passed away too soon, in July 2015.

Always we kept our eyes on the prize, *a community radio licence for Castlemaine*, although Barry Palmer said we were stupid to get involved in that and we should stick to Radio 88.

Stephen Atkins from ACMA was as helpful as he could be. He said he would get their engineers to see if they could possibly find a frequency for us. I felt that there was a feeling at ACMA that special circumstances applied to us in view of losing 3CCC and then KLFM.

By this stage we were questioning whether it was all worth it. We had copped so much stress that it was catching up. Maybe Barry Palmer was right?

* * *

Radio 88 was humming along merrily and we had several presenters, including Paul Thieman, Beverley Latham-Stephens, Faye Barker, Glenn Braybrook, Peter Seward, Barry Palmer, Julie Higginbotham, Len Cockerill, Marilyn and me. Later we were joined by Wilson Bunton, who made a significant contribution. I must further mention Peter Seward. Peter was a lovely man, a jolly round fat man, who found it most difficult to walk his way up the hill to the Old Gaol. Instead he got a taxi. He had trained as an announcer with Lee Murray in Melbourne, had never been on air, but was a fastidious presenter. His recordings were in mint condition and his presentation immaculate. His choice in music was ideally suited to our station. In fact he was a wonderful asset. Regrettably Peter became very ill and died quite unexpectedly. His death in a Melbourne hospital left a big gap in our volunteer staff. I had a high regard for him.

On the eventual departure of Paul Thieman, Wilson Bunton took over as treasurer, a difficult job that he did very well. It was a very good, friendly crew, all with the same wish for the future.

Radio88 soon gathered quite a large audience in spite of being a low powered station with a two kilometer range, and were thriving. Along the way we picked up the service, free of charge, of two of the top voice-over men in Australia; John Flaus and John Stanton. Both are first class Australian actors of stage and screen and well known to TV audiences as well. They reside in Castlemaine and when I approached them for the use of their voices they both agreed without hesitation Thus, with Col Herbert, Des Carol and Brad Bridger in the mix, we had superb voices delivering our sponsors' messages; as good as or better than any stations in the entire country!

* * *

I'm going back to 9 January 2006 now. I received a surprise call from Steve Atkins at ACMA with the fantastic news that a community radio frequency may possibly be made available and I should submit a detailed proposal. When ACMA say detailed they mean detailed! It was left up to us to identify a possibly available frequency; the cost of hiring professionals was a difficult $1500. Barry Palmer figured that he could do it himself by scanning the dial on his car radio from Gaol Hill. After hours and days of listening he found a spot that he was sure was vacant and to our surprise ACMA engineers accepted it. Things were going well. ACMA considered our detailed proposal worthy and we were advised to submit a formal application. It was a terrific time. Lodging the application was no easy task as it had to be accompanied by a further mass of supporting material, which was eventually completed.

The next step was an ACMA advertisement in the regional press inviting comment or objections from the public and existing broadcasters. A huge sigh of relief came when not a single comment came in and we were given a permit to conduct test transmissions. Test transmissions! It was our dream-come-true.

All went well with the tests and then, and only then, were we invited to apply for a Temporary Broadcasting Licence which, of course, we did.

Then we again waited anxiously, as there was now an opportunity for rival aspirants to apply. Happily nobody did. Then yet another anxious wait as ACMA invited public (and possible rival stations) comment and objections as they prepared a new Licence Area Plan. We survived that and we were delighted when issued a licence to commence full time broadcasting; our long wait was over. On November 11th 2006 WMAfm was born. Mazza and I then had to move back into the publicity plan that had worked so well for KLFM.

Chapter Twenty Five

WMAfm, The Most Outstanding Small Station in Australia, Choosing a name, upgrades, Optus, more helpers, the awards, E.R.P. upgraded, more helpers, pioneer presenters, board members, the right target

What's in a name? Why did we name it WMA fm? Simple. We wanted a call sign that identified with the area we served, the Mount Alexander Shire. Many alternatives were suggested; CCRfm, Localfm, Mainefm and Goldfieldsfm were a few we considered and rejected. We were also anxious to have the Mt. Alexander shire council on side. WMAfm was finally chosen to represent the entire shire. *Wireless for Mount Alexander.* It worked very well and was readily accepted by the community. The shire council proved to be very supportive, to the extent that, when CVGT left the council-owned Old Gaol, they offered free accommodation and power. It was a wonderful contribution that saved us thousands of dollars in the years ahead. Several years later, when the Old Gaol went into private ownership, the owners were equally generous and supportive although we now had to pay a small rental.

We realised that we had to start WMAfm on the right foot and we did considerable planning prior to switching on the new station. If we began with sloppy, non-professional presentation we would forever be branded as 'idiots'. The way we commenced was of paramount importance.

We knew that the population of Castlemaine was 48% aged over fifty and that's what we decided to aim for. In an era when most stations chase youth, WMAfm focused on the town's major demographic. We knew we had to maximize our audience. How else can a station in a town of seven thousand attract the advertisers necessary to survive?

We already had a substantial audience on Radio 88, accustomed to hearing older music that would follow us to WMAfm if we were careful, so we decided to start up with the Radio 88 style format. Experienced broadcasters know the danger of blowing up a successful format and starting over; we had to tread carefully. The plan was to gradually wean people off the 1930s, 1940s and the quieter type 1950s; so gradually in fact that our audience wouldn't notice it. It worked brilliantly, many of our audience followed us to WMAfm and not one complaint came in. We also adopted policies that limited talk to four minutes and ruled that three songs be played back to back. We knew that the majority of us turn off after four to five minutes of talk. The program policy worked well and was an important factor in WMAfm attracting a wider audience. We also knew that we had to present in a professional manner and trained our people accordingly.

A community radio station in a small town has to rely on a lot of goodwill from locals and especially local business people. We gradually built to over thirty business supporters, some small, some medium and one large. Whatever their contribution they were all treated alike and as well as we could. Our relationship with business people was warm and personal, an important part of our success. Without business support our means of raising money was very limited. We resolved to avoid the trap of bludging on grants as some stations do, which were not likely to be continuous. We knew of other stations dependent on grants and when they failed to be forthcoming the stations landed in serious financial trouble; some closed down.

We had support from other areas, too; for example from individuals like Gerry Pyne, Phil Rice and Jim Remedio. Jim was involved in indigenous broadcasting in Queensland and Northern Territory, and he sent us a second-hand broadcast desk, a valuable piece of equipment. We met up with Jim, who we knew from his time in Bendigo, at a CBAA conference in Hobart where he made the offer, which of course we readily accepted. Mazza and I believed in attending conferences where we learnt so much. We had made our way to Tasmania at considerable expense which we could not afford. It cost us about $1500 for the ship and accommodation alone, a fortune for us then, but the station helped us in a small way which was great. All the cost and bother proved to be very worthwhile this time because at this conference we were awarded the title of 'The Most Outstanding Small Station' in Australia. It was a great thrill for Mazza and me. It was an honour that we never seriously expected, but had maybe privately dreamed of.

When our win announcement was made at the gala dinner at the Hobart Casino, Mazza and I were thunderstruck and so excited. Mazza made her way to the stage and made a wonderful, heartfelt acceptance speech to great applause. It was like our very own Academy Award!

We grew to love Tasmania and thereafter visited there twice each year, including a visit each March to Longford for the annual WWII reunion of survivors of 'C' Company 2/3rd Machine Gun Battalion. As I mentioned elsewhere my half brother Ron served in the unit and died age nineteen on the Burma Railway.

WMAfm was going well by 2007. We had great sponsorship and the overall community right behind us. We had been able to buy a brand new broadcast panel, three computers, a top quality CD player and started to pay off some of the equipment and other gear advanced by Mazza and me to get us started. We even had a caravan which we set up as an OB Unit. CHIRP (Castlemaine Community Health) had a caravan, painted yellow, no longer useful to them, and we were able to buy it in mid 2007 for just $500, a bargain. Our first task was to cover the yellow with white paint donated by Lindsay Dale, local paint retailer. Wilson Bunton volunteered to help with the job as he had the spray equipment and he, Paul Thieman and I got busy with emery paper and prepared the surface. Three coats of paint later we had a white caravan, ready to go. It made its debut at the Lions Club swap meeting in April 2008 held at the Camp Reserve. For the uninitiated, The Camp is the local sports reserve, so named because it was the site of the Gold Commissioner's Camp in the gold rush of 1851. The exciting gold rush history of Castlemaine and Forest Creek (Chewton) is one of the principal things I love about the area.

Unfortunately the van was difficult to tow and park and the broadcasters inside were isolated from the people at any gathering. Nobody wanted to tow it and it was therefore a failure. As well, with modern technology taking over, it was soon rendered obsolete. Acknowledging that it was useless we sold it to an acquaintance of Roger Shillitoe for $200. I don't believe the buyer ever paid so it was a dead loss. Similarly we bought a trailer later on to transport bits of gear to OBs. Board member Bill Stephens did a great job on it. He built an all-steel, lockable canopy and painted it white. It looked great with our signs on the sides and we were pretty proud of it. Alas, like the caravan, it was rarely used as people preferred to toss the few electronic bits in the car boot, rather than tow anything. I do not know the fate of the trailer but suspect it went the way of the caravan.

As time went on it became apparent that the 100 watt effective radiated power we were allowed by the ACMA was not enough. We need to give our already large listenership a better service. In particular we were concerned that we could not penetrate well into Maldon, an important part of our shire. Our coverage of Castlemaine, Chewton and Campbell's Creek was good but Harcourt, Maldon and parts to the east of Castlemaine were missing out. So I got busy and lodged a detailed application for an upgrade to 1000 watts. In this I was greatly assisted by Ian Batty. We worked well together and I was grateful for his involvement and superior technical knowledge. I was also assisted on a good number of occasions by Bruce Leech, the hard working and talented volunteer Technician with a sister station, Goldfields FM in nearby Maryborough. We enjoyed a good relationship with that station, managed by two dedicated volunteers Jan and Alan.

We also realised that we needed a more elevated site for our transmitter and I made inquiries with Telstra for a place on their tower, overlooking the town to the south-east of the Old Gaol. I was informed that it was a possibility but first I had to fill out mountains of technical and other information. The other matter was the cost which was several thousand dollars a year. I decided to investigate other options and drove up a rough bush track to a huge tower perched high about two kilometres to the north-west of our station. I climbed through a barbed wire fence and took note of contact details on a small plate attached to the three metre high security fence. Eventually, after many phone calls, I was able to identify the owners as Optus.

I had had enough experience to know that you have to talk directly with the right people to get a response and to this end I made discreet inquiries through my sources and was given a contact name. Eureka! It was like gold. Several phone calls later I spoke directly to Karen, the person in charge of Optus towers Australia wide. She was extremely cooperative and helpful and assured me that she could see no problem in us locating on the tower. She forwarded documents that I filled out and returned. I was delighted when she rang me with verbal approval a few days later. By now we had established a friendly relationship but when she raised the matter of annual rental I was apprehensive. After earnest discussion she asked me to nominate a figure. I reluctantly suggested perhaps we could afford a thousand dollars a year, hoping not to insult her. She replied 'What about a dollar?' I was astonished! A dollar a year! Karen forwarded a ten year lease agreement which I completed and attached an electronic fund transfer for ten dollars. Surely this must be one of the all-time record lows for tower rental anywhere. Note that the one dollar per annum included supply of electricity. Optus would not allow unqualified people to climb their tower so Karen recommended two riggers who did regular contract work for them. They came from Melbourne and installed our new dipole on the tower. I watched in amazement as they defied death; walking on narrow steel arms and framework fifty metres above the ground. They were good blokes and gave us a hugely reduced rate. Unfortunately I cannot recall their names or a great deal about them, but I thank them sincerely. I rang Karen at Optus and offered to run regular on-air acknowledgements, but she did not consider it necessary. As a result Optus does not receive the publicity for support of WMAfm that they truly deserve.

More help came again from our community. Builder, Trevor Butcher built and paid for a magnificent powder-coated steel cabinet to house our transmitter and reception equipment. It was terrific. The problem of digging a trench to cable power to the cabinet was solved when young local electrician Rhys Ford responded to my call and did the entire job free of charge. He dug the trenches through the tough gravel soil typical of Castlemaine, laid the cable and set up the entire electricity system. He refused payment so I ran contra advertising for him for about a year, a small gesture considering his big effort for us.

We later found that the summer heat, when thirty-five to forty degrees hit, caused automatic protective transmitter shut downs. Bill Stephens installed an air conditioner, donated by Castlemaine Rotary Club, in the cabinet and it solved the problem.

* * *

I mentioned on air one day in our early days with the pre-WMAfm service Radio88, that I needed someone to relocate an FM antenna onto one of the Old Gaol chimneys. In a very short time I had a visit from John Jenkins who operated a small business, Star Electronics. John clambered onto the roof and did the job in ten minutes flat, supplying the necessary brackets and bolts. He refused to take any money and went on his way. I later had the occasional phone call from him over time but nothing more.

That was until our wonderful WMAfm IT man, David Sime had to retire. John immediately offered his services and, assisted by David, who showed him the often peculiar and particular methods of WMAfm technical systems, he stepped in. Mind you they were very big shoes to fill! David Sime came to us in much the same way; in answer to my cry for help on air. He and his wife Judy had recently retired to Castlemaine from his audio system job at Parliament House in Canberra. David was absolutely marvelous and his knowledge astounding. He set up complicated systems that I had no idea or understanding of whatsoever and we could never repay him for his totally volunteer work. Nothing was too much trouble for David. I would be constantly on the phone at all hours seeking his advice or help and more often than not he would drop what he was doing and come to my aid, either on his bike or by car. I cannot speak too highly of him and admire him greatly. His contribution to the establishment and growth of WMAfm was immeasurable. His wife Judy must have been very tolerant and understanding, too!

Ian Batty from Harcourt, mentioned elsewhere, also deserves an accolade for his fantastic contribution to WMAfm.

John Jenkins was and remains our good and true friend. He proved to be absolute gold – platinum even! Like David and Ian he was always available at the end of the phone and he spent many, many hours at the station doing voluntary work. Nothing was ever a bother to him and I am sure he neglected his business on many occasions to help me out of difficulties. I am a total dunce when it comes to computers and computer programs as well as the technical aspects of radio. John had it all and was a terrific asset to WMAfm and even more so to Mazza and me later.

Whatever Mazza and I may have achieved with WMAfm and since we could not have done it without wonderful people like these.

Back in January 2008 at our Annual meeting, we set our membership fees at $50 per year and Subscribers at $20. We copied KLFM and deliberately set the fee at this higher figure to discourage those who had no real interest or passion for local radio. It made it harder for a take-over by specific types and groups. We had seen this in a number of other community stations.

It was a pretty exciting time as we had just signed the lease with CVGT for the room at the south end and the adjoining kitchen and toilet. Barry Palmer, Nigel Lill, and I had completed the building and fit-out of our first studio.

Our studio had a Realistic brand mixer, a CD player, a cassette player, a four track reel to reel recorder, one microphone, a PC and a turntable, all owned by Marilyn and me, worth all-up less than three thousand dollars. The station was later able to purchase the equipment from us for half its current value. Above that, the most expensive item was our $600 antenna assembly. We were able to prove that flash studios and equipment were not necessary to produce good radio.

We also had a sparsely equipped office with a fax, phone, computer with internet and email. Not much, but it was heaven, knowing at last we were on our way up.

Our on-air staff back then was equally sparse with only Paul Thieman, Julie Higginbottom, Beverley Latham-Stephens, Barry Palmer, Len Cockerill, Faye Barker, Peter Seward, Marilyn Bennet, Alan Lane, his uncle Ken Lane and me. Len Cockerill had turned up in response to our broadcasts, first as an interested person then later as one keen to get on air. Len was a good bloke, extremely fit for his age and a keen tennis player. He tried very hard on air but could never have been a number one presenter. What he lacked in skill he more than made up for with his enthusiasm and willingness to help. Sadly Len passed away in 2012 following a stroke. Beverley Latham-Stephens called in one day expressing her long-held aspiration to be on radio. I was pleased to welcome her and to put her through our rigorous training program. She excelled and was soon on air. She was quite nervous to begin with but soon became a competent and popular presenter. She was a good person, well liked and very sincere in everything she did. Her husband, Bill Stephens, never once went on air but was a remarkable worker behind the scenes. He eventually served as a member of the board of management; his experience and business knowledge a great asset to the station. The same is to be said for Roger Shillitoe and his wife Josephine. Both came to serve on the board; Roger as a very good and thorough Treasurer and Josephine as an ordinary member. Both made a big contribution to our radio stations as time went by and, like Bill Stephens, not once appeared on the radio.

We filled most of the daytime hours with our limited staff, but the rest of the time was automated. We were happier to have good quality presenters rather than draw on the supply of plentiful but awful ones aching to be asked and so readily available. Local radio attracts them like moths to a flame.

Careful selection was to remain a deliberate policy when we expanded to WMAfm and we were getting great response from our increasing number of listeners because of it. In the early days of Radio88 we calculated that we had around four hundred local Listeners, not a lot, but a comparative percentage figure that any metropolitan radio station would be thrilled to achieve. Later, when WMAfm was up and running, we had somewhere near seven percent of the district potential audience of seventeen thousand. That equaled about twelve hundred listeners in the district, quite a good result. Realistically, it's unlikely that a small town radio station could improve above a maximum 10 percent. Cumulative, across a full week, it may get to a 10 percent in total but that's very optimistic. In Melbourne and other big city stations like 3RRR or 3CR, an audience of 2 percent is quite good. Two percent of 3.5 million is seventy thousand. In Castlemaine it is one hundred and forty! You may as well use a telephone!

It is possible to gain a fairly accurate assessment of the audience number with a calculated and selected phone survey of one hundred people. Making the one hundred calls is a pretty big job but one we thought worthwhile.

My experience taught me that to achieve a maximum audience it is necessary to target the right demographic. That's what we did at WMAfm and it worked. KLFM Bendigo is a good example of the success such a policy achieves. It is one of the most popular stations in Central Victoria. An idea held by a lot in Community Radio is the shot gun effect; the scatter approach. The wisdom is that if you fire off a scattering of shotgun pellets you'll be sure to hit someone. It simply does not work. Radio Listeners demand consistency.

Chapter Twenty Six

Growth, good people and bad, footy, you've gotta have rules, an expulsion, pirates, a jail break

WMAfm grew like Topsy as we gathered a collection of good presenters; people like Glenn Doriean, John Sawtell, Ken White, Eddie Ford, Ian Batty, the on-air Chewton duo of Glenn Braybrook and Bettie Exon, Kevin Daw (KD), Ken Ford and several others. Gus Reade-Hill was one I considered had talent for radio presentation, albeit at times a bit too talkative. We asked radio stalwart Randal Jones if he would like to join us, but he had to decline due to work commitments and travelling from his home in Bendigo was too difficult. Not that he had no transport; he owned a magnificently maintained full size Ford sedan, the envy of many. Randal had been around radio in Bendigo for many years; 3BO, 3CV and at KLFM. He was a first class announcer and would have fitted our station very well, his experience valuable. He most recently confines his on-air work to reading newspapers for Radio for the Print Handicapped in Bendigo.

Ken Ford was a terrific asset to WMAfm. An American, originally from New York, he had travelled the world, even lived in England for a time. His relaxed, warm and friendly style was a hit with listeners. Ken was ideally suited to the WMAfm style of radio. He finally left the station, then Mainfm, in mid 2015, saying nobody was listening anymore. A great pity as he was excellent on air with his friendly tone, funny stories, presentation of 'facts' and good selection of music. In fact he was a musician himself although I think he performed mostly in private. A good bloke.

I simply must mention Ray Applebee. Ray was a retired senior policeman, born in Tasmania and a seaman during WWII. Well into his eighties, Ray rose at six each Sunday morning to present a two hour show starting at 8am. He had to finish at 10am as he had to rush off to Church at the Salvation Army. He was a dedicated Christian and a true Christian. Ray's homespun presentation and selection of amazing jokes made his one of my favourite shows on Radio88 and later on WMAfm. He wasn't the most polished presenter that we had, but he had a great sense of humour as he casually yarned his way through his two hours, telling tall stories, playing Slim Dusty and Buddy Williams records and the occasional hymn; all very listenable. His Christian messages easily absorbed. I never missed a show. How fortunate were we to have such people!

We recognised the importance of football to country town communities and decided to get involved as much as possible with the Castlemaine Football and Netball Club (CFNC). Footy clubs are generally acknowledged as the heartbeat of the town in regional Victoria. Our approach to the CFNC President Tony Walsh and our suggestion that we broadcast footy was met with an enthusiastic response. First, however, we needed permission from the Bendigo Football Netball League (BFNL) and, importantly, people who were willing and able to be commentators. He spread the word and Stuart Dunn, a school teacher and footy club stalwart put his hand up. Stuart turned out to be an accomplished commentator. He was soon joined by builder, Trevor Butcher, accountant Brett Cole, hospital worker Brian Moon and then by John Hunter, the same John Hunter mentioned as a weary, youthful breakfast presenter on 3CCC years before, by now a police Detective Sergeant working in Melbourne. It eventuated that we had a truly first class team. We were very fortunate as such people are very hard to get and we finally had a first class on-air footy team.

Our next move was to seek broadcast permission from Stephen Oliver, the CEO of the BFNL. Mazza and I went to a meeting in Bendigo with him to discuss the possibilities and met with only limited success. For the first season we were permitted to broadcast only one match, a local event from the Camp Reserve, Castlemaine's home ground. Our team did a fantastic job on that, setting us up for much better things the next season. The broadcast was assisted by Barry Palmer who set up the technical side of it. Barry was always ready to help.

The BFNL was impressed and for the next season we were permitted to cover almost all the home games and for good measure threw in a heap of matches from the Maryborough/Castlemaine League. Our lads worked very hard and by the next season covered an impressive forty four district matches, a staggering achievement for these dedicated volunteers. A recently arrived volunteer presenter, Neil Woodfine, became the broadcast technician and did a fantastic job for a couple of exhausting years, another 'local hero'. Trevor Butcher was not only part of the pioneer footy broadcasts but always helped in other ways.

For the most part the broadcasts were successful. A notable exception was the scheduled broadcast of the MCDFL Grand Final from Maryborough in 2012. At the time we were linking by a mobile phone based electronic system. Because of the large crowd, many constantly talking or using their phones, the Telstra system could not handle the volume. As a consequence we (having not secured priority because of the larger cost) continually were dropped from the Telstra system. In the end we had to abandon the broadcast; embarrassing to say the least, but unavoidable. The Grand Final broadcast was a bloody disaster!

In the year following my departure the station failed to broadcast any Castlemaine Footy Club games, a bitter disappointment. I do not know what occurred to bring this about. Instead they focused exclusively on the Maryborough/Castlemaine League, covering their games. There was less interest in these matches than the BFNL, but it is nevertheless an important part of the footy world and they had the capacity to contribute financially.

By this time Stuart Dunn had departed after some disagreement and in 2015, just before the season began, the talented (and likely irreplaceable) John Hunter, disappointed with the lack of genuine support from management, quit. He accepted a position calling footy for The Fresh in Bendigo. Stuart Dunn's talent had also been recognized by commercial station 3BO and he went to work there. Brian Moon had family commitments that prevented him dedicating himself to the job and Brett Cole was indifferent to broadcasting, preferring to play the game.

The local footy was a great boost for WMAfm. There is no doubt it grew and held our audience significantly as more and more locals became aware of us. It also brought in a considerable amount of money in sponsorship; about one sixth of the station income in my final year. Without the support of footy and the money it generated, plus the listeners it attracted, WMAfm could not have functioned and grown as it did, it is that important. Hopefully footy will always be a respected part of the station.

WMAfm's daytime shows were generally music from '50s to '80s played three back to back and we strictly limited talk to four minutes without a music break. Not everyone stuck rigidly to this, and were not expected to, but most tried.

One notable exception was a particularly garrulous female who had no idea when to stop talking, espousing her knowledge of most things. Eventually we had to take her off air for continuing the practice. Our 'after five' shows, 5pm till midnight, were mostly alternative music styles and talk programs. This formula worked very well and was well accepted in the community and seemingly by our volunteers. This way we gave all sorts of people with all sorts of tastes a go on radio whilst retaining a good size, saleable audience.

The garrulous woman referred to proved to be a real trouble maker for the board. She regarded herself as an expert in governance. At a Special General Meeting called to bring our constitution into line with the ACMA requirements and to discuss a motion to increase the number of board members from six to ten; she argued at length that we were out of order.

As I usually did I stored the recording of the meeting, mainly to assist the minute writer. She quoted from her vast knowledge of most things but Mazza, the President at the time, had her measure and contradicted her at every turn. She ventured to claim that anyone who had paid the station a $10 fee as a Listener/subscriber was entitled to vote as a full member and that we had not notified these people of the meeting or its purpose. Therefore, she claimed the meeting was invalid. It was made very clear in a speech by Bill Stephens, a board member, that subscribers were definitely not members. The woman persisted, stating that all members had not actually seen and read the constitution, so a vote would be invalid. Marilyn then put it to a vote asking, 'Who wants to see the constitution before we vote?' Nobody put their hand up. It was all quite unpleasant and I admired Mazza's calmness, strength and firmness. The motion to change won easily and the vote on increasing the number of board members was soundly defeated.

This episode was a forerunner to a much more serious situation involving the woman. She consistently ignored the four minute talk rule and waffled on for up to twenty minutes without a breath expounding her knowledge and opinions on all things. Eventually she was taken off air for continually ignoring the rules, much to her annoyance.

Then rumblings began on the social media, claims that the board did not heed the voices of the members and volunteers. We knew without doubt that most members supported the board, or simply didn't care. We were then made aware of a social media message to all volunteers that the only way to be heard at WMAfm was to have the numbers. To this end she proposed a fundraising night at a hotel to pay for anyone who cared to become a member and therefore have a vote. The purpose appeared obvious. The board saw this, and other statements, as an act of disloyalty and detrimental to the organisation. She was advised that she would be expelled.

A special meeting was called at her request and there followed a most agonizing and stressful time. Mazza, as President had to bear the full brunt of the affair but again handled it with strength and courage at a Special General Meeting to vote on her expulsion. There was fierce argument from the person concerned but when the vote was taken she found herself expelled. In my experience she was the first person to be dealt with that way.

In an earlier nasty incident at an Annual General Meeting, the awarding of Life Membership to David Sime was interrupted as she strongly objected. The basis of argument was her belief that the board did not have the authority to award Life Memberships. Incorrect, of course, and again she was crushed by the strength of Marilyn. It was an embarrassment and spoilt the event for David. After her expulsion, there were a few parting shots on social media, but we had no more problems with her.

This extremely stressful episode had a damaging effect on all of us board members but Mazza worst of all as she suffered a heart attack a few days after the meeting. She survived and recovered well but her doctors told her to avoid such stressful situations in future. She was advised that the recent affair had likely been the cause of her illness. Great! Community Radio is supposed to be such a friendly activity to be involved in! Incidentally it is my view that so-called social media can be anything but social.

One day I was quietly working on a production when I had an unexpected visitor. I don't recall his name but I sure recall his purpose in calling in. He was an inspector from the ACMA and he explained that he was in town investigating a pirate radio station that was running. We had just been awarded our new frequency, 94.9MHz, and the pirate was using our former 107.5MHz. I had not been aware of a pirate station and was very surprised. The inspector said he had already spoken to two people about it, including a suspect, and had called on me as a matter of courtesy. We were definitely not under suspicion. It seemed that the operator had published some boastful details on Facebook or Twitter and that is how the ACMA became aware of the pirate. The ACMA had identified approximately where the signal originated from; somewhere near or in the centre of town. The inspector then went on his way saying he was calling on the Theatre Royal as he had seen a pirate flag fluttering from the top of the old, crumbling building. (The theatre was screening the Pirates of Penzance at the time.) I don't believe he had any suspicions but had to check it out.

I was shocked to receive a phone call a half hour or so later from the theatre owner, David Stretch, who went off at me for sending the ACMA to check if he was running a pirate radio station. He was not at all happy and neither was I that he had made a claim that I had dobbed him in. Of course I had not. The ACMA inspector had found his own way and for his own reason. That was the beginning of lengthy acrimony between David and me, but for different reasons.

We had a good number of adventures with volunteers at WMAfm. There seems to always be a problem one way or another and mostly we were able to sort out any problems, difficulties and arguments. A few times we had to put people temporarily off the air for breaking the rules. I hate rules but accept that you have to have them or have anarchy. We did not allow bad language or bad presentation. Our aim was to maintain a certain standard, even though community standards had dropped from what they used to be; swearing was common in conversation and on the streets but we tried to minimize it at WMAfm. Old fashioned but we believed it was still worthwhile.

Most offenders who were suspended, and there were very few, accepted it gracefully but a couple really opposed us. Two were late night presenters who used language that we found offensive. Their audience did not agree and we were inundated with objections mostly by email and Facebook. After a couple of weeks the board relented and they went back on air, promising to be good in future, which they were for a while.

Another individual, Ben, was the most defiant of all. Ben was a local artist, a bit of a local character, who rode an old motorbike and never wore shoes or socks. The Board had suspended him following a couple of warnings about inappropriate language in his morning show. He was put off indefinitely as he had offended before. His presentation style was also distinctly poor and mistakes galore his forte. For the first morning of his suspension I had installed an automated fill-in program. We always monitored the station from home about 18/7. That morning shortly after 8am as I sipped a coffee I was amazed to hear the unmistakable voice of Ben. He was apologizing for his absence from his show. 'I've been suspended for being naughty, but I'm still here,' he said.

How could this be? The Old Gaol was locked up tightly. I had been feeling uncomfortable about Ben, so late at night after the last presenter had gone home I drove to the station and changed the code on the front door lock. I felt confident that it being a jail it was not easy to get into, but Ben was definitely in there!

I hastened to the station, arriving just as Ben was leaving and heading to his motor bike. The exit door could be unlocked from inside. I was angry and yelled at him as he sped off. 'How did you get in'?

'I climbed over the fence,' he yelled before disappearing around the bend.

I couldn't believe that he could have climbed over the three metre chain wire fence that separated the Old Gaol proper from the governor's house yard. But he had done it! How, I will never know. Nor could I believe that he had the effrontery to so blatantly defy an order from the Board.

I later spotted him outside a café down the street and being in an angry state I gave him the mother of all tongue lashings; very bad language I'm afraid. He was banned for life after this episode, although, on reflection, there was considerable humour in it!

We had several changes in the board of management with good people like Roger Shillitoe, his wife Josephine, Barry Palmer, Beverley Latham-Stephens, Bill Stephens, Alan Lane, Ken White, Robyn Thomas, Rod Hadfield, Bettie Exon, Scott Sanders and Fergus Niall. Marilyn Bennet was our President for most of the time and I was also a board member as well as station manager. All of these terrific people served with dedication and gave willingly of their time and expertise. We were all good friends.

Mazza and I had established a good relationship with the Bendigo RSL and Vietnam Veterans in our time at KLFM. A number of times I was MC of the RSL annual dinners and Mazza and I were regular guests of Maurie Betts, Secretary of the Vietnam Veterans Association at their annual Cabaret. Unexpectedly I was approached by the President of Bendigo RSL, Cliff Richards, to produce a series of special programs for them. He had been impressed by my earlier efforts in producing war-based stories. Financially it was a big help and both Mazza and I worked on the project. It proved to be a winner and I gained more work with the RSL as a result.

I used to often be asked to act as MC or to do the commentary at functions or events like the annual show at Castlemaine and Maldon. Ken White and I shared the role a couple of times at the Maldon Show. This is a very small country show and filling in the day from 11am to 3.30pm when the Grand Parade ended the day was a bit difficult. There is a limit to what you can say describing the judging of the prettiest dog, or the one most like its owner, or the horse riding competitions. The Grand Parade of a few horses, a bull and five cows, a horse drawn gig and a tractor does not allow for an in-depth description, lovely to see as it is. The big event of the day was the sheaf tossing. This involved a series of contestants throwing a bundle of straw stuffed into a Hessian bag with a pitchfork, the aim was to clear a massive hurdle moved steadily upwards to up to twelve metres high. The contest went on for about an hour and describing it to those assembled was torture. But we got through; the sheaf tossers were absolutely amazing; their strength and skill awesome. The Committee treated us to great courtesy and we were given free lunches as well. The organisers were great country people. The salt of the earth.

A regular for me was the Castlemaine Show which I thoroughly enjoyed. One year I was unable to do it so I asked Ken White to fill in for me. He did so, but later swore he would never do it again. Poor Ken just could not handle it; describing the floats in the parade, the wood chopping, fleece judging, the side shows, the art and craft, the cakes and jams and sheep and cattle was simply too much for him. More often than not he stood flabbergasted, microphone in hand having nothing whatsoever to say. He said it was a dreadful experience and cursed me roundly for 'dobbing him in'. He later enthusiastically declined the opportunity to describe the Maldon Show by himself as I had retired. The Castlemaine Show didn't ask him again.

It's fair to say that we Board members were of the older variety, mostly people born shortly after the Second World War, but a couple of us were a bit older. Alan Lane was also a Vietnam Veteran.

Most likely we were resented by some for our age, being regarded as 'out of touch dinosaurs', but we had considerable business experience and, even more importantly, life experience. We were not out of touch but very much in tune with our community, we were representative of the major demographic of Castlemaine and came from a time in country towns, when everyone knew everyone and the struggles in the life of one effected the other; we had few, probably not any, people of power and influence. We were, we felt, the town's personality.

We were not of the Latte Elite, nor were we what locals derisively termed 'aristo-hippies' (derived from aristocratic hippies) those of better education and often, comparative wealth, mostly brought about through sale of overpriced suburban homes, pretending to be 'different' but at the same time bringing their city ways to our town. They were representative of the gentrification of our loveable town.

We board members were not university educated, just ordinary folk. To quote a fellow board member: 'Just because you have a piece of paper from a university doesn't mean you aren't an idiot.'

However, as it turned out, we were no match for them, idiots or not.

Chapter Twenty Seven

Gentrification, graves, the Old Gaol, the epic town division, interviews, new breed, coffee shops

For most of our time broadcasting from the Old Castlemaine Gaol we were the sole occupants. Many people were fascinated by our presence in an old jail but we thought there was nothing odd about occupying the abandoned 1850's prison. Undoubtedly it had been a place of horror and suffering for many of the inmates in the old days. Although classified as a heritage treasure I saw it as a monument to man's inhumanity. Ten men were hanged there in the period 1860–1890, their bodies buried in unmarked graves within the walls, where they remain today. There is considerable doubt about the guilt of at least one of the men.

The hanging beam and trapdoor were removed in the 1950s when for a time the place housed juvenile offenders, but the trap location is still quite visible; located on the first floor immediately outside the cell where the condemned man awaited his awful fate. I have read the graphic descriptions of the hangings, published in the Mount Alexander Mail, known later as the Castlemaine Mail and they are chilling.

I spent many evenings alone in the icy cold and damp old prison and it was never pleasant. I felt the presence of these men and of the many others who suffered there, but I never experienced a presence of actual ghosts. Perhaps they are there, certainly if ghosts do exist, you would expect they would have to be found in the confines of this awful place.

In 2011, we engaged a man suggested by Vin Cappy who claimed that he could actually devine the location of the hanged men's bodies with his length of forked wire. Out in the yard we believed we knew the approximate location and he proceeded to sweep the area with the wire. 'Yes,' he said, looking at the wire twitching downward, 'that's one of the spots for sure.' He repeated the action a number of times and assured us that the dead were where he indicated, right against the western perimeter wall.

Maybe he was right, maybe not, we never took the inquiry any further, but perhaps one day someone will. It would be fitting to see markers on the graves for these unfortunate men who today would not have suffered such a dreadful fate. Justice was swift and rough back then.

In all, there were ninety-four cells and until it closed in around 1990 the prison was fully occupied. The area our radio station occupied was the former warders' accommodation, where guards lived and raised their families. It was the original section of the building, opened in 1858.

Within the yard was the long abandoned and badly deteriorated Governor's home, a sturdy brick construction, as is the Old Gaol itself. The house has now been refurbished under direction of Heritage Victoria and the shire council, and is in excellent condition. Oddly enough the renovation did not include a kitchen, bathroom, laundry or toilet! So much for scrupulous heritage restoration; even in 1858 the governor's family surely had such facilities, at the very least a toilet!

When we first occupied our section we had a kitchen, laundry and toilet but, believe it or not, these were demolished in the early 2000s as part of the restoration plan for the building. It was said these buildings were outside the jail's 1850–60 era and had to come down. I believe they were circa 1940s. For the rest of my time there we had no kitchen, no water and we had to walk fifty metres to another toilet, rain or shine. Our water came in twenty-five litre barrels I lugged in from a tap outside the toilet and our coffee making was done on a rickety table outside the studio, of necessity, using paper cups. A small refrigerator for milk was donated by Vincent Cappy, a generous supporter.

The most frightening feature of all in the Old Gaol was the isolation cell area in the dungeon deep below. It was cold and damp and dimly lit from by two filthy barred windows. This area had served as the kitchen and laundry and also housed the handful of female prisoners incarcerated there. They did the cooking and the laundry in most dreadful conditions, their sleeping cells attached to the main kitchen/laundry section. At the furthest and darkest end of the dungeon were the two isolation cells. With the cell doors closed it was completely black; no sound or light could penetrate into the cramped seven by five foot cell. It contained a bucket and a straw mattress, nothing more and a person enclosed there must surely have lost their mind. Food was brought in twice a day, usually the traditional bread and water. I once shut myself in and in moments began to panic for release.

For a period, around 1870, the prison had adopted a new 'rehabilitation' scheme apparently derived in the U.K. For twenty three hours a day the offenders were locked in their tiny cell to be released into the exercise yard for an hour daily. These unfortunate men were compelled to wear a bag over their heads to deny them visual contact with any others. Man's inhumanity to man. More recently the Old Gaol has a new lease on life with new owners opening it up for weddings, gatherings, art shows, plays, a community market, and a variety of other uses including a coffee shop and café in the Governor's home. The Old Gaol served us well as our local radio station and continued to do so for some time.

One of my delights was standing outside the Old Gaol gate, on the hill overlooking Castlemaine, which nestled many metres below. I was always first to arrive at WMAfm and in the early morning, with the sun about to rise, it was a most peaceful and beautiful sight. I would often stand and simply gaze, often for several minutes as I absorbed the wonder of it all. In autumn,

March and April, when the hundreds of deciduous trees changed colour it was particularly beautiful and I was privileged to enjoy that in solitude. What better start to the day?

I went merrily on my way, managing the radio station, doing odd jobs and able to do what I enjoyed in spite of the pressures of managing the station. Being on air, broadcasting to my 'friends' three days a week for two hours, plus two hours on Sunday mornings, was what I loved and I enjoyed every minute of it. I read funny stories, cracked mostly awful jokes and spun yarns I made up about my gold diggings ancestors.

I enjoyed talking to people and carried out hundreds of interviews with locals. I have always believed that everybody has a story to tell, so I interviewed all sorts of people, mostly not famous but what we call ordinary. Often they were not pre-arranged, with people wandering in for a bit of a yarn. Typical was Ron Gartside from the Lions Club, a regular and Rod Hadfield a quiet achiever local bloke. Rod may have kept to himself but was however, world famous for his hot rods, car conversion kits, for building extraordinary motor vehicles, one equipped with a Rolls Royce Merlin engine from a WWII Mustang fighter plane. His car racing exploits on salt lake flats – both here and in the U.S. – are legendary. The numerous magnificent, world renowned cars that he builds in his shed at 'East Chewton' are on display at his Museum inside his massive shed.

I regularly interviewed Rotarians, religious leaders, truckies, painters (both house and the art variety), authors, doctors, councilors, counselors, club secretaries, nurses, musicians, artists, nurses, executives, labourers, mechanics, technicians, writers, politicians, senior citizens, unemployed, managers, water bailiffs, footballers, cricketers and just about anybody else. I thoroughly enjoyed it, and managed to mostly keep the live-to-air jobs within the four minute talk rule, with generous music breaks! I always pre-warned the person interviewed that we took music breaks after four minutes and without exception they were happy with this.

On one occasion one of my interviews was broadcast on the BBC in London. This came about when Allen and Ulwin, Alex Miller's publisher, contacted me and asked me to do an interview with him for the BBC. Alex lived in Castlemaine and had just won yet another major award and I was honoured to be asked. As a result I can claim to have been an interviewer for the mighty BBC!

One of my favourite interviewees was Sid Llewellyn from Chewton. Sid had lost a leg in a disastrous accident whilst cutting firewood with his father Mick at Sutton Grange many years before. The leg was severed to groin level by a runaway swing saw that they were using. A swing saw is basically large free-standing circular saw on wheels, the speeding blade fully exposed and dreadfully dangerous. Sid was working downhill from his father and glancing around he spied the swing saw, blade running, almost on him. It had drifted downhill, moved by its vibrating movement. Sid could not escape and the saw completely severed one leg and badly cut the other. His injuries were horrendous. His father ran to his aid and removing his bootlaces managed to tie a sort of tourniquet around the stump. Miraculously Sid survived and soon went back to cutting wood for a living. He was also the district grave digger and won fame as Chewton's one-legged grave digger. Try digging graves in this tough, stony country with no more than a crowbar and shovel! He continued to cut wood well into his seventies when he became too ill to continue. His father, Mick, is another amazing story, too long to relate here but deserving of a full coverage. Sid Llewellyn died in 2015 but the 'Sid's Woodyard' sign at Forest Creek, Chewton remains a memorial to him and is a local landmark.

I got to know hundreds of people and enjoyed a measure of popularity. It's important to recognize however that popularity is not to be confused with friendship, although many of these folk did become firm friends. Friendship is something different;

something special and hard to come by. But Marilyn and I have made and hold many friends.

What I have learnt is that one quickly fades from view and people's minds once you no longer are visible. Popularity lasts for as long as you remain in the spotlight, it's simply the way it is.

Castlemaine has been my home for many years, I expect that I shall die here and be buried here. There is no better place on earth than Castlemaine. However, my experience and attachment is more toward what I call 'Old Castlemaine', the quiet country town that it was before being 'discovered' by city people. Not that I don't like and accept city folk; they are, however, different to us oldies, especially in recent times. I feel that they have different ideas and different values.

Sadly, Castlemaine has been gentrified. Better off people, many bearing proceeds of over-priced house sales in the suburbs have moved in. Average incomes have increased, house prices are up correspondingly and pre-gentrification folk are being forced out. It's not an uncommon occurrence in the city. Probably some newcomers are victims of gentrification of their own suburb. Northcote is an example. Some of our newcomers do not want the town to progress; they want it to remain just as it was when they 'discovered' it. I don't blame them for that, but at the same time many bring with them the habits and amenities they had in the city; paradoxically attempting to turn their new town into almost what they came here to escape from!

I recognize that, by far, the majority of new people in town are good people. However, there is a certain number, who have, by various means, virtually taken over the town. My experiences with them have unfortunately, in many ways, spoiled the town for me and I am left with a bitter taste in my mouth which will probably never go away.

Once never imagined, Castlemaine now has around twenty coffee shops and numerous high priced restaurants and hotels. Dining el fresco, weather permitting, and unheard of ten years before is now the norm. Breakfast at a café is the done thing. Wherever one goes, one stumbles through a collection of tables and chairs on the footpath, some of them displaying No Smoking Here signs. Oldies are becoming less and less visible; they became known as The Invisibles. Some people will disagree, but it's said that many stay at home not wishing to mingle with people they view as alien. I believe it is at least partly true.

Many 'oldies' only emerge when something really troubles them. For example, in 2012 they demonstrated clearly that they were still here when the council proposed using a reserve in the middle of town to construct a new swimming pool. Over fourteen hundred angry residents, mostly 'oldies', me among them, attended a protest rally organised by my good friend, the late Felix Cappy and Robin Taylor, both former councilors. One puzzled newcomer wrote in a trendy local (now defunct) online publication, 'Who are these people? Where did they come from? I have never seen them before.'

The proposal for the new pool on that site was dropped.

In 2012, the town was torn apart when a group of fifteen hundred, mainly 'older' residents, supported the establishment by the Maryborough Highland Society of a new community club containing electronic gaming machines. The society proposed to spend around four million dollars on developing a decrepit and abandoned railway goods shed into a community club. Most of the town was happy with the plan; a club was long overdue. I became embroiled in the fight when I was interviewed on ABC TV in support of the club. There was a strong reaction toward me from the EPIC group who bitterly opposed the plan. This dragged the radio station into it with considerable impact.

The catalyst for Mazza and I making full commitment to The Club concept came when we, along with a couple of hundred like-minded people, attended a public meeting at the town hall called by Maryborough Highland Society (MHS) to explain their proposal and answer any questions.

What happened at that meeting will stay with me always. I have never seen such a display of such bad manners and lack of courtesy to visiting people. The behavior of the EPIC group was inexcusable; a total lack of respect. The question time was taken over by the EPIC group and, in a deplorable display of bad manners, a number of the EPIC supporters stood and turned their backs on the speakers. It was all I could do to restrain myself from sinking to the level of the opposition.

About thirty of us gathered outside the hall after the meeting feeling ashamed to be Castlemaine residents, expressing our anger and disgust at what we had seen. It was then that Mazza and I resolved to do all we could to support the club. A long and spiteful battle was set in motion that night

It seems, in the eyes of EPIC, that as radio station manager, it was very wrong for me to express an opinion on TV not in line with theirs. I copped a barrage of flak, mostly by email and it was seriously suggested that WMAfm be boycotted. I was judged unfit to manage the radio station and it was said I was not deserving of my Australia Day award. Our volunteers were divided on the issue as well and several began to make their views known on air, which threatened to split the station. The Board voted to put out a notice forbidding any on-air comment on the subject. It was a worrying time.

Never in local memory had Castlemaine been so bitterly divided. Friend turned on friend and neighbour on neighbour. The town was plastered with signs proclaiming 'No More Pokies' and car stickers 'Enough Pokies in Castlemaine' appeared on numerous cars. The social media was choked with anti-club propaganda. A fearful social media attack was launched on a legendary Aussie entertainer who had enthusiastically signed up as the Club's 1,000th member. Eventually, reluctantly, he was forced to resign, fearing damage to his reputation such was the vitriol directed at him. The group was cleverly led by David Stretch, the proprietor of the Theatre Royal entertainment centre. A club venue would almost certainly have impacted on his business offering music and other entertainment, but he denied any connection. He was named as the contact for a boycott by musicians and others who pledged never to perform at the new club. Two years on I understand that David had moved his family to another town.

Amazingly, alas, our Shire Council voted to support the EPIC group and asked VCAT to overturn the VCGR decision approving the club. It was later revealed to general astonishment that the Council's Social Impact Study, prepared to go before VCGR and VCAT was prepared by a senior council officer who was a member of EPIC!

It was a dreadful time and was not resolved even though the appeal to VCAT by the shire council, aiding the EPIC group, ended the Highland Society's plans. The VCAT decision did nothing toward repairing the damage done to the fabric of the town. The bitterness and resentment will take years to go away. WMAfm was an innocent bystander, but I was its manager and therefore the station had to pay.

The Castlemaine we first moved to was populated almost exclusively by true-blue working class people who worked hard at all sorts of menial jobs. Our big employers were Thompson's Foundry, Castle Bacon, fondly referred to as The Pig Factory, and Victoria Carpet Factory known as The Mill. Every morning the town came alive to the shift start whistles. They were preceded by a steady stream of people, many on pushbikes and some men with Gladstone bags perched on the handlebars, making their way to work. This was repeated in reverse at knock-off time in the afternoon. A lot of the men (few ladies went to the pub then) called into one of the numerous pubs for a couple of beers before closing time at 6 o'clock. Often they would buy a couple of long neck bottles to place in the Gladstone bag for later. That was how life went on back then.

In the 1970's a change came over Castlemaine as an influx of hippies made it their home. These odd sorts of people, foreign to any seen in the town before, were readily accepted as they quickly and quietly blended into the existing framework, becoming almost invisible over time. But they did in fact bring change, opening our eyes to another world that existed out there. They brought music, fun, happiness and a carefree attitude. They showed us how to relax and enjoy ourselves more. They brought food ideas that changed our ways. They also brought marijuana, lots of it, a bit of a shock to some, but soon accepted as part of the norm.

This was the Castlemaine I loved and enjoyed. So did Marilyn and we were simply one of the crowd. We fitted in perfectly, minus the hippy clothing and the marijuana!

Chapter Twenty Eight

Surprises, awards, a rooster today, a feather duster tomorrow, a sad farewell

I have won a number of personal awards for broadcasting over the years, all highly valued, but none could equal a couple of surprises in the 2000s.

I was friend of respected Castlemaine family, the Cappys; Felix, Joe, Vincent (Vin) and their mother Cath. The family father, Joe Cappy Senior came to town in the late 1930s, an Italian immigrant. He was on his way to inspect a small business for sale in St Arnaud when he stopped over at Castlemaine. He was impressed and instead of going further north he chose to buy a small café on Hargraves Street next to the old Theatre Royal. Joe worked hard and built a business, which laid the foundation for the family businesses that were to come later. I came to know the family quite well, especially mother Cath, who was one of my staunchest Listeners. I always referred to her as Mrs Cappy, never her Christian name, out of respect for her. I will always remember her frequently requested song, 'I have a dream' by Abba. This, from a woman in her nineties at the time, showed me that you are never too old to have dreams.

Joe Cappy Senior, who died before I got to know him, was known around town as Joe 'Cappy', an abbreviation of Capicchiano, which Aussies found too difficult to pronounce. So Joe adopted the name Cappy and it remains today. Officially it is still Capicchiano.

When my friend Felix Cappy died, Castlemaine lost one of its finest sons. His dear mother had passed away quietly about a year before. Felix had appeared weekly as a guest on one of my radio programs. His wit and humour were brilliant for radio and his knowledge of the town and district history astonishing. Our Listeners loved him and so did I. I recorded my last session with him at his kitchen table in his beautiful home in Hall Street. He was far too ill to come to the studio.

Felix had a huge funeral in St Mary's Catholic Church, which was filled to capacity, followed by a huge wake at the church hall. He had many friends and had been a shire councilor for several years. At one time he ran as a Liberal Party candidate in the state election. He lost, but came close. Our political views were slightly different but mostly we thought the same about most issues. We were simply good friends. If ever there was a small 'L' liberal it was Felix Cappy. To add to my list of good things about him he was, like me, a staunch republican.

I speak of the Cappy family, not only because they are a leading family in the town, but because they were regular and generous supporters of our radio stations. One day Vin Cappy rang me and invited Mazza and I to a Rotary Club evening at a local hotel. We were of course delighted to accept. I was not a member of Rotary but we had previously been guests on several occasions and twice Maz and I were guest speakers at Club dinners. On this occasion it turned out to be a special dinner, where the club awarded selected people, usually Rotarians, Paul Harris Fellowships for extraordinary community service.

To my amazement I was called to come forward as Vin stood before the microphone and read a list of items related to my activities in Castlemaine and Harcourt districts. That night, to my pride, I was made a Rotary Club Paul Harris Fellow, one of a few who are not Rotarians.

On Australia Day 2012, Ken White, Mazza and I were conducting a live-to-air broadcast of the celebrations from the beautiful Botanical Gardens. We had been broadcasting this event for a number of years and always got great response to it. As the official part of the program began we sat quietly, microphones open, making the occasional comment. The compere began reading out the awards. He came to the announcement of a special award struck that year for Service to the Community and I heard my name. I sat puzzled for a couple of seconds and it hit me. 'Shit!' I yelled into the mic. 'That's me.' Not the sort of language I normally used on air! It was another very proud moment in my life as I accepted the award from Mayor Janet Cropley. I knew I had been nominated but I did not imagine I would win.

    I am of course very happy to have these awards decorating my walls at home but I emphasise that anything I achieved in my career in local radio was because I had the unswerving love and support of Marilyn. I simply could not have done it without her. Nor, I must add, could Mazza and I have achieved the building of two local community radio radio stations without the wonderful generosity of the business people, about thirty in all, who supported Mazza and I in our efforts. Community radio depends on local support for its existence. Some rely on government and other grants and manage to survive, but to be truly successful I believe that a station must have the local business and full community support, not just a section of the community, but the full community. Otherwise, they are broadcasting to a select few and the true purpose of the station is lost.

    Over the years I had some great Listeners who really stuck by me, some regarding me as someone special. Of course I am not special, I am an ordinary bloke who loves presenting on radio. In this Great Listener category one person stands out like a beacon, a Castlemaine woman named Gwen Coupland. I have known Gwennie for over thirty years; in fact she was one of the nurses who cared for me when I was so badly burnt in 1984. She has followed my career from station to station and her support for me in some very difficult times was unwavering. As I write Gwennie is around eighty-five years old; she still listens to my broadcasts and our station every day, the most loyal one of the estimated four hundred Listeners our current little station has.

She rings us at least weekly and never fails to say 'I love you two', referring to Marilyn and me. We love her too, and she is one of our dearest friends. Another favourite is Jessie Crew who with her late husband David, were long time supporters of the radio station. In later years she moved from Maldon to Campbells Creek, remaining as staunch as ever.

They say all good things come to an end; it is true of life – even of time in radio! I suppose I always imagined I'd retire with acknowledgement of my time and contribution from my colleagues and peers. I figured maybe a testimonial dinner, a gift of some sort; a gold watch even! I thought that there maybe would be a few speeches and a few reminiscent laughs. I was to be disappointed.

My final time at WMAfm and therefore in community radio, was painful. Marilyn had already experienced a heart attack and she became distressed again by events. I was in poor shape too, my blood pressure was up and my doctor told me to walk away. Our President, Ken White, suffered a serious illness, was hospitalised with heart problems and then pneumonia. The remaining board members suffered in a variety of ways.

In July 2012, I celebrated a milestone birthday and decided it was time to retire from management to focus on what I loved; presenting radio programs. Being the Manager was a multi-skilled job: responsible for all day to day operations, selling sponsorship, a big responsibility, therefore careful choice of a successor was necessary.

Our Board, which now included relative newcomer Scott Sanders, appointed a volunteer from our ranks, Martin Myles, who appeared to be suitable for the job. We contracted with him on a six month trial, agreeing to pay him $150 a day for three days a week – days to be of his choosing. We agonised over the payment amount, a huge step for us. We emphasised to Martin that a major role for him was maintaining sponsorship income. Martin assured us that he would actually increase sponsorship to around $120,000 a year; we thought it an overly optimistic figure but he appeared confident. I stayed on for about a month to teach him the job.

Sadly after a few months our treasurer advised the Board that we were heading for financial shipwreck. Our Manager was not up to expectations and income was falling away. As an example our footy broadcasts brought in between $6,000 and $8,000 in sponsorship each season. For the fast approaching season it was nil. In addition, he was refusing to take instructions from the board, stating at an awkward meeting with Ken and me, that he would 'morally and ethically refuse' to obey particular orders and he would not be 'micro-managed'. He was changing the station format without authority and we were in a quandary. To put it mildly there was a misalignment between the station policies and its Manager.

An example of Martin's disregard for our policies is clearly demonstrated by one particular incident. I had asked Ken Ford, one of our best performing volunteers, to take home about 780 songs on a disc to put them through the editing process. This is a time-consuming job involving removing silent pieces at the start and end of a song and levelling the sound to consistency. Each song takes around four to five minutes. By the time Ken had finished the work Martin had taken over as Manager. Ken told me he showed him the USB stick containing the processed songs, asking what he should do with them. Martin said something like, 'Throw them in the bin. They don't suit the station format anymore.' Ken was extremely disappointed and angry but complied, destroying several months' work.

We then received an email from Martin stating he would attend no meetings with the Board unless he had twenty-four hours notice in writing and could bring a companion. Next thing we received a doctor's certificate placing him on two weeks stress leave.

The situation was as toxic as it was untenable and the Board made the only decision open to it. The Manager had to go.

With Martin still on leave we consulted a local solicitor, anxious to act correctly. An appropriate letter was prepared and mailed by the lawyers. The letter advised him he was placed on garden leave; he would continue to be paid to the end of his contract but was not to attend the station.

Unfortunately he apparently did not receive the letter before the day of his return to work and this led to an unpleasant confrontation.

Within days we were notified by his legal aid solicitor that we were to be called before Fair Work Australia in Melbourne charged with wrongful dismissal.

At the hearing we argued that Martin was on a contract and wrongful dismissal could not be considered. We tried to compromise, offering a considerable sum in settlement, but it was refused point blank. He demanded not only to be reinstated, but his term extended by three months! There was no way we would agree to this so the hearing was adjourned to a future date.

Martin's legal action prevented us from making any statement to explain our actions. All we could do was publish a statement in the local paper and in emails to volunteers explaining the legal situation, but it said nothing of substance; we could not reveal the facts.

Meanwhile Martin's supporters began an assault in the press and social media demanding his re-engagement. I was on the end of a barrage of emails and letters, all roundly condemning me for sacking a person they claimed was an excellent manager. On May 17th, a particular person wrote in praise of Martin claiming that any of WMA's recent achievements were due to Martin's work and the board failed to speak of this. He also claimed 'irregularities – with respect to recent committee activities', urging readers to take up membership. This was pretty heavy stuff!

We were disappointed when he and another man began a drive to recruit members, obviously intending to vote the Board out. In just one day we received forty-seven applications, more than doubling our membership. It was clear to Board members that we were heading for a special meeting where we could not survive a vote and with a certainty that Martin Myles be re-instated.

So much damage had been done that even if the Board succumbed to Myles' demand we could not work with him. It was a most distressing and unhappy time. We were also deeply concerned at the waste of hard-earned money on mounting legal costs, whereas Martin was receiving free Legal Aid counsel. This is not readily given but sometimes available to the poor and disadvantaged depending on the circumstances. To fight on we would be further stressing ourselves, creating more health damage and increasing the legal cost. Outnumbered, we had to raise a white flag and with great reluctance we decided to resign en masse. We knew that this meant handing the station over to Myles and his supporters. We had an alternative, but we didn't even consider it. Under the Constitution we had the right to refuse the membership applications without explanation. We could have sacked any dissenter; we could have bled the station dry in legal costs. This would have destroyed the station, by acting as we did it could survive, repugnant as surrendering was. Additionally, we could simply bear no more pressure.

On 23 May 2013, we called a Board meeting which was attended by about twenty Myles' supporters. I had been warned in a phone call from a coup leader to expect trouble and was uneasy. The meeting began with regular business being suspended and there was considerable surprise when one by one the Board members resigned, me first. We did it in a calculated and orderly fashion to ensure that the station could continue without interruption. We quietly and quickly left the meeting.

I don't know what actually happened next but it was apparent that John Rowland took over as President. John had earlier spoken with some board members suggesting he take over as President, stressing he had the business experience to keep Myles under control. He now had the opportunity. Without delay Myles was reinstalled as Manager.

Our Board members, Ken White, Robyn Thomas, Fergus Niall, Bettie Exon, Rod Hadfield and me had suffered enough. Marilyn by this time had retired but was badly effected as she had continued to be the strength behind us all. Robyn Thomas, in the absence of President Ken White through his dispute-induced illness, acted in his role and was absolutely marvelous.

And that is how I finished my thirty-five years in Community Radio.

The End

Epilogue

*Any jackass can kick down a barn, but it takes
a good carpenter to build one.*
Sam Rayburn

The coup at WMAfm is not the first time a Community Radio station has been taken over by a particular group. When all the work has been done, there are often those who think they can do it better. Because of the usual structure of community radio, taking control is a relatively simple operation.

Proudly, we left WMAfm in great condition with $50,000 in the bank, over $30,000 in committed sponsorship, first class equipment and potential to grow further.

The new group promised to 'Put the community back into radio', but in fact they did the opposite, catering for a non-representative group, with 3RRR/MBS style programming. It is not small country town material.

Martin Myles stayed on as Manager for around a year and then resigned; the details of his departure were never revealed. It proved however that the disruption, stress and unhappiness, all done in his name, was for nothing.

I was surprised to receive a letter from the WMAfm President suggesting that we were pirating their sponsors in favour of our Radio88 service. It contained a thinly veiled hint that I would be expelled from Castlemaine District Radio Inc. for disloyalty! Pretty severe treatment for Mazza and me, both Life Members. The suggestion of pinching sponsors was false of course as our sponsors had been with Radio88 from day one.

The ultimate insult to the founders came when the station was renamed Mainfm, one of the titles our committee had rejected years before. In effect, WMAfm was obliterated, closed down and consigned to history. In its place an entirely new station, Mainfm, emerged.

The old board was treated with scant respect by the new. For example, I wrote to the new group asking that some commitments of the previous board be honoured. The request for a plaque on the studio wall to honour Faye Barker was rejected with the reply that it was not in the budget. A miserable, maximum $50! This showed no respect for the person or our history. The request that an appropriate board, costing maybe $300, be mounted on a wall with the names of Life Members in gold leaf was completely ignored. They then proceeded to spend a whopping $40,000 on new studios! That was a very puzzling decision; there was no long term and secure rental agreement with the Old Gaol owners. They then bought a caravan, had it signwritten and fitted it out as a mobile studio. This was a particularly odd decision as we had previously bought and then sold a caravan, finding it a rarely used white elephant.

Early in November 2014, Mainfm President, John Rowland had dispatched an email to volunteers and members which contained startling news. Mainfm was moving to the former hospital in Myring Street, the site that we had investigated and rejected several years before. In December 2014, the station was dismantled and moved. It seemed a rental agreement could not be reached with the Old Gaol. Judging by an email and a statement to the local press it seemed the blame was directed at either the Old Gaol owners or the Shire Council. Who knows where the facts lie? But whoever or whatever caused this move it is best described as a calamity.

Mainfm changed; it did not-reflect the new slogan 'Putting the Community back into Radio', except a certain section. The audience built over six years was lost. Sadly, WMAfm is only a memory held dear by those who began it and who enjoyed listening to it.

* * *

Mazza and I still own Radio88 which you'll recall we had purchased from CDR Inc when WMAfm began broadcasting. Once we had recovered somewhat from the anger and disappointment of our removal from WMAfm, we focused on Radio 88 which had never stopped running. Of course with a power limit of one watt we could not hope to cover anything but a portion of Castlemaine, perhaps 75 percent of it. A large audience was not a possibility. However, we felt that Radio88 for Seniors was worthwhile with the significant population of senior residents in the town, so we set out to enlarge the audience.

Not wishing to share the accommodation at the Old Gaol with WMAfm (Mainfm), although it was offered, we gained permission to relocate our transmitter and studio to the town's hospital building.

In the end it all worked out okay and these days I enjoy going on air when I feel like it and have friends join me from time to time. We talk about the history of the town, the good things in life, recall the good old days and the things I know our locals like to hear. And I don't have to be looking over my shoulder for the next attack. We even have a professional news service!

Prior to the coup d'état, the Board had approved $500 for the purchase of a pastel work by local artist Christine Browning for presentation to Mazza. The work is of some of the farmyard chooks for which Christina is well known. The sign above the chook house door reads 'Mazza and Ian's home sweet home'. It wasn't until after the coup was finalised that we were able to arrange a time for the presentation. Four volunteers and several friends gathered at The Five Flags hotel for the occasion. It was sad really; not a fitting end for Mazza's years of devotion to community radio. Robyn Thomas and Ken White presented Mazza and me with a beautifully mounted Shure microphone of 1950's vintage. Both gifts are proudly on display at our home in Castlemaine along with a lot of memorabilia of the good times we had in radio.

I have learnt something of human behaviour; personality disorders for instance. I have heard it said that a person in politics for a number of years can become narcissistic or grossly egotistical. They can exploit others, have a sense of entitlement, a need for attention, a pre-occupation with their own importance and show a lack of empathy for others. I think it may well be an adequate description for some people in radio. At times this story may appear self-serving, but if the truth is such, so be it. I have made many mistakes of course, but the biggest ones were being so passionate about radio and putting my trust in certain people.

At times my writing reveals bitterness. It is true that I was unable to conceal it at the time of writing when old feelings surfaced. However I now realise that those who made life difficult for me played but a minor role. They mean little to me now. The friends I made remain so.

I'll continue to broadcast as long as I am able and hopefully retire gracefully.

Finis

www.ingramcontent.com/pod-product-compliance
Lightning Source LLC
Chambersburg PA
CBHW051543010526
44118CB00022B/2561